BRETHREN

ROBB PRITCHARD

Dedicated, as is everything else, to
Jana Goetzova.

I write and think of many things that are just fantasies.
You came true

Names

Ordo-wik (plural: Ordo-wiki)	is the possible Brythonic pronunciation of the Latin Ordovice
Dogs	Deceangli tribe

Locations

AD 77	*Today*
Crow Hill	Dinas Bran, Llangollen
Deva	Chester
Dinorwig	Dinorwig hillfort, near Caernarvon
White Walls	Caer Drewyn hillfort, near Corwen
Bastard's Hill	Penycloddiau hillfort, near Denbigh
The mines	The Great Orme, Llandudno
Fort on the Chief River	Caerhun Roman fort, near Conwy
Chief River	River Conwy
Mona	Anglesey

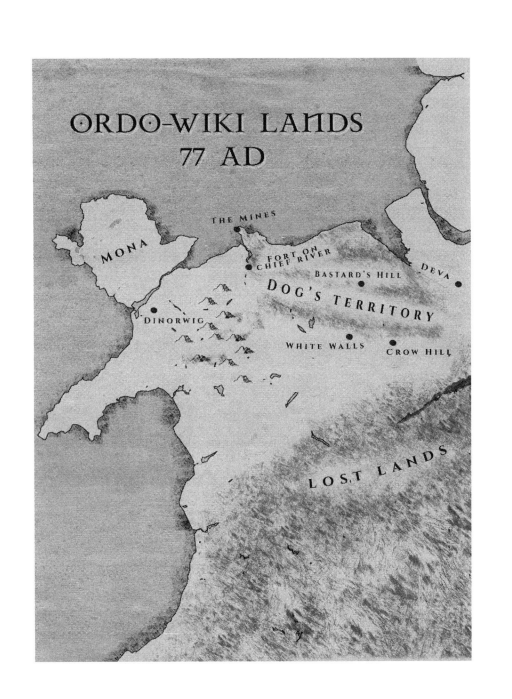

ORDO-WIKI LANDS
77 AD

MONA

THE MINES

FORT ON CHIEF RIVER

DEVA

BASTARD'S HILL

DOG'S TERRITORY

DINORWIG

WHITE WALLS

CROW HILL

LOST LANDS

"Do you not know that a man is not dead while his name is still spoken?"

Sir Terry Pratchett

ONE

U P ON THE hillfort ramparts, Cadwal tugged the rough wool cloak around his shoulders. His companions on sentry in the incessant wind were a pair of weathered skulls perched on posts. Old warriors of the Ordo-wik tribe, even in death they still protected the fort.

The larger of the two had been Rotri, a fierce fighter. The light of the towering mid-summer fire cast dancing shadows in the empty eye sockets. It was an unnerving sensation, and Cadwal had to shrug off the idea of there being some life in the bones.

The living worried him more, though.

He drew the knife from its patterned sheath. Ground on the whetstone for days in readiness for its purpose this night, the edge had never been sharper. It had been his father's and his father's before that. Old enough it was poured molten from the forge in the days when a tribe only had other tribes to fight before the land had known anything of Rome. His father had been killed half a year before Cadwal had been born so in honour of the man he'd never known, he'd carried and kept it oiled all his life. The precious metal had never been used to kill.

Until tonight.

With a coldness in his chest, he remembered that, come the next dawn, his own sons would likely be without a father.

He tasted blood. He'd bitten his lip too hard again.

As he felt the weight and balance of the blade, he told himself again that what he'd set himself to do was for the good of the Ordo-wik tribe. Killing his enemies might cost his own life, but if that was to be the price, he would pay it. Until the very last drop of his blood had been the words of his oath.

The boys would be brought up, and one day made into good, strong warriors, by his brother, Tamm. The thought helped harden his resolve for the killings to come.

With the urgent rhythm of the festival drums reverberating through the palisade planks and thumping in his chest, he turned to look inside the fort of Crow Hill. Under his breath, he cursed at how the wind-whipped flames blew sparks perilously close to the thatch of the nearest roundhouses. Swirling embers were the least cause of his gnawing unease, though.

1

Spinning in wild circles, blue spirals of woad paste daubed over cheeks and brows, the dancers seemed closer to the realm of spirit than that of man. But how they could wave their arms and toss their hair with abandon, as though the enemy wasn't already inside the walls with them, he had no idea.

He scanned through his dancing clans folk, trying to spot the newcomers. Outcasts from a nearby tribe, or so their story went. Cadwal hadn't believed it since the day they'd prostrated themselves at the gates, begging for mercy. The teryn, the young daughter of the king who had absolute rule over the Clan of the Crows, believed them, though, and that had to be good enough for everyone else. But Cadwal's bones told him the men were from the enemy tribe, the bastard Dogs, and nothing they'd done in the passage of a moon had changed his mind. And if they were Dogs then they hadn't come to Crow Hill for sanctuary, they were here because they intended to kill everyone he held dear. How, he wasn't sure, but he knew he had to kill them first. Whether they were the teryn's guests, held under sacred protections, or not.

He could see only a couple of them in the crowd, but not their companions. One against two were odds he was happy with, and with a twist of his heart, knew the time had come. Knife sheathed, he made his way down the ladder.

Down in the half-maddened crowd, a couple of girls swirled around and reached out to interlock arms. Seeing it was him, though, they recoiled. Without realising it, he touched the jagged scar at the base of his skull. It was a curse to be knocked out by a slingshot stone before the fight had even begun, and not since that day had anyone listened to his concerns as nothing but bad luck could come of taking advice from a man the gods did not favour. Cadwal couldn't disagree about that; as he'd lain on the ground his wife had been killed. There could be no greater curse in the world than that.

Deeper in, buffeted out of the way at almost every step by sweat-soaked bodies, he pressed through the heaving throng. In the haze of smoke and kicked-up dust, it was hard to see who was clan and who was foe. Then he saw the wide shoulders of a man moving a little stiffer than others, as though he was only pretending to lose himself in the beat of the drums, as though he was thinking other thoughts than dancing.

He crept closer. Tightening his fingers around the leather wrapped hilt, he drew the knife free and held it in such a way that the blade was covered by a fold of the cloak. So close to a kill, a familiar calm washed over him. The drums, and the people around him, seemed far away. One stab in the back of the first man, close to the spine but far enough away from bone that the blade wouldn't be trapped. Then it would be embedded in the throat of the second man before he even wondered why his friend was crumpling to his knees. Two quick movements, two enemies dead. The thought was as natural to him as the farmer knowing how to sow seeds in the fields.

He was ready to strike, a single breath away, knife angled and aimed. He drew back his arm, muscles tensed but before he could thrust, a girl spun in front and pulled the nearest outsider away for a dance. The moment of hesitation was all the other Dog needed to spot the threat. A fighter just as well trained as any Ordo-wik, Dax didn't miss the intent in his stance, but reacted with nothing but a challenging sneer. Blue circles over his face, eyes wide and tongue sticking out, he seemed like some maleficent creature risen from the Otherworld. Knowing it was a Dog inside the fort, Cadwal didn't think that was too far off.

Cadwal's chance of surprise was gone, but Dax was unarmed and, warrior or not, flesh against sharpened iron was an unequal match. He checked his grip on the knife again and took a step forward, but before he had a chance to stab, another girl rammed into him. By the time he'd pushed her out of the way, Dax had disappeared into the crowd. Cursing in frustration, he followed, moving like a fox slinking through the hedgerows between the dancers, ducking under raised arms and weaving around bodies in his own dance. But one of death, not celebration. Heartbeat now indistinguishable from the drums, he was lost in the blind panic of thinking that any of the men standing on his toes or swinging their arms around without a care was a Dog about to sink a blade between his ribs.

He stopped and forced himself to catch his breath and look around. But with nearly a hundred people all making exaggerated movements and the fire causing flashes of bright light and deep shadows, he couldn't see either of the Dogs anywhere. And after coming so close not once but twice, he couldn't help the unnerving feeling it was the action of some god that had stopped him. He dismissed the thought, because why wouldn't the gods of his Ordo-wik tribe want their enemies dead? It made no sense.

He forced himself to loosen his white knuckled grip on the knife. It was the reaction to having something vitally important slip through his fingers. About to sulk dejectedly back up to the rampart to mull over what he could do next, a sharp pain on his shin made him stumble. Still seething from the missed kills, he was about to vent his rage at children being so careless to play-fight with toy hammers in the middle of a festival, but stopped when he saw whose children they were. Suddenly he was lost in the sense of relief of being with them again. With an overwhelming need to protect his sons, he was about to drop to a knee and wrap them in his arms, as secure as the fort gates closing at night... but something about how his eldest was fighting his little brother made him stop. Cadwal watched captivated as Owyn held the small hammer lightly with two hands; the best position to be able to quickly choose which way to strike. Feet planted firmly, knees slightly bent, Cadwal was amazed to see how he moved with a little flinch before he swung. Owyn wasn't simply trying to beat Arwel, he was indicating what was coming, so Arwel could offer a more confident block. Much more than merely an older brother, he'd taken on the role of teacher.

Having just been a moment away from killing two men, Cadwal's heart was still racing, but now it was gripped in anguish because in the void she'd left, he saw they were reshaping themselves to fill in the space that had been hers. Hunting Dogs around the mid-summer fire suddenly not so important, he watched their beaming and carefree smiles while trying to hold the pieces of his heart together. Once more he told himself there was no fault in their happiness.

He caught sight of Trenus striding purposely towards him and realised too late he was still holding the knife. He tried to cover it with his cloak and step to the side but Trenus barred his way with his barrel chest. "What are you doing?" he snarled. "A *knife*! At the festival? When everyone thinks you are cursed? Give it to me!"

Cadwal hesitated but couldn't argue that he needed it to kill the guests. The teryn's counsellor was no man to argue with. He also he knew Trenus was doing him a real favour as he could have simply called the guards, and that would have been that. Reluctantly, he turned it around and handle first, handed it over.

"If your father hadn't been my blood-brother..." he said, shaking his head. "We'll talk about this in the morning."

Allowed to go, Cadwal hustled the boys over to the nearest roundhouse. With the wall at his back he could more easily watch for anyone coming up on them.

"Da!" little Arwel exclaimed excitedly. "I killed Owyn five times!"

"What did I tell you about fighting in the middle of the festival?" Cadwal shouted loud enough to be heard over the drums.

His victory denied, Arwel looked crestfallen. He had his mother's sky-blue eyes, and Cadwal saw her in them sometimes, especially when he was daydreaming. He also had her radiant smile, and it was a cruel bitterness that whenever his son was happy, Cadwal was stabbed with the agony of losing her again.

Owyn, two summers older and a head taller, wasn't too impressed though. "I killed you *twenty* times!"

"No, Da!" Arwel wailed. "No, he didn't!" In a quick fit of anger, his youngest ducked down and swung his hammer in a short arc. Off guard, Owyn couldn't react in time to stop it whacking into the side of his leg.

Cadwal had a momentary pang of fatherly concern. But in Owyn he saw a clear image of how a child trying his best to look tough in front of his father would one day be a man defending the tribe. It would take years of training, of being knocked down as easily as Arwel, until, as he got a little stronger each time, one day it would be a warrior who stood back up.

As Owyn readied his hammer, he wondered if he'd now get to experience the greatest honour; that of bringing his boys up as warriors. The Dogs still needed to die tonight, though. One way or another.

With gritted teeth, Owyn looked for permission to strike back. Cadwal nodded and with two deft and hard strokes to open Arwel's shield, Owyn jabbed him in the chest with the head of his hammer. Only a lump of unseasoned wood, it was still substantial enough to knock Arwel to his backside at Cadwal's feet. "Ow!" he cried, clutching where the bruise would come. "Not fair!" But he scrambled back to his feet and, staring up with his big innocent eyes, asked, "Da? How long will it be before I am brave?"

"Brave? I don't need you to be brave," Cadwal said. "All I need is for you to learn how to stay alive."

"Why?" he asked, rubbing his chest in a way he hoped wouldn't show how much it hurt.

"Well," Cadwal started, but realised it was going to be a hard answer for a six-year-old. He would speak no lie though, especially on a festival day when the gods were watching. "Beyond the borders of our lands, we have enemies. People who want to kill us."

"Like they did with Ma?"

Words suddenly failing him, Cadwal could only nod.

"But why?"

He sighed. "Because they are not us. Not Ordo-wiki. They're a different tribe and they want our land for themselves. And our sheep."

"They want to kill us for our *sheep*?"

Having the words to calm a child had been Gwen's gift. Before he could mumble an inadequate reply, Arwel asked, "Can I only fight enemies who are little like me? Ones with only wooden swords?"

Building walls, digging ditches and teaching their children how to kill, such was the way of the world. As he tried to find the words to explain why they fought the Roman invaders and neighbouring tribes, ash from the fire fell around them like snow. The drums slowing to a double beat of a slowly pounding heart saved him from needing to answer. He looked up nervously to see what had caused the sudden change. The sight of two druids, white clay painted on their faces and smudged dark circles of charcoal powder around their eyes, made it feel as though things normally found in a month-old grave were crawling over his skin. Druids and bad news often travelled together, so the saying went. And the fact their arrival had been a secret was far from a good sign.

Any chance of killing the Dogs this night was gone, but had his plan to kill the teryn's guests been found out? Was he about to be ripped from the boys' arms? The fear of being betrayed by magics unknown felt like a cold hand crushing his chest.

Minura walked out, as aloof as only a teryn could be, and blew the horn. For those always poised to fight from the fort of Crow Hill, right on the edge of Ordo-wik lands, the bitter note was as effective for getting their attention as a slap in the face. The sound stopped the drummers in mid-beat and brought an abrupt pause to the festival. People stopped dancing and patted their friends on the back to get their attention. The last ones, having spent so long lost in the beat of the drums, came back to the world and unsteady on their feet, looked around slightly embarrassed. More than a few were slumped against walls of the closest roundhouses. Not too unusual in such a festival, but the horn should have roused them.

In the respectful silence, Minura called, "Clansmen!" Her hair, the colour of summer morning sunshine, was braided and tied up in knots as complicated as any artisan could paint, carve, or cast. With a pair of fox skins draped over her shoulders, positioned so that the two fists of the torc at her throat glinted in the firelight, she was dressed to impress the gods, never mind the clan.

With a wave of a delicate hand, her muscled guards dragged a trussed and hooded man to her feet.

"What's happening, Da?" Arwel asked as a strange silence descended.

"A sacrifice," Owyn said in awe.

"What's *that*?" Arwel piped.

Most men wouldn't dare make eye contact with a druid, never mind fight in their presence, so with no threat of an outsider brandishing a weapon in retaliation, Cadwal deemed it safe enough to lift Arwel up to sit on a shoulder. "It's when we offer a life to the gods. To give our thanks or to ask for something."

"They're going to kill him," Owyn smiled.

"Kill?" Arwel whined.

"For the gods," Cadwal nodded.

Another big man bounding over gave Cadwal a fright again, but it was Tamm. "Here, take this!" he said, slightly breathless and ruddy-faced from dancing. He held out a battered old ram's horn of ale.

Cadwal's hand was halfway to it before he checked himself. "I'm on sentry duty!" He left unspoken the punishment for a guard found inebriated.

Tamm scoffed. "You really think any bastard Dogs would come out for a raid tonight? On Alban Hefin? This is a *sacred* day!"

With his blood-shot eyes and fool's grin, his brother Tamm looked far too drunk to bother arguing with. "For us it is," Cadwal agreed. "But who knows what gods the Dogs follow now."

"*Roman* gods, you mean?" He coughed up a weighty ball of phlegm, and to demonstrate his disdain, hawked it an impressive distance. He tipped his head back to finish the ale and trails of it ran down both sides of his unkempt moustache. "A man can't just choose what gods he honours! That's just not right! Or..." he asked with a playful smile, "you still think they're all in here with us?"

Cadwal ran a finger through the long hairs that flowed from his upper lip down over the sides of his chin. In the glow of the firelight, Tamm's long locks looked even redder than usual, and he felt the familiar jealousy over his lousy mouse-coloured moustache. "I don't trust them," he shrugged.

Tamm tried to stifle a laugh, but it came out through his nose in a snort. "Still? They've been with us near enough a full cycle of the moon! Tell me, how do you see enemies in men who spend their days fixing fences and go hunting deer to give us fresh meat?"

It made no sense to Cadwal either. And yet the four of them were here.

Tamm grabbed the back of Owyn's tunic and in one hand hoisted him to his shoulders. Arwel squealed as Owyn waved his hammer at him. "Oi!" Cadwal snapped, trying to convey the respect needed in the presence of the teryn and the druids.

"Ah..." Tamm sighed, suddenly sounding as wise as an Elder druid. "Gwen. That's why your heart is in darkness on the day of light. You've been speaking her name to Lleu, the god of light all day."

Cadwal shrugged. Better Tamm think he was missing his wife than knowing how close he'd come to killing the teryn's guests around the festival fire.

"Brother of my clan and my blood, hear me while the fire burns for the gods, so you know the truth of these words I speak. Gwen's death was not your fault. It was a trap, an ambush, and we all walked into it. She was supposed to be safe with the wagons."

"She still died, though!" Cadwal snapped and as he said it, he could feel her unavenged death dragging on his shoulders as heavy as a soaking wet cloak. Arwel's hand balled up in a lock of his hair.

"Aye, she did. With too many others. But I've said it before, if someone is to blame, then why not look at the teryn?"

"Tamm!" Cadwal scolded, horrified his brother would say such a thing with so many people around, especially the boys. "She'll take your tongue!"

"She took your *wife*!"

"You're drunk!" Cadwal scolded.

"Aye, I am. Must be a damn strong batch of ale, this. I've only had two horns and I'm ready to drop. Like them." He indicated those passed out on the ground and gave the inside of the horn a suspicious sniff. "But that doesn't mean I'm talking horse shit. Tell me, who led men where us warriors had told the teryn not to go? Who sent us off the wrong way to charge some empty woods?"

"She'll *banish* you!" Cadwal seethed.

"Bah," Tamm shrugged and Cadwal took his brother's impressive belch as a statement of disdain. "Being the daughter of the king doesn't make her a warrior. And if it's a lie that passes my lips, then let Lleu himself take my eyes so I never see the light of truth again."

Cadwal was about to growl another retort but noticed how the newcomers had been ushered into a line and made to kneel in supplication before Minura. They were in a perfect position for someone to lop their heads off, but Cadwal suspected the teryn was about to do something much worse than execute them.

He touched his cut lip with his tongue and tasted blood again.

"Nearly a moon ago," Minura said to the silent crowd. "Some strangers came to us wanting to keep faith with our gods instead of their people's new ones. Since that day, they have shown us nothing but honour and dedication..."

She let the words hang and a heaviness settled in Cadwal's stomach, as though he'd swallowed a large pebble from the riverbank. She was about to invite the outsiders into the tribe. Enemies were about to be called brothers. He almost gagged at the thought of having to share mead with men he'd just tried to kill.

Before yelling out his objection, he had to remind himself she was just eighteen summers old, sixteen when her husband, chief of the clan, was killed in another fight with the Dogs from the north. Despite her youth, she had the responsibility of the whole surviving Clan of the Crows resting on her delicate shoulders. He'd heard it said that such a thing must be heavier than the thickest *torc*, but wondered if Tamm was right. Could it have been her inexperience and petulance in asserting her new rule over hard men that had got his clansmen and wife killed? And if she'd made that mistake, who was to say that inviting the strangers into the hillfort wasn't another awful misjudgement.

"So tonight, on Alban Hefin, the day the Great Wheel of the ever changing seasons turns another spoke, and in the presence of the gods, from this night on, I welcome them as Ordo-wiki, free to marry, to work as they choose and to fight as our brothers. And to mark this joyous new growth of our clan, I offer a blood sacrifice!"

A few in the crowd cheered their approval.

She pointed at the man held by her guards and flanked by the druids. Hearing his fate, he began to struggle but with two strong men holding him, there would be no escape.

"Yesterday this thief was caught from a group of Dog sheep raiders."

At the mention of their most hated enemies, Arwel squirmed.

"Oh, that's clever," Tamm grinned.

"Clever?" Cadwal asked. "How?"

"Think about it," he said, his voice noticeably slurred. "It's a Dog lying there about to face the threefold death, right? If the newcomers are from a tribe to the south like they say, they won't care when she takes his hood off. But if they recognise their clansman and try and fight to save him, they're as good as dead, aren't they!"

"And then what?" Owyn called down.

"And then we'll have some nice new heads to hang over our doors," Tamm laughed.

"Can *I* have one?" Arwel chirped.

Cadwal set him safely down and said, "Stay with Tamm," with a tone forceful enough to make sure there would be no misunderstanding.

To get a better look at the newcomer's faces, he moved to the side. Not for the first time he wondered if one of them had found Gwen's body in the grass and had ridden home with her severed head slapping against the side of his horse's flank. Cadwal saw how Dax's eyes flickered nervously as he searched through the crowd. Was he looking for the man who'd come so close to killing him?

The drummers started pounding again and increased the tempo to better attract the god's attention until the beat was as fast and frenzied as the feet of a horde of Ordo-wiki charging at the enemy.

The flickering light of the fire gave a strange effect to Minura's face. In one moment, Cadwal could see a young girl terrified of such responsibilities. Half a heartbeat later, though, he saw a flash of a hard woman, steel grey eyes, in charge of her destiny and all of those in the clan. Be that for better or worse.

As she whipped the hood off the prisoner, Cadwal stared at the kneeling men, willing them to leap to their clansman's rescue. A couple looked shocked and perhaps it was recognition he saw in their eyes, but none got off their knees to defend the prisoner. The teryn's test passed, only the one Dog would die this night.

At a wave from Minura, the drums abruptly stopped and the druids took the sudden silence as the signal to do their grizzly work. With a short cudgel, one cracked the bound man on top of the skull, the other put all of his strength into pulling on the rope around his neck and Minura leaned in to slit his throat. As the sheep thief's life blood spattered over her clothes, she threw her head back and laughed.

The man was dead instantly, but Cadwal revelled in the sense of satisfaction seeping into his heart. It was the first time he'd witnessed the death of an enemy for many moons, and as the body slumped lifelessly to the ground, he wanted more.

But while he struggled to temper the burning need to rip the heads off the kneeling Dogs with his bare hands, he was appalled to see his clansmen clasp wrists and slap shoulders with them. The women gave them hugs and kisses. The same ones who'd been reluctant to even make eye contact with Cadwal.

He was still standing in mute dismay, hand on Arwel's head, when Dax approached. Smiling and holding out a horn of ale, he said, "So, we are brothers now?"

Cadwal's hand went for the knife but found only the empty sheath.

Tamm took the horn gratefully and downed a long swig. Dax then offered it to Cadwal. "You should drink," he said. "The gods watch us."

Cadwal couldn't believe a man whose throat had come so close to welcoming his knife could act so calm, as though nothing had happened. The man was either a fool or judged Cadwal to be as much danger as a puppy nipping his heel.

Wetting his lips with an enemy's toast was the last thing he wanted. It might as well have been poison. "I'm on sentry," he replied coldly.

"Ah. So you think your enemies are on the other side of the wall?" Dax grinned.

Tamm laughed heartily at that. "Drink for me then!" his brother insisted. "Drink to this strange future we go to together."

"The one that starts this night," Dax beamed.

Reluctantly, Cadwal took a couple of sips. It tasted slightly bitter and very strong. If that was what everyone had been drinking all night, it was a wonder not more had keeled over.

"So, we celebrate, my new brother?" Dax said to Tamm. He put his arm around Tamm's back and turned him away from Cadwal.

"Come," Tamm called over his shoulder.

"I'll put the boys to bed," Cadwal said dismissively, the first excuse he could think of.

"But Da. I want to see the dawn," Arwel protested.

"You saw it this morning."

"But I want to see another!"

"Ha!" Tamm roared. "The wish of a warrior!"

The sight of Dax laughing with his brother filled Cadwal with rage, but he'd have to wait another day to open Dax's veins. And he'd have to get his knife back from Trenus first.

He picked Arwel up and grabbed the back of Owyn's tunic. "If you wake up in time, then you can climb the wall and see the sun," he said as he hurried away.

He expected them to be full of questions from what they'd witnessed, but having been awake all of the night before as well as most of this one, they were asleep in just a few moments. Cadwal sat next to them. Their soft snores were deeply relaxing. It was as though he could feel all the worries of the world flowing out of him. The feeling was as welcome and warming as blood draining from the corpses of his enemies.

He reflected on coming within a heartbeat of this being his last day with them. His father's knife covered in blood and four Dogs dead and him next was how he'd envisioned this night would end. Instead, he had four new brothers and his boys in his arms, and had absolutely no idea what to do about it.

Muted sounds of the celebration he wanted no part of came from outside and he began to imagine a battle where every last Dog and Roman lay dead as far as he could see. And that same evening he would put the boys to bed, just like this.

Such a day would be far too much to dream of.

TᴡO⊙

Sᴛᴀʀʟᴇss ᴀɴᴅ sᴛɪʟʟ, the night was so thick it felt to Brei as though she was breathing in darkness.

At the end of the long slope from the fort of Dinorwig the whole clan was gathered in a wide circle around the readied pyre. Dressed for battle, their faces were painted with spirals and swirls, and well-polished weapons glinted in the flickering flames of the torches. She rested the shaft of her spear against her shoulder so she could wipe her sweaty palm. There was to be no bloodshed under the moonless sky, but if she was facing an enemy this night it was the gods themselves.

At her side, Heulwen kneaded her tunic in little fists. She let the king's youngest daughter snuggle into the crook of her elbow, hoping the girl could find some reassurance behind the shield. Only seeing her seventh summer, she would have no real grasp of what had just happened to her uncle. But in all honesty, neither did Brei.

In a wide circle around the pyre, stacked up taller than head height, everyone waited in strained silence for King Bleddyn to perform his duty and set it alight. A few shuffled impatiently. With a sure certainty, every man in the land knew it was in no one's best interest to keep the gods waiting but none dared to speak their unease to the king of the Ordo-wiki. They had stilled their tongues with the life-sworn vow that to dishonour the king was to dishonour the gods.

Unlike Brei.

Standing next to the king she'd come to despise, she took her last look at his nephew Maidoc laid out on the pyre. For a few hope-filled moons he'd held the fate of the tribe in his hands. Son of Gwain, the former king she'd been queen to for seven blessed years, he could have called enough fighting men to him. In all of her thirty-something years in this harsh world, no grief had ever weighed so heavily on her chest as the sight of his body laid out ready for the flames. Not even the tiny pyres she'd made for the babies she'd carried and birthed, but had never taken a breath. As painful as those fires had been to light, those deaths had been her own tragedies. With Maidoc gone, not only were her hopes for the future about to be consumed by the flames and turned to ashes, so were those of the whole tribe.

Gripping the spear for support, she thought again of the horrors of the Black Year, some seventeen summers before, when the Twentieth Legion had marched to the sacred isle of Mona, the druids' place of learning. The savage pain of seeing everyone she knew and loved cut to pieces or nailed to trees was as raw now, more than half her life later, as in the days when the fires still smouldered and she'd thought the world had ended.

In quiet moments like this, the desperate cries still echoed in her soul. The first had been from the women as they tried to raise some battle passion into the men. She recalled how many brave warriors had been struck dumb as they watched the Roman cavalry horses swim across the straits towards them, ignoring the strong currents. Afterwards the screams came from the slaughter that followed, and it was these that still haunted her dreams. For years she'd only heard them when she slept, but now they were beginning to bleed into her days.

Now, the legion had almost finished building their huge new fortress at Deva, just a couple of days ride from where she stood. There was absolutely no question that it would be an impenetrable base to launch attacks from, just as the Silures to the south had suffered and she knew exactly what the men of the legion would do if they were allowed an unopposed march back to the sacred isle. Her whole body twisted with disgust as she imagined the glee of five thousand identically uniformed murderers and rapists putting a final end to the devastation they'd wreaked a generation before. It was a fate wrought on peoples who dared to stand against Rome.

And yet, for a reason she'd not yet fathomed, the king remained stubbornly blind to it, insisting Rome's plan was to target the Brigantes to the north.

To stand any chance of survival, someone had to raise an army to form some kind of defence and so she and Maidoc had broken the sacred blood-oath of honouring the king above all else. Displeasing the gods to try and save the tribe was a risk they'd decided was worth it... but with Maidoc dead in such a way, the gods had seen otherwise.

Knees so weak she had to hold onto her spear for support, she wondered if they were about to kill her as well. And how? As quick as a blast of lightning? Or as quiet as a stilling of the heart? Or maybe from dark shadows, Arawn, god of the Otherworld, he who lurks in the shadows as a child coughs, he who stalks every battlefield as eager as the crows come to feast, would reach out and pull her into the folds of his thick cloak.

From beside the king, the appropriate position for her high standing of counsellor and healer, she turned to the man who would rather rot of old age on the throne than bring his people together for a chance to defend it. In the hand that had gripped the edge of the ancient seat much more than it had ever done a hammer shaft or sword hilt, Bleddyn held a burning torch. In the brief lulls of the blustery wind, it flared bright enough to show the white beginning to streak his long moustache. Brei was close enough to see the long years that had written themselves into the lines around his rheumy eyes.

His chest shook again. No sob for the loss of the nephew he'd called heir, though. As the clan's healer, Brei knew whatever was causing the bleeding in his lungs would soon drag him down to the Otherworld. During her ten long years of instruction in the Laws and Ways from the druids on Mona, she'd never seen a person recover from such an ailment. She wasn't expecting him to be the first.

With his hunched shoulders and pallid features, she wondered who else suspected how ill he was. Whether he led men to face a legion or not, this would be the last summer he'd see. The moment a couple of hot-headed men decided the throne was within reach and took up arms against each other, would be the moment the tribe had already lost everything to Rome.

In the stand of trees down by the stream, an owl gave a plaintive cry, and a cold gust wrapped around Brei's legs. It whipped the end of Bleddyn's thick cloak and caught the loose strands of his hair. Thankfully, he seemed to take it as a breath of the gods' mounting displeasure and finally bent over to hold the torch to the kindling. But not without a snarl... and Brei's relief quickly turned to concern that the gods had noticed such a show of contempt. It was their blessing the tribe sorely needed, not their wrath.

With the first flames, sparks from the damp wood shot up towards the silver wheel of stars, and smoke began billowing into the faces of those down wind she caught the scent of sage. Heulwen, already adept in the knowledge of herbs and their uses, despite her young age, had spent the afternoon stuffing thick sprigs into the gaps.

A few places to the side in the crowded circle, she saw Gavo, the chief of White Walls, the stone-ringed fort on the eastern edge of their land. He had come to plead for more men to secure the border against ever more confident raiders and had inadvertently found himself attending a funeral. With as many white hairs in his moustache as ginger these days, his round face was set into an expression as stern as those carved on trunks of the sacred oak groves. Gavo had been blood brother to Gwain, the former king and the husband she missed now more than ever, and she trusted him more than any other man alive.

He caught her eye and dipped his head in a knowing nod. So much she had to say, to ask, but these moments were Maidoc's. The last before he'd be no more than a memory, a name in songs that would never sing the story that should have been.

One of the most invaluable lessons she'd learned from the druids was reading the secrets in people's faces. Men could lie with their words, sometimes even with the gods invoked, but if you knew what to look for, an unguarded expression could tell what thoughts someone had on their mind even better than words. In Gavo's tightly clenched jaw, she saw contempt, and in the brow, which was as furrowed as a field in spring, there was grave concern. His hillfort, White Walls, was close to Deva. In the flames, she supposed he was imagining long lines of Roman legionaries marching up the valley.

Brei looked through the crowd again for the one man left in the world who could bring a big enough army of warriors together to stop that. But as soon as Maidoc's younger brother Helig had learned of his death he'd saddled his horse charged out of the gates. He still hadn't returned. Now the survival of all she loved depended on a man too weak to watch his brother's body burn.

She was glad for the one grace that at least no one else at the pyre could read the helplessness on her face.

The wind changed and the pyre's heat was enough to flush her cheeks, but she forced herself to stand firm. The gods had seen fit to give Maidoc an honourless death in his sleep, like a sickly baby or a weak old man, and she wouldn't add to the shame by taking a step away.

Once the fire had taken a proper hold, licking up towards the shroud-wrapped body, the carnyx blowers raised the ornately sculpted horse heads up against the night sky. The flames reflected off their polished bronze faces, making it seem as though they were living creatures. It was a beautiful sight, but the moment she had been quietly dreading had come.

The men filled their chests with the crisp night air and with a nod from Bleddyn the shrieking sounds ripped through the night's sombre silence. Every hair on her body pricked up, and from the top of her head, a shiver of fear and awe surged all the way up her spine. She'd heard the otherworldly, blood-curdling cries many times in battle, as fighting men had raced headlong toward enemy fighters. But even just calling out for the attention of the gods as Maidoc's spirit rose to them, it seemed the noise was enough to tear open the sky.

One by one, like the first drops of rain before a heavy storm, the warriors in the crowd began beating the shafts of their hefty hammers and sword hilts against their shields and the crescendo soon grew to a thunderous roar.

With her spear, the polished metal tip higher than her head, palm sweating so much it was hard to grasp the wooden shaft, Brei joined them by beating it against her shield. Heulwen shied away and pressed into her hip again, trying to muffle the sounds by burying her face in the folds of Brei's shawl.

Together with the eerie cries and screeches of the carnyx, every god must have turned from whatever held their attention to look down on them. From Taranis, he of rumbling thunder, to Blodeuwedd, found in the delicate meadow flowers. And so, as they took the spirit of the man she'd been conspiring against the king with, Brei stood under their awakened gaze. Despite the fierce heat of the fire, the fear was cold enough to make her shiver.

The cloth-wrapped bundle of straw above Maidoc's shoulders, in place of his head, which would be mounted above the hillfort gate, caught and flared up in a bright flash. Soon the dead flesh began to hiss. Brei wouldn't turn her face away but let her gaze lose focus until all she saw was the dance of blurry flames burning the future away. In them, she looked for a sign or message, even though the Twentieth Legion had cut short her druidic training long before she'd had a chance to learn such skills. Besides, it was the flames themselves that were the message.

And yet she still lived. Spared by the gods. For now, at least.

It felt like an age before the centre of the wooden platform gave way, but finally the logs collapsed, and, in a huge fountain of sparks, Maidoc's spirit was freed from its earthly bonds. He was gone, the ceremony was over... and Brei hadn't been cast down by a displeased god. The relief felt as though she hadn't taken a breath in a hundred heartbeats. She lived, so could still fight, as Ordo-wik warriors often said to each other.

Bleddyn didn't allow her to relax for long though. "To the Great House!" he boomed. "A king needs an heir!" He turned around so fast he had to push his way through his men.

Brei almost wept aloud. For the death of an heir to the Oak Throne there should have been days of mourning, long nights to feast and drink and to tell tales of his heroic deeds. Days in which she could try and work out a way to stop men fighting each other and letting the legion simply march back unopposed through Ordo-wik lands to Mona.

It was with a genuine reluctance that she followed in the king's wake up the gentle hill back towards the fort. Heulwen, now tired and sullen, tripped from dragging her feet in the sheep-cropped grass. Brei almost did the same. Not from tiredness, but from an all-consuming sense of dread.

"The wolves are getting hungry," Gavo said over her shoulder, and she turned to see her haggard-looking friend. He smiled at the shock on her face. "Seems I am not the only one with the magic eye to peer into the souls of men."

"Henny, run and get the hearth fire lit again," Brei said, pushing on the little girl's back with a little encouraging pressure.

"But I want to walk with you," she moaned.

"I can say please, or..."

"Or?" the young teryn challenged.

"Or I can tell your father about such behaviour. And I don't think the king is in a mood to listen to such a surly little girl."

"Can I carry your shield?"

Brei let the young girl unstrap it from her arm and tried not to laugh as she watched her run clumsily with it up the hill.

As she disappeared into the darkness ahead, Gavo chuckled. "The daughter of a king acting like the daughter of a king. At least some things are as they should be."

"A pity nothing else is," Brei said but looked nervously around to make sure no one was close enough to overhear. In the clatter of weapons swinging on belts and dozens of feet trudging up the soggy path, she judged it safe enough to talk.

"That's a truth," Gavo sighed. "But my sad old heart worries that Maidoc might not be the worst news of today."

"Oh?" she gasped, not sure if she was ready to hear how much worse things had become.

"News from a trader who braved the valley up from Cornovii lands. The new governor of Britannia to replace the bastard Frontinus, won't be stopping in Londinium..."

"He's going straight to Deva?"

"Aye," he growled.

With the sheer size of the fortress the Romans were building just over the eastern hills, they'd feared it was going to be the empire's main base in the lands already lost to Rome. But hearing that the new governor would have his command so close to Dinorwig felt like a kick with a hobnailed boot to the guts.

Gavo spat to the side. "We made the mistake of giving them no fight in the Black Year, so they think that expanding their empire over our land will be easy glory for their emperor. My bones tell me they'll go straight back to Mona to finish killing the druids they didn't manage to last time. If I'm right, it means we're sitting, scratching our arses, right in the middle of the legion's path."

The frustration at having a king who refused to see what threat was being amassed right at the border of his land came out in a loud sigh. "What can we do?"

Gavo scratched his chin. "If we're to have any chance against them at all, we have to find out what their route will be and when they will leave their fortress. Enough of us together and we can harry the legion while it's on the move, attack their supply wagons, stop them from building one of their marching forts to hide inside of. Or, if the gods will see fit to help us, even catch them in the forest like Boudica did with the Ninth Hispana."

"Boudica." Brei spoke the name of the warrior queen's name with the respect it deserved and imagined what a thrill it must have been to bask in the heat of burning

Roman settlements, an inferno she'd ignited herself. A fiery vengeance for all the blood the Romans had spilled and all the land they'd taken. But the story of Boudica's last day, against the same Twentieth Legion that had raced away from Mona to face her just a few days earlier, had been told around hearth and festival fires for half her life. It was not a happy tale. "How will it be different this time?" she asked, hoping for an answer she could find some strength in.

"Because it *has* to be," Gavo said. "We are the last now. If we lose the next fight, there will be no one left in the land to speak the names of our ancestors. But if we end up facing a line of Roman shields across a meadow..."

He didn't need to say more. No tribesman stood against a testudo formation and lived to tell their children about it.

"Maidoc was almost the answer," Gavo said sadly. In his voice, Brei could hear the same disbelief that the gods had taken him she felt. "A son of Gwain the Great wanting to defend our lands, people would have followed him before they stood behind their king and we'd have scouts at every pass."

"Would have." Reminded of what Maidoc's loss meant, she struggled to hold back the yawning sense of hopelessness. Born to former wives who'd called him husband years before she had, none of Gwain's boys had called her mother, but Maidoc's burning pained her as though it was the body of her own child they'd turned to ash.

"And how far are we from getting an army ready?" he growled. "Instead of just a few poorly trained lads who've never even seen a Roman."

Brei turned to take a last look at the burning pyre. Through tear-blurred eyes, it was just an island of bright light in a sea of darkness. "A lot further than a day ago."

Gavo spat again and with more iron in his voice said, "I will not die sitting on my hands waiting for a Roman to put a collar around my throat. Bleddyn can pretend the empire will just somehow decide to leave us alone, but I will meet the gods with a hammer in my hands. They have seen my blood when I made that promise." He held his hand up but it was too dark to see the scars on his palm from the blood-oaths he'd made.

"I have heard similar words from many men," Brei said, but didn't add that there were far from enough of them.

Up ahead, she heard Bleddyn curse and grumble. When her brother, Tegin the Druid arrived, she hoped to give the king a few more thoughts to contemplate; his death being one of them.

They rounded the outer wall and followed the curving path between the two high earthen banks of the fort. A welcome shelter from the wind for those who lived inside. A killing ground for any who wished them harm.

Gavo tilted his hammer in the direction of Bleddyn's back and sighed. "Before we can defend our land and lives against Rome, first we have to fight against our own king. Who cast such a strange and ill fate for us, huh?"

Brei had to hold onto her spear shaft to stop from stumbling. "The gods..." she hissed in warning. "So close to the pyre!"

Unconcerned, Gavo scoffed, "One thing I've learned as chief of a clan is that it's better to fear the ways of men more than those of the gods." In a hushed tone, he added, "But as you have mentioned them, the gods are another thought of mine. A troubling one, and certainly not one a man would usually dare claim."

"You can speak it to me," she said, although not without apprehension.

"I am just a normal man with no ideas about the happenings of the Otherworld. But Maidoc was for war, wasn't he? So, wouldn't Camulos, god of *war*, be glad of that? Wouldn't he support a man who would spill the blood of enemies for him? Not let a warrior die in his sleep?"

"What are you trying to say?" she asked, questioning if she'd heard him right.

"Maybe I'm going daft in my old age, but I'm starting to wonder if in whatever distant lands they dwell, the new Roman gods have had some battle with our gods... and ours have lost. Maybe that explains how the Romans can build a fortress at Deva, and the outposts that ring our land, with impunity?"

"Gavo..." she seethed. "For much less scandalous words men have taken a walk with druids. One that ended at the wrong end of a garrotting rope!" If it was anyone other than Gavo speaking, she'd have been tempted to relieve them of their tongue herself. But to such unexpected words, all she managed to answer was, "That's... a question for an Elder."

"Well, we have the Elder Branogwic standing above the gate of White Walls night and day in all weather, putting the fear of magic into the hearts of those thinking about raiding our fort. How she does that with arms and legs as thin as sticks, I have no idea. But I thought there might be slightly less chance of getting my brains smashed out with a staff if I spoke to you."

"You're talking about one of the most powerful and revered people in the whole land!" Brei seethed.

"Just an old man's thoughts," he chuckled, but his laugh did nothing to dispel the weight of his words. "You are much more qualified for such contemplations than I, to know whether it warrants merit, or not. But it seems we had better hope Helig makes it back soon. He is a son of Gwain, so perhaps not all is lost. Unless the gods have taken him too... Which is another thought..."

"I think you've had enough thoughts for one night!" Brei said in a harsh whisper.

"If it wasn't the gods that took Maidoc... who, in our realm of flesh and blood, stands to gain the most if he is not the heir to a dying king?"

"You think Helig killed his brother? That's more unbelievable that saying the gods have lost the realms of the Otherworld!"

"Not Helig! What if *both* of them are dead? Who would be next to the throne?"

"Derog?" she almost laughed.

"The last of Gwain's loins. It's always been thought there was something less about him than normal men. I've often heard him called a runt, but in White Walls, we know him as Half Seed. If he's got a sniff of the throne, what would a man like him, who couldn't win a sword fight against a boy, have to do to get it?"

"Poison his brothers?" Brei spoke the words but couldn't believe them.

"Would you put it past him?"

Again, she had no idea what to say.

"And despite how much Bleddyn just wants to sit on the Oak Throne... he might not be there for too long..."

"What do you mean?" she asked guardedly, as something in her chest constricted.

"The years by themselves are enough to take a man to his pyre, but often there are... circumstances that help him get there."

"What are you trying to suggest?" she asked, unsure if she was ready to hear him say anything else.

"Bleddyn is dying, isn't he?"

She walked a few more slow steps around the curving path on weak legs, but there was no use in denying it. "He is."

"And if I can see it, then others can too..." His sigh was so long it seemed she heard the last of the hope leave him. "A glorious death in a battle in his prime, strength intact, and no one would question his choice of successor. But getting a little weaker every day, it won't be long before a young hot-head comes in for the kill. For the glory of sitting on the throne, gods be damned, half of the men of the tribe will fight to the death for it."

In one sense, Brei was reassured to know she wasn't alone in her fears. But on the other, that someone else could understand so well what she had believed was a secret was a little disconcerting. "That can't happen," she said. "Whoever calls himself king after we've fought between ourselves, will end up ruling over nothing more than a pile of bodies bristling with Roman spears."

"You can fight men, but you can't fight men's nature," Gavo mused. "We may be noble, and the only creatures in nature to know the gods by their names. But call ourselves chiefs and kings all we like, we're still animals."

As chief of a fort on the border, he must have seen more of what horrors men are capable of than most. Brei wondered if that's how he could speak with as much wisdom as a druid.

"So, a Roman legion, our king, the gods, and Gwain's last son... anyone else we need to fight, or is that it?" He laughed, but they both knew there was a terrible truth to his words.

The path curved around the other side, where they turned the tight corner to face the skull-adorned gate. In the light from the torches, Brei saw the space Maidoc's would be set in once the carrion crows had pecked it clean. Next to Gwain's. The dozens of fallen warriors from generations past that protected the fort usually gave her comfort, but tonight it seemed there were more of the dead mounted on the gate than there were living behind it. As she passed under, she knew that to stand against what was coming they'd need more than bones and spirits.

Inside the circular inner wall, a dozen large roundhouses huddled together, high peaks of their thatched roofs pointing up at the night sky. She was greeted by the familiar aromas of wood smoke and animals, the smell of safety, and the knowledge that loved ones were near.

"I'll put Heulwen to bed and join you in the king's house in a moment," she said.

"I will save you a horn of mead," Gavo smiled.

In the soft light of the sentry torches, she watched him walk away, a slight limp she hadn't noticed before, and wondered what to do with the words he'd given her. The Otherworld, full of victorious foreign gods, was not a thought she was ready to contemplate. Neither was Derog killing his brothers for a chance at the Oak Throne.

THREE

CADWAL JOLTED AWAKE. Heart painfully strained, his whole body was covered in a sheen of sweat. The bed creaked as he pushed himself up. In the dark, he felt for Arwel's small head and the rustle of straw in the mattress as his youngest stirred, gave great comfort.

But something was wrong, much more than just a bad dream.

With a sickening wave of panic, he realised he'd fallen asleep instead of going back to guard duty. But it wasn't the prospect of what the teryn would mete out to his back that was causing the deep unease. With a primal instinct any father knows when something threatens his children, he rolled into a crouching position, heart hammering as though the war horn had been blown next to his ear. He reached for the sword from beside the bed and, with a soft hiss, like that of a lover's sigh, freed the long blade from its scabbard. But even with it in his hand, he had no idea who to wield it against.

Willing his heart to slow down, he tried to listen over the assorted snores of his blind drunk clans folk asleep on the floor, but for all the noises they made, he might as well have been in a pigsty at feeding time.

He felt groggy, as though it was the morning after he'd drunk a full bucket of ale. He remembered taking a few sips from Tamm's horn. Remembered the strange taste.

He ruffled Owyn awake. Moaning in protest, he tried to roll over but, feeling the hard handle of the dagger against his chest, he sat up with a start.

"Stay here and look after your brother," Cadwal said in a harsh whisper.

"What's happening, Da?" he asked, voice tight with bewildered fear.

"I don't know. I am going to look. Stay here until I come back." And then he added, "If any of the newcomers come close, kill them."

"Me? But..."

He shushed his son quiet and said, sternly, "Stay here and look after Arwel."

In the central hearth, the last of the embers glowed faintly under the cauldron but didn't give enough light to see. Creeping carefully to the door, he pulled the skin to the side, unsure what threat waited in the dark. There was only fresh air and absolute silence, but the strange silence was just like the moment a breath has been drawn in and the scream is about to come.

He found the foot of the nearest person and shook it, but there was no response. He shook harder. Still nothing. Feeling his way up the prone body to a hairy face, he slapped it hard. Whoever it was stayed steadfastly asleep. He did the same to the other men, but no matter how much he shook, punched, slapped, or even kicked, the best reaction he could elicit was a sluggish groan.

Whatever was wrong, he suspected the newcomers were behind it, but *magic*? A sick shudder of disgust coursed through him.

Alone, he slipped outside and shivered at the cool air on his clammy skin. The ancestors, the silver band of the warrior horde, were visible in the sky, marching down in a great arc toward the western ramparts. He held the sword up so the hundred generations that had come before reflected on its polished iron surface to help guide it to the heart of the enemy.

He needed the whole clan to be awake, and magic or not, no Ordo-wik could possibly sleep through a long blast of the war horn. It was with Nye on the wall, so he started to run... but slowed when he saw that the torches above the gate were out. They were supposed to burn through the night to illuminate the ground in front.

His first step up to the rampart creaked loudly, which should have alerted whoever was on duty to call down a warning. At the top, the cold wind blew from the valley, catching his hair and moustache. He took a few cautious steps but fell over the slumped form of the guard. With a bare foot, Cadwal nudged him, but he seemed as spellbound as the others. He knelt down and began slapping the man's face, and almost cried out when his fingers slipped into the deep gash across his throat. Nye was dead.

Suddenly it wasn't a lashing for abandoning his post he was in fear of, it was his life.

With a coldness in his heart, bleaker than any mid-winter gale, he fumbled around for the horn, but couldn't find it anywhere.

Frustrated, he tried to calm down enough to think. There'd been no fight at the gate, so the fighting was on the inside. It could only be the newcomers. He'd been right, they really were Dogs. And they were in control of the fort.

And he'd left the boys alone.

Stifling a scream, he prowled back towards the house almost on tiptoe, willing every step to silence. Gripping the sword in both hands, he was ready to swing it in any direction at an enemy it was too dark to see.

But he wasn't alone in the space between the houses.

Whoever it was running up behind him wasn't as quiet as they thought they were. Either over-confident or untrained. It didn't matter which, their carelessness was about to be the death of them.

He slowed a little to let them catch up. Closer, closer. When, from the muted footfalls, he judged they were within reach, he spun around. The muscles in his lower back and shoulders protested in pain at the sudden explosion of movement as he dragged the heavy blade around in a killing arc. It swooshed as it cut through the air and Cadwal braced for the impact... yet it sailed around without connecting, almost pulling him off his feet with the unexpected momentum.

Spirits then, he thought as he staggered for balance, or the gods themselves, and he fought with the terror of not knowing whether to scream or to drop to a reverential knee.

"Da?" the decidedly ungodly voice asked.

In a wave of both relief and blinding panic, he dropped the sword and pulled Owyn to him, patting his body to feel for wounds, knowing full well the blade had come within a hand's width of cleaving his head clean off.

"I told you to stay and look after your brother," he hissed.

"He's sleeping."

"You've left him unprotected!"

"I wanted to help you!"

"I almost *killed* you!"

"Who's there?" a gruff voice asked.

"Da!" Owyn gasped as Cadwal found himself on the ground without knowing how he'd fallen. A strange buzzing sound filled his ears...

At the doorway to Brei's house, Heulwen was stroking the old ginger cat she'd cheekily named Gavo. As Brei gently rubbed behind his scabbed ears, he meowed appreciatively. With arthritic back legs, he wasn't the fierce rat catcher he used to be, but he'd fathered enough hungry kittens to prowl the granaries to earn an assisted retirement.

"Can he sleep with me tonight?" Heulwen asked.

"Don't you already have enough fleas?" Brei smiled.

"Pleeeease?"

"All right. But if he brings a little squeaking and bleeding gift to say thank you for the warm place to sleep, you need to keep it away from me."

"I promise," Heulwen giggled. The cat gave a wheezy meow as she picked him up.

Ducking under the thatch, Brei set her spear in its place by the door. If the horn blew, it would only take one movement to have it battle-ready as she ran out, ready to fight.

"Don't be alarmed," a soft voice spoke from behind one of the big weaving looms and both she and Heulwen screamed. Heulwen cried out again as the cat tore itself out of her arms.

"It's me, Helig."

Heulwen, her fright instantly replaced by excitement, ran to throw her arms around his legs.

Brei breathed out in relief as she put the spear back down again. But like a blacksmith quenching a glowing blade in cold water, the happiness of seeing him alive was quickly extinguished by the anger that he hadn't stood at his brother's pyre.

"Brei, daughter of Kelwyn, counsellor and healer of the tribe. Queen of Gwain the Great..."

"You can spare the formalities," she chided.

He dropped to a knee, a gesture of respect that made it easy for Heulwen to wrap her arms around his neck. "Forgive my intrusion," he said, weaving in and out of Heulwen's furious little kisses. "I have come to beg your counsel."

"You've been gone soooo long," Heulwen complained. "We were all worried about you!"

"Only a day. But I am back now, little cousin."

"But are you staying?"

"I'm not going anywhere," he said in a serious tone.

Brei understood that the statement was directed at her. "Henny, would you go to the well and fetch a bucket of water?" The gods were known to look through the eyes of children. Children also tended to have looser tongues than the adults whose lives depended on the secrets they kept.

"But he's only just come back. He can tell me a story?"

"It wasn't a question," Brei said sternly.

"But it's dark outside," she protested, arms still locked defiantly around Helig's neck.

"You know exactly where the well is!"

For wasting such precious moments when she needed to talk about the very future of the tribe, Brei was close to grabbing the young girl by the scruff of the neck and getting her outside with a boot to the behind, king's daughter or not. Helig though, with loving patience, said, "Pleeease... I am really thirsty."

With a beaming smile, Heulwen picked up a leather bucket, but before she left, Brei held out a hand to stop her. "You cannot tell anyone you saw Helig here. Understand?"

"I know. I'm not *stupid*," she snapped. Chin raised haughtily high, she huffed her way out.

Helig chuckled at the little teryn's behaviour.

"Well, if it's my advice you seek," Brei said, trying to keep her voice calm. "I would have said that riding out when you were needed here was a very bad idea. Do you know how much rests on your shoulders now you're the eldest of Bleddyn's nephews?"

"I'm sorry," he shrugged. "When they woke me up to tell me about Maidoc, it just seemed as though all the walls in the fort were pushing in on me. I couldn't breathe, I just had to get out in the open air."

"You needed some fresh air instead of sending your brother to the gods?" she asked, incredulous.

"It seems like a madness now, but I just couldn't think. I had to ride even though I had no idea where I was going. I can't explain it."

She wondered if he'd been given a lower dose of the poison she suspected had killed Maidoc. From what plant it could have been made from, she had no idea, and that was worrying. No one in the land could use herbs to heal as well as she could, so who could know better than her how to harm?

But it seemed Gavo was right about someone wanting both brothers dead. Maybe he was right about Derog.

As Helig stood back up, proud and very much alive, her fury and worry dispelled a little. Taller than Maidoc but with a much softer face, he had deep and dark eyes so similar to Gwain's, it sometimes felt like the great man was looking at her across the hearth.

"What would you ask me? We don't have much time," Brei said. "Bleddyn just called a gathering to name an heir..."

"Now?" Helig gasped. "In the middle of the night? With the pyre still burning? Couldn't he at least have waited for Maidoc's ashes to scatter to the winds?"

"I know," she sighed. "But as an omen, his heir dying on the day of the turning season couldn't be any worse, so he needs a new one as soon as he can. And a strong one that no one will contest."

It was Helig's turn to sigh in dejection. "And that will be me? Taking Maidoc's place on the same day he was sent to the Otherworld."

"Many men would be more than honoured to have such a position bestowed on them."

"Not those who would spit at his feet when he says he will not offer any defence towards Rome!"

With such words, the warm relief of knowing Helig was still in the land of the living turned to a chill of dread and Brei leapt towards him to cover his mouth with her hand. "Not in the fort! Not in my house!" She looked around, but with the fire so low, the alcoves around the curving wall were draped in darkness.

"It's just me here, I made sure," Helig assured her. "But you know as well as I do that peace with the Romans starts with tributes, but then they'll take so much grain and cattle to feast their fat faces that half of us won't see it through the winter. After we've destroyed our own weapons for them, they'll take our sons away to fight in far away wars in their name. And then all that's left of us Ordo-wiki will be some half-starved old men ready for the Dogs to pick off, as helpless as though we're lying wounded on a battlefield. And I know the new fortress at Deva means death is coming to all those who oppose Rome, so, I ask this of the counsellor of the king, am I wrong?"

Brei wished his words were an exaggeration born of fear, but it was the truth he spoke. All the tribes to the south had succumbed, either by blood or a signature on a parchment, and now the legion was back at their border. "You are not wrong, no. But the ceremony is only just over, so the gods are close. Speaking ill words of a king has been a death sentence for men before."

"The gods," he said, looking up to the rafters. "Camulos, the god of war himself can hear me say that I despise Bleddyn's weakness for not wanting to fight."

Brei's skin prickled at how ominous it was that she'd heard two men say such forbidden words to her in just a few moments.

"So," he continued, "the chiefs and warlords who were ready to fight under Maidoc, will they follow me?"

"I have been wondering the same thing from the moment we found Maidoc dead in his bed," she said, "But I cannot know for sure."

"And I'll lead fighters who'll all be defying their king," Helig sighed. "All terrified they'll be struck down for going against what they believe is the will of the gods. And I would count myself among them."

"The responsibility of betraying a king can weigh heavily on a man," she said through gritted teeth.

"I know."

"Which you should have thought about before laying with the queen..."

Seeing a warrior, not just one trained by Gwain, but sired by him, look so embarrassed was a sight to savour, even through all of her fears.

"I swear by every one of the gods, and on the ashes of my brother's still burning body, and on the head of Heulwen, who doesn't know she's my daughter," he said, putting his hand over his heart. "I will lead the tribe to battle to defend their lives and take your counsel as my own. If the gods want to strike me down for that, then let them do it now."

Brei wondered if maybe the gods had waited for the two of them to be together before striking them from the world of the living. They both looked up nervously towards the pitch-black apex of the roof where the supporting poles came together, but the ceiling of hanging wood smoke a little above their heads remained undisturbed.

"Brei..." said a soft voice from behind her and her heart twisted as though it was a wet cloth being wrung out to dry. Slowly, she turned to look at the cowled figure of Arawn, who was holding out a cold hand to lead her away...

"The king asks for your presence, counsellor," the young messenger said with such formality that in any other circumstance, she would have laughed. "And I am to look for you as well, Helig."

Brei raised her finger and tried to draw a breath into her paralysed chest. "Efan, tell the king I am tending to his daughter and that I will be there in a moment. But I beg you not to mention that you saw Helig with me here."

"But..." he stammered. "I just saw her outside. At the well."

"It's important," she said, but so was keeping his tongue still. The change of persona from healer to threatening druid was like donning a heavy cloak. She even heard how her voice deepened. "You remember I tended to your mother when she was struggling to birth your sister?"

"Yes," he gulped. "You saved her."

"I did. And now I will take my payment."

Eyes wide, Efan looked suitably terrified.

"I am not asking you to lie to the king, just not to speak the whole truth. You do that for me."

"Yes," he said, with a seriousness beyond his years.

He did well not to burst into tears, just as Brei did by not running over to offer him comfort.

"If you don't," Helig added, "your mother dies!"

Brei was about to shout her outrage at him, but the security of knowing Efan would stay silent outweighed the guilt and shame of threatening a child so terribly.

Once the white-faced boy had left, Brei turned back to Helig. "We are on the very edge. If Bleddyn finds out we're plotting against him, we could be trusting our lives to children."

"Is that better than trusting them to the gods?"

She shrugged. The words Gavo had spoken earlier, now gnawing like a tooth at the first sign of an abscess, would need some real consideration. But that was for later.

"So I have to accept the king's offer, with the gods invoked, even though it is the king we need to fight?"

Brei smiled. "It takes more than the right blood and a hammer to become king."

"But what about the gods?" he asked.

"Let me worry about them."

He nodded. "What do you need me to do?"

"Go now, offer Bleddyn your finest words and I'll follow in a little while, so no one will know you came to me before the king."

Out in the clear and cool air, Brei stood in the deep darkness under the close hanging thatch between a couple of houses and tried to calm her racing thoughts. Gavo hadn't asked a question he wanted an answer for, he'd only spoken his mind. Yet his words pressed for her attention, like Heulwen in a stroppy mood. But warring gods or not, her fight this night was with men. One man. The king.

Stepping into the light spilling from the door to Bleddyn's house, she paused to pull her shawl open at the throat. To expose the fists of her golden torc, she adjusted the palm-sized gold brooch, all ornate swirling and interlocked knots, at the left shoulder of her shawl. Every little gleam of the sun's metal would count towards the image of authority she needed now more than ever before.

Inside, the smoky air was thick with the smell of unwashed men and ale, but the mood was far from jovial. No one was telling stories of Maidoc's life to the raucous laughter of his heavily drunk clans folk. No one was sloshing mead-filled horns and cups together in toasts for the departed. He hadn't fallen bravely in battle and there were no songs to sing for those who just didn't wake up one morning. In the solemn atmosphere, men talked among themselves in hushed voices and women stood stony-faced. If any listened to Bleddyn, they did so disinterestedly.

"My brother, Gwain, was the bravest man I have ever known," the old bastard slumped on the Oak Throne said. "He swam out from the isle of Mona across the straits with his hammer on his back. And you all know what swirling demons lurk in those waters..."

Telling heroic tales about his long dead brother as if they were his own turned Brei's stomach. Not for the first time in the long years since she'd felt Gwain's huge, calloused hands around her waist, she wished it was still him on the throne, the house still filled with his booming laughter. If Gwain the Great was still here in the land of the living, she was sure he'd be ranging through the land mustering an army to stand behind him anywhere the Romans chose... All through the long years since his death, she'd wondered for what reason the gods had seen fit to let him fall in an unimportant fight and let Bleddyn take the throne. And she wondered again now.

Everyone had heard the story Bleddyn was telling a hundred times, even wildly different versions of it, but with each telling, Gwain's name was kept alive, so she tempered her displeasure.

The long hearth was big enough to spit the largest boar over. At the far end, the coward king sat on his heavy throne carved from the trunk of a single ancient oak. Splayed out at the base, gnarled roots as thick as a strong man's thigh, still reached down into the earth. It was so ancient that the house had been rebuilt over it at least twice, but not even the oldest Elder knew when it had stood as a tree. All up the sides the curving and interlacing knots depicting the infinite cycle of life wound up the frame to the wheel over the king's head, a knot-embossed circle intersected four times by two crossed straight lines. The four segments depicted the four seasons. The uppermost one, high summer, had just been crossed. The day Maidoc had been taken away.

The head of the immense battle hammer named Gordd-ap-Duwia, Hammer of the Gods, rested beside it. How Gwain had swung it, knocking down men like wooden pegs in a children's game, seemed just a distant memory. He'd often joked he could feel its thirst for enemy's blood. If it needed to drink again, it wouldn't have to wait too much longer, but it wouldn't be Bleddyn who would satisfy its wish.

Brei glanced around the glum crowd of about thirty men and a dozen women. Across the hearth stood the stout and stern-faced Dillona from the sea fort of Dinas Dinlle to the west.

Like Gavo, she was here to request men to defend her walls, and equally as important, the salt flats. Now that the Romans had cut off all trade to Ordo-wiki lands with the ring of auxiliary forts to the south and east, her few bags of sun-dried sea salt were vital for preserving meat and making leather. With Maidoc gone, she too would probably be left without help. Her sad eyes showed despair.

But then she caught the sly smile on the face of Derog, Maidoc and Helig's youngest brother. It only flashed from the upturned corners of his mouth to his eyes for a heartbeat, but in it, she read a sense of real satisfaction. In such a mournful moment, it was so out of place she knew to keep watching, so slipped behind the backs of a couple of men to spy without being noticed. He spoke close to the ear of a friend, who sniggered, then cast another glance at the troubled king. The sickly thrill of being a step closer to power wrote itself clearly on the tongue touching his upper lip, as easy to read as the clouds of a storm gathering over the mountains.

She wondered if Gavo could be right and Half-Seed did have something to do with Maidoc's death. She frantically searched her memory for every detail of what she'd seen at Maidoc's bed. There had been no obvious signs of poisoning, no blue lips or frothing at the mouth, and no one who slept near him had mentioned any convulsions. So, if Derog had slipped some poison into his brother's drink, she couldn't guess what concoction it could have been. Or perhaps even more importantly, where he could have got it from.

If Derog was capable of such an abhorrent act, there now stood only one man between him and the oak throne. The tiny expressions on his face, that only she could see, screamed to her that Helig was in danger.

Bleddyn banged his empty wooden cup on the arm of the throne and the din of dozens of voices, as subdued as they were, began to quieten. "Helig ap Gwain, son of my brother, you have come back to us at last! And not a moment too soon," he beamed, the last of his drink running off his shaven chin. "A good omen in this dark night. The eldest bearer of my family's blood, come to me."

Silence fell on the crowd and as Brei expected, a tell-tale scowl of disappointment fell across Derog's face.

Helig had been listening from the far end of the hearth, and when he walked, his head almost touched the wispy layer of smoke hanging under the roof. The others shuffled down the bench that lined the edge of the fire to let him take the seat to Bleddyn's right.

"The gods know I would have had it another way, that Maidoc was my chosen heir. But their will is ever a mystery to us mortal men." He tried to move Gordd-ap-Duwia over so it stood on its shaft between them, but struggled with the weight of it. "It is known that you don't agree with me on some things, even though I am your king. But I am old enough to know that wisdom comes with age, so if you accept my ways, if you will stand proud as guardian of my legacy, I will name you heir."

As she listened to him speak, Brei was so certain of his impending passing that it seemed as though his voice was echoing off the walls of the Otherworld.

Helig slowly nodded his head. "It is a great and weighty honour you extend to me, my king, and brother of my father," he said, but then no more words came. In the quickly widening silence, Bleddyn sat up straighter and a few men shared worried glances.

Helig took a long swig of ale from his horn and slowly wiped the foam off his moustaches.

"Well?" Bleddyn demanded. "Do you care to offer any reply for such an honour? Or do the gods have your tongue?"

"The gods..." Helig started. "The ways of the gods of which you speak... Maidoc believed in your ways, did he not?"

"Yes, of course he did!" he snapped impatiently. "What of it?"

"Maidoc gave you honour and swore to uphold your legacy."

"Yes! Right here. From the very seat in which you sit."

"And while he slept in his bed, the gods took him to the Otherworld."

The collective gasps from the crowd were like Gordd-ap-Duwia had been slammed into the chests of everyone present.

"On the day of the turning of the seasons," Helig continued. "Just a soft last breath in the middle of the night that no one heard. My concern is that if I give you my word, who is to say that the gods will not come to take *me* in *my* sleep?"

Another wave of murmur washed through those watching. Derog looked confused, but it was Bleddyn's face Brei watched now. Not so much the expression, but the shade of red it had turned.

"What are you saying?" Bleddyn growled.

"My king. Forgive me for putting words to it, but the omen could not be any clearer."

"Be very careful, nephew of mine," Bleddyn growled like a dog warning it was about to bite. "I can give you this throne, or... I have the power to banish you to wander the lands without clan or name."

Brei turned to Derog again and was unsurprised to see the look of absolute glee spreading from ear to ear. He knew how close he was to sitting his bony arse on the throne. But then he looked around, and as soon as he caught her eye, his expression turned instantly ice cold. To Brei, his guilt rang out as clear as a cry of the carnyx... and so she had an enemy in a man she'd known since he was a baby mewling in his own soil.

"The Romans have almost finished building their fortress at Deva..." Helig continued.

"Just consolidating their lands in the plains, far from our land," Bleddyn snapped impatiently. "It's long been known that the Romans have no need for anything this side of the mountains. The Dogs gave them the copper mines on the coast and so they have all they need."

Brei had to bite her tongue to stop from crying out in frustration. He was talking about the Romans and Dogs as though they were a neighbour grazing his sheep on the next pasture.

"Maybe so," Helig said. "In which case, if they stay in the east and offer us no threat, I will agree to be your heir and honour your legacy."

Brei almost applauded at how he'd managed to twist the king's will to announce to all who stood listening he was for mustering an army to stand and fight the coming threat. He was more competent at the dirty and dangerous game of politics than she'd given him credit for, and she saw that a few other men understood how brave he'd been.

The king cleared his throat and her attention swung back to him. He put a hand to his mouth and, as he made an effort not to cough again, she watched as his face flushed to an even deeper hue. If he allowed himself another, he wouldn't be able to stop until he was spitting up blood and gasping for air, begging for her herbs.

As she willed it to happen, she imagined that the blood building up in his chest would feel like drowning, just as someone spluttering for breath in a river. She was impressed at the sheer strength he had not to show his weakness.

Helig had put him in a difficult position. Apart from fighting for breath, if his nephew declined to be his heir, he would look untenably weak. "Only if the Romans are the aggressors?" Bleddyn croaked. "Only if they seek to take our lands?"

"Only. If they stay out of our mountains, I agree."

"Agreed," Bleddyn forced a smile and rapped his tankard on the arm of the throne three times, and in the cheer that followed, Brei squeezed Gavo's arm. He leaned over so she could speak close to his ear.

"He's for war."

"Seems a clever boy," the chief smiled.

Helig was more than just clever. Not only had he become heir, he'd done it while proclaiming his stance to all those who wanted Roman blood on their swords and hammers. For the first time since they'd found Maidoc's body, she felt something she recognised as hope.

FOUR

THE PAIN WAS so intense it took a while to come properly into focus. From the stabbing throb in the back of his head, he wondered if he'd been kicked by a horse or had fallen off the rampart. His limbs felt so heavy that for a moment he panicked he'd been dumped in a peat bog as a sacrifice. He opened his eyes and what he saw wasn't any worse than being a victim of the threefold death. The prone bodies of the Clan of Crows were strewn on the ground and he saw his old nightmare of waking up on the battlefield with everyone else dead.

He tried to get to his feet, but something around his neck hindered him. Instinctively, he tried to pull whatever it was off, but it was locked on tight, almost as if someone had fastened it there. It felt like a metal band.

He couldn't understand.

"Gwen!" he called out.

"Quiet!" someone shouted, and the accompanying kick to the back of his leg was hard enough to remind him of all the harsh training lessons at Gwain's feet when his body refused to do what he wanted.

He rolled over to get his hands under him but was stopped from pushing himself up by the gleaming point of a spear at his throat. He looked right past it though, because the real horror was behind. He was on the even ground at the bottom of the steep slope under the fort where traders came with their wares and supplies were transferred from carts to backs, to be lugged up the hill. But instead of a wagon full of goods, he lay next to one made with a sturdy frame of bars. In it were the unconscious bodies of everyone he knew and loved. Some were naked, some barely clothed, but with no blood or injuries on them. It looked like they hadn't fought at all, as though they'd just been pulled from their beds and thrown inside while they were still asleep.

A chain clinked nearby, and he turned his spinning head to see Drust with a collar locked under his wispy white moustache. It was attached to a chain coiling from out of the back of the wagon. A pair of naked-faced men picked him up and bundled his small body into the back.

"That's the last of the miserable bastards," someone announced.

Cadwal recognised the voice as one of the newcomers', and a sickening realisation dawned through the fog of pain and confusion. They'd been inside all along, just as he'd feared. Just as he'd tried to warn. The fort of Crow Hill was lost.

The crushing sense of dread felt like a druid had split open his belly to read the omens in his entrails. But another thought hit him even harder. *The boys.* Owyn had been out with him. He wouldn't have survived such a hard crack to the skull.

He tried to get up to call out their names but a kick to the chest knocked him back to the ground again.

"What about this one?" the man standing over him asked.

"The bastard almost knifed me last night," Dax spat.

"He can walk!" whoever was in charge replied.

"Let's go!" someone called out, and with a cry, the horses were whipped into motion. The wheels of the wagon creaked as it moved forward.

Cadwal only had a moment between looking at the short chain uncoiling and realising that it led right to the collar locked around his neck. There was no time to react, and with a pain that was blinding in its intensity, it snapped tautly and dragged him along in the dirt. Choking and gasping for breath, he kicked at the ground and rolled over, desperately trying to get to his feet. When he managed to scramble up, a ring of fire around his throat, it was to the sounds of the Dogs laughing.

He limped to the back of the wagon, put an arm through the bars, and desperately slapped heads and faces. "Wake up. Wake up!" he cried, but slumped on top of each other, arms and legs sticking out between the bars, they only moved with the motion of the wagon. "Owyn!" he cried out. "Arwel!" But there was no reply.

Still struggling for breath, he called out at the nearest Dog. "Where are my boys? What did you do to my sons!?"

"Who knows?" one of them smirked.

"Fight me, you godless cowards!" he shouted and began clawing at the collar, trying to force it open with his bare fingers.

"We *did* fight you!" one of the others replied, his wide smile turning into a full laugh. "You just didn't notice!"

Full of fury, Cadwal leapt towards him, but like a guard dog on a short tether, he only managed a few steps before the chain pulled tight. Again, he was jerked helplessly towards the gate. The Dogs had turned their backs and paid him no attention.

He tried swinging the chain around to yank it free from whatever it was attached to, but even as he did, he knew it was useless. The wagon's pull was relentless and digging his heels into the earth did nothing at all to slow it down.

And then he saw them. Bound in rough rope, Owyn and Arwel knelt in a line of similarly restrained women and children. A few of the younger ones were screaming hysterically, and the sound was almost enough to shatter Cadwal's heart. Arwel looked confused and was quiet, but Owyn, with a cut lip, was shouting.

Over the noise the others were making, he couldn't hear but saw how his eldest's mouth worked around the words, "I'm sorry."

Cadwal was about to call back that it wasn't his fault, but the chain yanked him off his feet. When he'd managed to catch his breath, he cried, "My boys! I will come for you!" He had no idea if they could hear him or not.

He didn't know for how long he shouted, but when he stopped, his throat hurt and they were so deep in the morning mist that he couldn't see the fort.

High up in the heather, above the pastureland where the sheep grazed and the last of the trees, Cadwal turned to look back at his home. The hump-backed Crow Hill, ringed with ditches and wooden walls, was an island over the soft morning mist still filling the valley. He'd hoped to see the houses burning, but the undamaged pointy thatch roofs looked as they did on any normal morning. No alarm of rising smoke meant no band of warrior brothers would be chasing them up the track to free them. And it was too late now anyway. As they turned to climb up the valley, sunlight catching the top of the scree cliffs he'd explored as a boy, they were already in Dog territory.

The most immediate concern, apart from falling and not being able to get up again, was water. The pain at the back of his head from where they'd knocked him out had radiated down his neck and into his teeth, and the sound of the wagon's wheels clattering along the track seemed loud enough to split his head open.

Tamm was the first to come awake. Slowly, he swept his shaggy red hair from his eyes and shook his head as if to clear the nauseating sensation of movement. He found the chain that led up to the collar on his neck and spent a while pulling at it. It was when he saw Cadwal, that Tamm realised this wasn't a drunken dream. It was very real. His shoulders sagged as he said, "Horse shit. I guess you were right after all!"

Cadwal shrugged.

"Aye, you told us. None of us listened."

As much as he could move with the chains restraining him Tamm searched through the bodies. "Where are the women and children?" he asked.

"Lined up, tied together, back in the fort," Cadwal replied.

Tamm's cry to the gods brought tears welling up in Cadwals's eyes and he stubbed some toes on a few rocks in the road.

"What did they do? Poison us?" his brother asked.

"I think so."

"On Alban Hefin!" he spat. "The ale was too strong. I remember telling you that."

Cadwal remembered the people he'd seen sleeping on the ground before the sacrifice. He'd watched the Dogs' attack happening in front of him... and hadn't suspected a thing.

Tamm set to work trying to wake the others, slapping faces so hard it made Cadwal wince. But one by one, cousins, friends, and clansmen came around. Fighting the chains in panic, as though they were snakes they'd found in their beds, cursing the Dogs for the bastards they were, their reactions were mostly the same. And equally futile. A few tried to formulate plans of escape. A couple didn't wake up at all.

The chain that linked each man to his neighbour's iron collar was attached to a thick ring set in the middle of the wagon, but even with the hands of four men straining at it, it wouldn't budge.

"I think it might be as bad as it looks," Tamm finally admitted.

Kenion, a young sheep herder, wasn't as resigned to his fate as Tamm. He pulled himself as close to the back of the wagon as his chain would allow, and yelled at the pair of riders behind, "You bastards of dogs!" as though he were charging into the midst of a battle. "What fatherless cowards are you? What did you do? Poisoned us to make us sleep? Spineless cowards! *Bastards*! The gods are pissing on you now! *Pissing* on you! Our tribe will see the houses burning and will be coming for your heads and I will piss in your skulls, you scum!"

Gwil tried to calm him down, but to no effect.

"We are the Clan of the Crows. You know why? Because we bring your death to you on the battlefield. The crows feast on your eyes!"

He kept shouting, white spittle running down his chin, as the Dogs rode up. Dax, the heads of the teryn's guards bouncing against the saddle, pulled his horse alongside. With his spear aimed through the bars of the cage, he pushed hard. The tip went straight through Kenion's throat, just under the collar.

"Hey! Don't waste them!" the other shouted, annoyed. "It took us a month to get them all as slaves."

A few moments later, a trail of blood started dripping out of the back of the wagon.

By the afternoon, the trail wound down from the moors towards the great plain, the fertile farming land long lost to the foreign invaders. Cadwal worked out that if he pulled himself up on the back of the wagon, he could rest on his forearms. It would help take some weight off his now agonisingly bruised and bloodied feet.

Drust lay with his head close to the bars, tears glistening in his deep wrinkles.

"What will they do? Send us to a mine somewhere?" he lamented. "Beat our backs until we can't stand any more, then dump our bodies in a ditch for the crows? What god would notice a death like that? And who will there be to remember me? Who will say my name for the gods to hear?"

"What is your name?" Cadwal asked.

Drust looked down with his haunted and empty eyes. "Has your head gone daft? You know my name. I've known you since the day you were born."

"I would have you say it to me."

"What does it matter?"

"If we are still alive, we can still fight."

"Alive, but in chains," he spat and shook his head for emphasis. "That seems more dead than alive to me."

"If a man is remembered and his name is spoken, he is not dead," Cadwal said. "So speak your name."

"My name is Drust," the old man said with the beginning of a smile. "My father was Hywel, Clan of the White Walls. He fell at the battle of Caradog with his hair as white as mine. His father was in the Otherworld before I was born. His name was also Hywel."

"Drust Ap Hywel of Crow Hill," Cadwal said. "I will remember you."

A bitter smile crept across Drust's face. "And how much longer do you think you will live to remember me for, huh?"

"Oh," Cadwal smiled. "Until my beard will be whiter than yours."

Drust chuckled but looked around at the others chained up with him. "Might be that you will be a very lonely old man then."

A little before dark, their captors pulled off the road and stopped at a small, abandoned settlement. In utter exhaustion, Cadwal sank gratefully to the damp grass. With what felt like the very last of his strength, he gathered some handfuls of weeds from under the bushes and tried to clean out the wounds in his feet. If, as he suspected, they were going to Deva, he'd have to do the same distance again the next day. The thought of falling and not being able to get up again, being dragged along the ground as the skin was flayed from his body was almost enough to make him sick with dread.

The Dogs busied themselves setting up a makeshift camp and started a cooking fire.

"You still alive, brother?" Tamm asked. "Did you see which one of these godless bastards has the key to the door?"

Cadwal had been in such a panic about being forced away from his boys, he hadn't noticed.

"Can you find some piece of metal from somewhere to try and force the lock open?"

The chain didn't give much more than a couple of arm's lengths of movement, but he pulled himself under the wagon to see if there was anything useful he could reach. There wasn't.

"A rock, maybe?" Tamm suggested.

"If they hear you bashing they'll stab us in the face like they did Kenion," someone warned.

One of the Dogs dipped a bucket in the stream that ran on the other side of the road and set it down in front of Cadwal. But Dax didn't pronounce it ready to drink from until he'd taken a long piss in it though. It was with a warrior's skill of self-control that none of the prisoners tried to protest, even while his friends howled with laughter. Cadwal dipped his hand in it and took a couple of handfuls, the first and last drink of the day.

Once their captors had eaten, and only after the smell of their food had tormented the captives, a few bread crusts and chicken bones were tossed into the wagon. Starving hungry, several men started grabbing at them until Tamm shouted for them to stop.

"We are not animals," he snapped. "Let's not make our suffering into our enemy's entertainment." He took the bread, asked how many still lived and broke them into roughly equal chunks. Drust passed Cadwal's portion down to him.

Before it was fully dark, another wagon pulled up through the ruined gates of the farmstead. Chains clinked as men got up to call out the names of their wives and children.

Cadwal just about managed to push himself up to his knees, heart pounding with the hope of seeing the boys. There was no one inside. The wagon was full of the Ordo-wiki's personal items like spits from the fires, iron cauldrons and sacks of wheat from plundered grain stores. And what Cadwal thought were bronze shield bosses, but surely not even the Dogs would smash sacred battle antiques of ancestors just to get the metal off them. But, as the wagon trundled past, he saw something that made it feel as though the world had given way beneath his feet and he was falling through the air. Hanging off the back with chords threaded through the empty eye sockets, were the severed heads of the two druids who'd performed the threefold death on the sheep thief. Cadwal would have been less shocked to see the heads of Owyn and Arwel there.

"I told you so!" Drust croaked. "That's how much these bastards care for all that is sacred. If they can do that to druids, then truly it is the end of our days."

Cadwal sat with his back against one of the rear wheels and felt himself shaking. Not from fear or anger, or even shame, just a feeling of utter helplessness. The Dogs were their enemies, just as they had always been, ever since the days before his grandfather when they'd come from over the western sea and taken a third of Ordo-wik land for themselves. The way it had always been was that fights were for the battlefield, where the winners were simply the side with the bravest and god-favoured warriors. That was in the past. Pretending for almost a whole moon to be friends just to sneak in past the fort defences and cutting down druids as though they were trophies of war, really meant that today the world was a different place.

As different as going to sleep a warrior and waking up as a chained slave.

With not even a scrap of cloth to keep the chill off, for most of the night Cadwal huddled under the wagon as much out of the thick drizzle as he could. Listening to the lamentations and curses of his clans folk above and imagining his boys bound and being led away by dogs, his hatred roared as furious and white hot as a metal worker's forge. The memory of Owyn mouthing his apology burned so much he had to fight with himself to not try and drag the wagon back to Crow Hill by his neck. He remembered the last words his sons had heard him shout... and wanted the gods to hear the same oath.

He pinched a bit of skin on his palm between his teeth and bit down until it bled. He felt no pain. He held his hand out and if any god who hadn't cursed him cared to notice, he promised to rain death down on the Dogs and see his sons safe again. But it was no god he saw before him, accepting his blood oath. Thin blue dress hanging over her breasts and hips, Gwen stepped towards him, hand out-stretched. He pressed his bleeding palm against hers.

"It is witnessed," she sighed before he saw the blood pouring down her chest from the gaping wound in her throat.

He awoke with a cry, with no idea how he'd managed to sleep. Dawn was creeping over the eastern horizon and there was movement around the makeshift camp. Like a startled dog, his first instinct was to fight, but chained and unarmed, that would serve no good. Inside, he tempered his raging fury and hatred of the Dogs down to a smoulder and covered it in ash, ready to be ignited when the time came.

He took the edge off his terrible thirst by licking the dew off clumps of grass in the arc the length of chain allowed, making sure that none of the captors could see him acting like a sheep.

Above, all the anger had dissipated from the group, yet with it, so had hope. When one of the Dogs threw some bread in between the bars it was passed silently around from person to person who each took their fair share.

Two parts came down to Cadwal again. "Take mine," Drust said. "I have no need of it."

He didn't argue and wolfed it down.

The wagon creaked as it began to move, and at the sound, he forced himself up. On cut and bruised feet, stomach lurching in fear of the day to come, and how it would end, he stumbled forwards.

Hands grasping at the bars, standing to spare themselves the worst of the wagon's jolting and jarring as it crashed over the uneven rocky track, the men had nothing to say so the morning drew on in desolate silence. Shock, grief, the after-effects of the poisoned ale, and knowing that they were all as a good as dead, weren't topics conducive to either conversation or banter.

Cadwal probably couldn't utter a word even if he'd wanted to. His throat was parched and what was left of his strength had almost left him. He didn't notice when he was pulled into the water. Only half way across the ford he realised why the sound of the clattering wagon wheels had become muted and his lower legs were cold. With a cry of gratitude, he sank to his knees and scooped up a blissful handful. On his cracked lips the muddy water felt like a gift from the gods. But the collar snapped taut and the brief moment of relief was followed by a blindingly painful fight for life as he was dragged along by the chain under the current. A refreshing drink turned into a choking nightmare.

He struggled up, coughing and spluttering, and saw the chain was in Drust's hands as the old man had tried to fish him out. Hands pushed through the wagon bars to help grab him, but he pulled an arm free. So desperate for every drop of water, he ground his teeth on the grit and silt trying to catch the water running down his face.

"That was the last hope," Tamm sighed a little while later.

"Why?" Gwil asked.

"Don't you know what river that was?" No one replied. "That was the *Aerfen*. Aerfen! If the goddess of fate and war has nothing for us, then the crows are already gathering for our bodies."

Cadwal turned to look back at the crossing. Dax and the other Dog had stopped in the river to let their horses drink, a luxury they had denied him. Tamm was right. It was the sacred river which wound through the valley at the foot of Crow Hill. They'd crossed it so they were in the Lost Lands now. If Aerfan had let her warriors wade through as captives then their only hope of survival lay ahead with whatever fate awaited in Deva. As Cadwal struggled to put one foot in front of the other, he knew any mercy from the men of Rome was far too much to hope for.

They came to the huge Roman road that cut through the land like a giant scar. For as long as he'd lived he'd never seen anything so unnaturally straight. It was wide enough for two wagons to pass and was laid with smoothed cobbles rather than loose stones, although with the damage already done to his feet, he could feel no real difference. The wagon didn't buck and jar as much as it did in the mountains, but it went faster. Once he turned to look back and saw his bloody footsteps trailing away behind and imagined a rescue party being able to follow them from all the way back home.

Half delirious from thirst, he didn't pay much attention to the surroundings, but what he did see gave his heart no uplift. His fears about what the Romans would do to the land were heightened by the swathe of devastated nature they rode through. Until recently it had been a thick forest, but everywhere he looked there was nothing left but stumps poking out of a rough carpet of severed branches. With so much wood taken for building material, the size of the fortress they were constructing at Deva grew in his mind until it reached terrifying proportions. But he wasn't sure he was going to get to see it. Every time he stumbled and dropped to his knees, the tops of his feet began to get more scuffed and scratched. And to get up again, he had to fight the savage and almost unbearable pain of the collar dragging him along. One limping step at a time, he managed to keep going, but knew he was getting closer and closer to the point of being slowly flayed alive on the road.

He looked at the scab on the palm of his left hand, where he'd made the cut for his blood-oath, but the promise of seeing the boys safe again wasn't enough to keep him alive. Somehow he had to believe he wasn't going to die today, that he'd find some way of making it back to Ordo-wik lands to save them. Otherwise he could just stop putting one foot in front of the other and get it over with.

It was Dax who saved his life by giving him the impetus to keep walking. "There he goes," the bastard laughed. "I told you he wouldn't make it! You owe me an ale!"

"No, look, he's got some life left in him," his friend chuckled. "You've not won yet!"

With no strength left, it was spite that kept him going.

Eventually, they came to a halt and as soon as the chain stopped pulling him forward, Cadwal collapsed to the ground. It was all he could do to not to pass out. He was sure it was the end now, because if the wagon started again, there was no way he'd be able to get back up.

Through the thick swirling of confused thoughts in his head, he was dimly aware of men talking. As he fought through the odd buzzing noise in his head, he realised it was his brethren spitting out the vilest curses and insults. It sounded like the snarls of cornered animals attempting to scare a predator away. When he forced his eyes open, he saw why. Roman soldiers. Instantly alert, he recoiled in fear and disgust, and tried to shuffle back as much as the chain and his tired muscles would allow.

They wore shirts made entirely of thumb-sized scales of metal as though there were some strange creatures risen from the depths of the sea. Each polished piece dazzled him as it caught the sun. It looked like every soldier wore more iron than was in the whole fort of Crow Hill. And worse, as they strolled purposely around the wagon talking casually to the Dogs, he heard they were speaking the tongue of the land. He listened intently as they discussed making slaves of their own people.

A huge horse was positioned behind the wagon, and with the uniformed guards holding spears at the ready, the door was opened. A Roman soldier reached up and, ignoring the curses, reached in for the end of the chain. This, he hooked to the horse's harness and when it was slapped forwards, the men were dragged out by their necks in a line like livestock, much to the amusement of all who watched. Some were dead, and the living tripped over their dragging limbs as they fought to stay on their feet.

One of the Romans drew his sword. It was much shorter than anything Cadwal was used to wielding and it took a few sickening hacks to sever each head of the men who hadn't woken up. Trenus' head rolled back the way they'd come from. The direction of Crow Hill.

A round faced man, wrapped in a white robe, curiously similar to a druid Elder, but styled differently, walked up to the line looking each man up and down. He knew to stand well out of reach. As he spoke in his twisted language, Cadwal was sure he must be an outrage to the gods.

The soldier translated that the men were worth five hundred denari.

The Dogs suddenly looked nervous.

"Ha!" Tamm laughed. "Five hundred denari? I'm worth twice that on my own!"

Despite their dire situation a couple of the clan laughed.

"I wouldn't take any less than two thousand for us. Plus some extra for the transport and hospitality, of course," he added.

The Roman official looked aghast and, with a nod, ordered one of the soldiers to jab Tamm hard in the stomach with the butt of his spear. With the chain pulled tight between the wagons, he couldn't double over.

"Do you like that?" the soldier asked.

"A bit higher up to wind me properly next time," Tamm said.

"I can turn it around," the soldier said as he aimed the pointed tip at Tamm's chest.

"That's nothing," he smiled.

"No?"

"No. I could turn you *inside* out."

When the Roman got to Cadwal, he waved for him to get up. They could have hit him with spears all they wanted, there was no way he could stand on his bloodied feet and wasted legs. The Roman dared to step close enough to look at the soles of Cadwal's feet and grumbled. Not with any human sympathy, just the same disappointment of finding a sheep had gone lame. He spat a curse or an insult. The translation came back as 'worthless'.

At spear point, Drust was taken out of the chain and made to sit with Cadwal while the others were forced back into the wagon. The Dogs went to mount their horses but the Roman soldiers stopped them. "No native can cross the river," one said.

"Only in chains," the other sniggered.

Tamm laughed. "Seems you're not so different to us! Allies of Rome, my hairy arse!"

"Will you still be laughing when you're in the mines?" one of the Dogs shouted. "Take your last look at the sun today, because you won't live to see its light again!"

"We'll meet again one glorious day, brother!" Tamm called out to Cadwal as the selected men were wheeled away. "There will be much mead and vengeance. The gods will be pleased and our names will be remembered!"

Cadwal managed to raise a hand.

"We shall be heroes! And will die in the sun!" Tamm roared as the wagon was pulled over the bridge.

Waking in the dark and cool, Drust welcomed him back to the world of the living with a ladle of water. The touch of it against his parched lips and swollen tongue felt like a gift from the gods and he gasped in joy and relief. He tried to slake it all down in one gulp.

"I thought you might like it," the old man chuckled. "Seems the Romans are kinder to us than our cousins. I needed water so badly, I would have drunk the Dog's piss straight out of their cocks. I was just sitting on my bony ass in the wagon. I can't imagine how you must have felt."

Cadwal drank another two full ladles before his stomach clenched in protest and he threw it back up.

"Slowly. Drink it slowly," Drust soothed. "That's the way," he encouraged as Cadwal took a single mouthful.

"Where are we?" he gasped.

"I'm too old and you're too broken, they said."

"What?"

"To be slaves. They only want strong men for the mines."

The vaulted roof they were under was part of no mine. "Where are we?" he asked again.

"Where did Gwain threaten to send you if you didn't eat all of your dinner, or if you didn't practice slinging stones enough?"

"The arena?"

"Aye. Not quite as big as I'd imagined, mind, but it's an arena all the same. Maybe we won't have to die in chains, or from thirst, after all. Maybe we can go to the gods fighting in the sun."

A man not deemed worthy to be a slave would not be long for the world. Cadwal drank as much water as he could before his belly protested again, then took some more. "Not today," he said.

Drust held out a bony hand to help the cup to Cadwal's lips. "Come now, you don't think there is any way we're going to get out of here and see our homes again, do you? There's no song I ever heard a bard sing where someone got to walk away after being sold to a Roman."

"I promised my boys I would go back for them," Cadwal said.

Drust sighed. "Better believe they're dead and that you'll be with them soon."

Using some of the water, Cadwal bent his stiff legs and cleaned out the cuts and blisters on his feet as best he could. Then he poured some on the raw chaff the collar had made on his neck.

"Do you think they have lions out there, like in the stories we tell the children?" Drust asked a little absently. "I think I'd like to die fighting a lion. It would be a good story for someone to sing about one day." He chuckled to himself in the near darkness. "Something I can tell my boys when I see them again. Do you know how to fight a lion?"

Cadwal took another mouthful of water. "You can't fight a lion. You think they'll give you a spear or something to defend yourself with? They'll just want to laugh as they watch us being eaten."

Drust scoffed. "And the Romans call *us* barbarians! Still, probably better than what the Dogs will do with our women."

Cadwal retched again.

"They'll be with child soon enough," Drust lamented. "Then they'll go with the men to live on Crow Hill. And one day they'll forget about us. But actually, I think I would rather fight a lion than have a Dog cock in me."

Cadwal supposed that many of the poor women he'd seen bound would share the same sentiment.

Drust found Cadwal's hand and squeezed it. "Remember me, Cadwal Ap Madog."

"I will. I give you my word."

"And remember Tamm too. He made me smile on my last day. I want the gods to know that."

The sounds of jingling metal getting louder meant a soldier was making his way down the corridor. As he unlocked the door, he snapped, "On your feet," in a thick southern accent. He held a nasty looking flail with knotted strands and shook it threateningly. "If you want to keep the skin on your back, do as I say. Right?"

Cadwal couldn't bear to put any weight on his feet, so took one last long swig of water and crawled out of the cell on hands and knees.

"The sun is shining," Drust said as they headed up the steps.

Cadwal felt the same inexorable and dreadful pull away from everything he loved as when he'd been dragged out of the fort. "I will speak your name," he said to Drust. "Because today I will not die."

From behind, the guard scoffed.

Before his eyes adjusted to the brightness, Cadwal heard the uninviting sounds of mocking laughter. Although Drust was looking forward to being mauled by a lion, Cadwal was glad it was just men he saw waiting for them. But when his eyes adjusted to the light and he realised it was some eager looking boys they were being led to, he knew there would be no glory to satisfy the gods this day.

Their instructor, with a broad torso as gnarled with knotted muscle as an old oak tree, threw a wooden sword to the sand in front of them. Drust bent stiffly down to pick it up.

Cadwal held the small bite wound on his palm up to the sun. It seemed such an inconsequential mark to signify something as important as a blood-oath to his dead wife. He lifted it to his mouth, felt for the scab with his tongue, and bit it again.

He intended to live, but with a quickening sense of panic, he looked around at the curving wall that ran all the way around the inside. It was only about half his height, but given the state he was in, there was no way he could scramble up. The only way out was the passage they'd just come through. The guard stood at the entrance, whip in one hand, the other resting casually by the hilt of his short sword. It seemed the only way out would be as a dead body.

The boys' commander cursed Drust to at least put up a semblance of a fight, then shouted at the recruits to form a line with their shields.

The old man nodded a sad-eyed farewell to Cadwal, then turned to face his meaningless death, nothing more than for the young boys to have their first taste of barbarian blood.

At the thought of Owyn and Arwel growing up as slaves because he'd died for something as pointless as this, disgust rose in the back of Cadwal's throat with the taste of bile.

The instructor barked at the boys and they stepped forward with their short swords poking out of the gaps at the sides of the shields. They had a peculiar look on their faces, a combination of revulsion and lust.

Drust must have fought in dozens of battles and skirmishes with the Dogs over his long life, but now a white haired old man with sagging skin was no match even for the youngsters. Another command, and, in unison, the boys stepped forwards. A sword was shoved forwards, aimed at Drust's chest. Despite his age and his useless weapon, he parried it easily, an Ordo-wik to the last. But another jabbed him from the side. Cadwal watched helplessly as the wrinkled shoulders hunched around the pain of the blade and could only hope they would finish the poor man quickly.

The biggest of the boys, chubby muscles taut as he swung his sword, hacked halfway through Drust's neck. As the old man slumped to his side, the boy stood with a sickly smile of satisfaction on his face.

The commander kicked Drust to his back and chose a student to step forward and stab him in the chest. The nervous-looking boy pressed down on his sword a few times, but only on the third attempt, when he pulled it up high enough, did it crack through Drust's rib cage. In its last gasp, his heart spat out a gush of blood that splashed his killer in the face. His friends all laughed.

With a foot to the back, Cadwal was shoved forward. Ready to face his sad fate, he crawled to the place in the sand they wanted him to die. The blood-stained sand of a half-finished arena was far from the battlefield of clashes and cries a warrior is supposed to dream about. Being beaten to death by a group of boys not much older than his children was not a final day he'd ever wished for himself.

The commander kicked the wooden sword over, but it was smaller than even the ones Owyn and Arwel played with. Under the blue sky, he dragged the 'blade' across his palm and held the unmarked skin up to show that there was no edge. The significance of showing the gods that his killers should claim no glory for his death was lost on his audience.

Timidly, a couple of the boys stepped closer. A man unable to stand with nothing but a toy sword couldn't have seemed much of a threat, especially as his friend had died without so much as a curse on his lips.

Cadwal took a deep breath and allowed nothing in his mind but the scene in front. If his death was to serve as a lesson, at least it would be one they wouldn't soon forget.

He held up one hand, looking to someone who knew no better like he was begging for mercy, but when he fell weakly to the side, he grabbed a fist of sand. He watched the ugly fat boy step closer, wanting his turn for blood. Cadwal easily twisted out of the way of the short sword and, off-balance, the boy tumbled forward over his shield. As he did, Cadwal scrambled to his feet and let the embers of hatred he'd subdued that morning flare up into an all-consuming flame. Where the flash of strength came from, he didn't know, but in one swing, he brought the toy sword across the faces of most of the other boys in the line. As they were knocked over, or tried to twist away from the blow, he stamped down on the neck of the fallen boy and was about to throw the sand into the instructor's face, hoping to blind him for long enough to fight the guard with one of the discarded swords... But a massive blow from the end of a staff smashed into his wrist, then snapped around to slam into his lower back. He was knocked to the ground dazed and breathless.

Before sand was kicked into his eyes, he saw that the guard had barely moved a muscle.

Then came a torrent of booted feet kicking and stomping, but at least they were so close it would be hard to get a weapon into the medley, and that would allow a few heartbeats to beg forgiveness to Gwen and the boys for breaking both his promises to them before he died...

FIVE

ROM THE UPPER platform of one of the squat gate towers, Brei looked at the clouds over the western horizon. The undersides were lit by the setting sun, cast in the same yellows and deep reds of a burning pyre. "Ember red sky, king's house on fire," went the child's song. Sky the colour of Rome. The omen couldn't be any clearer.

Neither could the news of what had happened to Crow Hill.

The messenger's half-dead horse, steam gently rising from its back, sloshed about in the trough trying to drink faster than it could swallow. The man who'd almost killed it riding all the way from one side the Ordo-wik lands to the other was in the king's house explaining the horror that had befallen the Clan of the Crows. For Brei, the news had come as no real surprise and she didn't need to know the details. It was enough to know that some of the toughest warriors in the most well-defended fort in the whole land had fallen.

A break in the clouds and the low sun shimmered off the thin straits separating the isle of Mona from the mainland. Since the Twentieth Legion had left, a generation ago, the land had known a type of peace. Many were glad of it, of course, but for Brei, it was only the lifeless quiet of a tomb of the Old Ones. She could walk among the stumps of what had been the sacred oak groves, or spend time with the handful of priests who had survived the slaughter, but not without reeling from the pain of what deprivations Rome had inflicted.

Shaking the floor of the gate tower, a trio of serious-faced riders stormed out on Bleddyn's best horses. They were obviously heading to Crow Hill, but Brei shook her head. At best, it would take three days for them to return, even with the fresh horses which would be soon ridden out behind to meet them on the way back. She wasn't sure if the tribe even had three days. But of course the coward king wouldn't take the messenger for his word and would waste days of inaction waiting for his men to pointlessly verify what had happened. She'd spent years listening to the old fool dismiss every report of Roman activity as no cause for alarm. Even as the legions butchered the southern tribes into submission, even as they built forts along their border to block trade and make salt scarce. Not even the massive fortress being built at Deva could persuade him to action.

She still hadn't decided if his refusal to listen stemmed from a blind need to cling onto his power for as long as he could, or if he truly couldn't see the threat. For a man on the Oak Throne, both could be the death of the tribe.

Taking a long, deep breath, she relished the familiar smell of smoke wafting through soggy roofing reeds. A comforting aroma of ages past. Grounding. The shrill song of a blackbird caught her ear. More special even than the greatest lyre or flute player, such music of nature helped her touch some inner peace deep in her heart. Calming the emotions was one of the very first lessons the druids taught, and was one of great importance. When she spoke to Bleddyn next, it would be much better for her words to come from the cold rock of calmness rather than the part of her aflame, ready to scream with rage. The king didn't much appreciate being looked at the wrong way, what she was thinking of saying could make him burst. With luck.

Helig ducked under the thatch at the door of Bleddyn's house and strode across the muddy ground. The glum look on his face told her he understood death could lie in the delay.

More than a head taller, he had a presence so like his father it made her legs weak, especially as he wore Gwain's fox fur cloak draped over his shoulders. Under it, he wore his finest chequered shirt. The different coloured square patches proudly displaying many different yellows, blues and reds of his family's lines. At his throat, the twin fists of his hefty torc would catch the light of the fire when he spoke the sacred words that would soon make him king. He was resplendent, and looked every inch the king Maidoc should have been.

He grimaced at the hue of the clouds. "We are fighting for our very existence this time. We have to meet them at a pass, choose our ground to fight. We have no hope otherwise."

Most people in the tribe were wise enough to understand that. Just not the king. But no army the size they needed could be called together if the king didn't command it.

"Defeat, invasion, and conquest. That's the usual procession of a legion, isn't it," Helig said ruefully.

"With a few variations for pillage and rape," she nodded.

"Maybe, if we're lucky, we can choose death or slavery."

It hurt her heart to hear possibly the only man who could lead the tribe speak such defeatist words. "We're not totally helpless," she said and saw the seed of hope spread across Helig's face.

One of the most sacred rules of the druids was not to interfere in matters of power. Their job was to counsel, so the king ruled under the Laws and Ways, but anyone trained in those Laws and Ways was forbidden, often on pain of death, from trying to influence things for their own reasons. "I've spent years trying to persuade the king of what is before his eyes, what is coming over the horizon. Things that are as plain as day to normal men. I judge that in this blindness he had broken the oath he made to protect his people against any threat. If I break mine in return, is that not restoring the balance?"

She spoke more to the gods than to Helig but as she expected, the sky remained calm and the gate tower foundations held strong.

"What are you going to do?" Helig asked.

"Kill him."

Helig looked aghast. "How, by every god in the Otherworld, do you think you're going to do that? You're just a *woman*!"

"I hope one day to teach you that apart from just bashing someone's brains out with a hammer, there are other powers over life and death.

"There are other ways to kill a man than with sword or hammer."

"How?"

"With *words*."

"Magic?" Helig gasped.

"Normal men might call it that, yes, but not you or I."

But before she created the chaos to come, which she hoped would end with Helig on the Oak Throne, she needed him to know of another enemy. One a lot closer to home than Rome. "Yesterday, we burned your brother's body," she said softly. "We've just found out that the final war has already begun, but there is another threat that worries me just as much."

"What could be worse than the legion marching towards us?"

Finally giving voice to the awful truth, she said, "I believe ill came to Maidoc by Derog's hand."

Hearing the same thing about her brother, she would have been floored by such a betrayal, so she was surprised that despite what storm of thoughts must have been thundering through Helig's head, he just asked, "Why?"

The answer was as simple as it was unbelievable. "To be heir."

"And then to be king?" he finished.

She nodded.

"Derog as king? I honour him as a brother, but the boy can't point his own cock to piss where he wants it. He can't lead an army." He was far calmer than she'd anticipated. Almost kingly. "He really thinks the tribe will follow him?"

"He has Gwain's blood. With you out of his way he'd be the last connection to the hero everyone wished Bleddyn would be. Don't underestimate the power of what such a thread to the past is. Especially in times like these."

"But I live, so his plan is finished."

"Not completely. The tribe was ready to follow Maidoc despite the king, not you. We will have to start almost from the beginning and people will be frightened that Maidoc was not god-favoured."

"But how do you know for absolutely sure that Derog did what you accuse him of?"

"From..." she started, but realised how strange the words were going to sound. "From the way he looked at you last night when you took the seat next to Bleddyn."

"And how did he... look?"

"Like he didn't want you to be there..."

Helig shook his head. "You can accuse a man of killing his own brother just from a look on his face? That's some powerful druid magic!"

"Not magic. Just a skill I was taught."

"This is no time to joke," he scoffed, annoyed.

"I'm not. You would say that you can easily tell when a man is angry, or scared. I learned to read more subtle signs, that's all. But I tell you, on my word as counsellor of the king, for whatever that is worth after today, I am sure he plans the Oak Throne for himself. And that means you are in great danger."

"How?" Helig said after a few moments. "He's my brother. *Maidoc's* brother. You were married to my father; how could a son of Gwain do such a thing?" His expression turned thoughtful. "How could he kill Maidoc in his sleep without leaving a trace? I've never seen a healthy man dead without a spot of blood, or even a bruise."

"Poison, I think."

Helig's shoulders slumped. "You *think*?"

"Many plants powerful enough to kill a man grow near here, if you know where to look. Hemlock, wolfsbane, deadly nightshade. But it was none of them."

"How do you know?"

"Because with a concoction of any of those, a man would wake half the fort with his convulsions before he died."

"A small mercy, then."

"I suppose so."

"Strange though," he mused. "Where else would you get poison apart from the druids or the Romans?"

At that, Brei's heart turned ice cold. *It couldn't be!* If Derog had got poison from the men of Rome to kill the man who should have been king... It means everyone in the tribe was already as good as dead.

Helig reached out to steady her and spoke calmly. "When you married my father, I was the same age as Heulwen is now. And although there's only a handful of the season's turns between us, when I was young you were like a mother to me. You were queen then, and now counsellor to the king, so I trust your word over any other man. But if I am to kill my brother in front of the gods, I will need more proof than just a *look* you caught him giving."

Before she could think of a way to catch Derog out to admit his guilt, Helig asked, "Can I ask a question?"

She nodded.

"Is Bleddyn dying?"

Stunned for the second time in as many moments, Brei had no idea what to say.

"I wasn't sure," Helig grinned. "But that look on your face was shock, so now I do."

Despite herself, Brei couldn't help but smile. "You're too clever to be just a warrior. You should have been sent to Mona to learn the Laws and Ways."

"Well, I am *just* a warrior... Which is why I'd also like to know how many men you and Maidoc got to agree to fight?"

"Sworn to Maidoc, against Bleddyn, about two thousand."

He breathed in quickly. She wasn't sure but it looked like he was trying to stifle a laugh.

"Not much for two moons of work, risking everything," she admitted.

"Remind me. How many make up a Roman legion?"

"Five thousand. Plus the auxiliaries."

Helig sighed. "Men will not fight for a lost cause. Not even the gods could win with those numbers."

The night before, her terror had been that the gods would snuff out the light of her life as they'd done with Maidoc. With the seed of doubt Gavo had planted now taken root, she was worried there weren't any gods left at all. But hers was the realm of man, and the very first thing she had to do was to somehow get the king off his throne. If they were to have any hope at all, she had to do it fast. Half an idea floated around like a dandelion seed on the breeze, but how it could be done without invoking the wrath of the gods, she had no idea.

With heavy legs she made her way down the ladder and towards Bleddyn's big house, walking side by side with the real king she wanted to be sitting on the Oak Throne.

At the door, she paused to adjust the top of her shawl. Now, more than ever, she'd need the fists of her torc at the nape of her neck to catch the firelight, making it look like a little part of the sun was shining as she spoke. Bleddyn probably wouldn't be asking for her counsel, but by the gods, she intended to give it.

"We all respect your words more than we do those of the king," Helig said as he watched her. "Do you really need to be concerned about such details?"

"Sometimes, the appearance of things is more important than the truth about them."

"Another druid secret?"

She stared him in the eye long enough for his quizzical expression to be replaced by a respectful one of worry, then said. "Yes."

In a gesture so painfully reminiscent of his father, Helig reached out to gently arrange a fold of her shawl so the torc would be even better displayed. "We just need him to name me heir," he said.

"I know."

"And then he can die."

At first, she almost laughed, but then the dire seriousness of the situation hit her like being doused by a bucket of cold water. It was unseemly for the counsellor to hit the heir to the throne, especially at the threshold of the great house, but Helig needed to understand the importance of what she was about to do. "Do you not realise what is at stake now?" she hissed. "We fight so that Heulwen has a land to grow up in, instead of being tossed into a slave pen!"

"I know," Helig said apologetically, rubbing his chest with his large hand.

Grip on the much needed calm somewhat loosened, she ducked under the lintel. Expecting to enter in the midst of two dozen outraged men loudly planning counter-attacks to the raid of Crow Hill, the stony silence was unnerving. Brei stood taller than no man apart from Derog, but because of her years of druidic tuition and the respect that afforded her, the men parted as she made her way up to the far end of the long hearth.

Someone reached out to brush her arm, a touch of reassurance, and with such a tiny unspoken gesture she knew that some would still be with her, whatever Bleddyn was about to say. Selyf gave a light squeeze just above her elbow to tell her she could count on him and his sons to fight, even though the youngest was only twelve. Hadyn, a hunched man, hurt in the Black Year by a spear in the back, gave a nod so small no one else would have noticed. The thirty men and women he led were fierce Silures come north after what the legions had done to their land. They knew exactly what happened to those who opposed Rome and they would line up against them for their revenge.

She pressed cautiously through the last of the men and took her seat at the top of the bench, to Bleddyn's left. With its outstretched tongue, one of the iron fire dogs around the hearth seemed to mock her.

"My heir and my counsellor, both here at last," Bleddyn smiled, but she was instantly alert to his far from welcoming tone. He leaned over on the throne as though he couldn't contain his excitement, or as Brei realised with a sinking feeling, his anger.

Derog in a breath-taking display or arrogance, sat opposite, in Maidoc's old place. She didn't need to look at his face to know with what reluctance he moved down to let Helig, take his spot at the top of the bench, closest to the king. She took her place to the king's left.

Bleddyn didn't speak, so to end the nervous silence, she asked, "So, my king, what is to be done about the messenger's news?"

"News? A hundred people magicked away without a fight, gates still standing, not a building burning? It sounds like a story we tell children. Gavo rode back to White Walls and I sent my men after him to see Crow Hill with their own eyes, and verify the story. Or not. And then we shall know the truth of the messenger's words."

"It will take several days for them to return."

"And they will return with the *truth*! Do I need to remind you that my daughter is the teryn of Crow Hill? If the Dogs have done anything to her, I will send a raiding party to their lands the like they have never seen."

"Dogs?" Brei asked, confused. "Surely you mean Romans? No tribe could take all the people of a fort without a fight!"

"*Romans*?" Bleddyn snapped. "Who said anything about the Romans? See something in your dreams, did you?"

Derog sniggered, but the smile was wiped from his face when Helig turned to him with a stern look.

"The messenger said..."

Bleddyn cut him off with a dismissive wave. "It must have been the Dogs! Romans fight in tight lines of formation, everyone knows that. They don't go sneaking into forts in the dead of the night to steal people away. Besides, their armour would make too much noise!" he added, but no one laughed. "For how long have I explained that the Romans don't care about how we live here in the mountains? Like a nest of wasps, if we don't go poking them with a stick, they won't come to sting us. That's the reason no one has seen a single legionary in these lands since the Black Year."

Apart from the ones building forts around their lands, she thought. "So, what will we do?" she pressed.

Bleddyn stared at her, eyes gleaming with malice. "My dear counsellor." The last word was laced with so much contempt it made her stomach lurch. She didn't need a druid's magic to know that whatever was about to happen before the Oak Throne this day it wouldn't end well.

"Care to give some druid-taught advice? You have plenty... seeing as you've been offering it around freely. Going behind my back, talking to *my* men against me! That is nothing more than the most sorrowful betrayal."

A public accusation of a capital crime. She hadn't been careful enough and had spoken to the wrong man. The fire of life, the heady mixture of hope, fear and the sense of belonging that living on the land of the ancestors had always given, drained out of her like an upturned ale skin. She felt so weak it was an effort to stay sitting up straight. By druidic lore her life was protected, so from banishment she was immune, but it was the others she lamented for. For much less than the crime of conspiring against the king had many been handed to the priests, their lives given to the gods as a sacrifice, their bodies to the still waters of a bog.

And if he suspected Helig of the same crime, would he banish the only man who could assemble an army?

She took a quick look around and as expected, interspersed between the semi-circle of men gathered around the opposite side of the hearth were three of Bleddyn's personal guards, all with hands on the hilts of their daggers. Another stood near the door, covering the only way out. There would be no escape. At least not one attempted with weapons. She would have to fight another way.

Heart pounding, she said, "Sometimes what is best for the king is not best for the tribe." It was the verbal equivalent of swinging at him with a hammer. Several men gasped.

What she needed was for him to cough.

"The king *is* the tribe!" Bleddyn growled, hands gripping the arms of the throne, knuckles turning white.

A splatter of blood on the palm of his hand as she spoke such shocking words would be an omen no one could misunderstand. With every fibre of her being, she willed it to happen. "He leads the tribe, that is the truth, and the way of the gods," she replied. "But what if he leads the tribe towards great danger? One that his people can see clearly, yet he can't? What should they do then?"

She expected his guards to seize her. She also expected a few men would rise to her defence, Helig among them, and she wouldn't be able to prevent the sanctity of the great house being soiled with spilled blood.

Instead, Bleddyn asked, "And what would you have me do?"

The question hung in the silence, but everything was happening so fast she couldn't decide if he'd really deferred such power to his counsellor or was trying to catch her out. To sit on the Oak Throne for so many years, a man has to be shrewd... and ruthless.

She was fully aware that if he kept breathing easy, she might be speaking her last words as counsellor, so she decided to make them ones to be remembered. "Five thousand soldiers of the Second Legion are building a fortress just three, maybe even two, days' march from where we stand." She spoke calmly, but loud enough to be heard by the whole thronged assembly. "Remember the Black Year, and how Paulinus Suetonius led the Twentieth Legion like an arrow through smoke to Mona and painted the world red with the blood of our warriors and priests?" Her voice almost broke at the memory. "It has always been said they will come again. The only reason they haven't returned until now is because there simply weren't enough of us left after the Black Year to bother fighting."

A few nervous murmurs of agreement spread through the men.

She looked for any sign on the king's face that he was about to cough. The bastard still sat on the throne, unnervingly calm. Maybe her healing herbs had worked better than she thought. There was a glint of something in his eye that she couldn't read, but too far gone to stop, she carried on. "Their last governor, Frontinus, defeated the Silures to our south and so now the legion have moved north. To us. Our borders are *already* ringed with auxiliary forts that cut off all trade, and salt, so there cannot be any question of what their intent could be. And now, there is news that a new governor is on his way to their new fort!"

As she'd hoped, this was greeted with a few gasps of dismay.

"She speaks the truth!" someone called out.

"And we can suppose he will be keen to impress the emperor Vespasian by expanding the borders of their empire. Mona, despite the devastation they wrought seventeen years ago, is still where druids learn the Laws and Ways. Guardians of our culture and rites, it will be Rome's first target. And because we gave them no fight on their march last time, they will assume going back will be as simple as plucking a ripe apple from a low branch."

She wanted the crowd to be a bit rowdier so the coward king would know that there were many in his house who were unhappy with his inaction. But she could blame no one for being either too frightened or respectful of their king.

Bleddyn looked poised to speak, so before he could offer a measured reply, Brei quickly added, "Either the coming battle will be the most famous that ever happened in our land... Or when the Romans leave here again, there will be none left living to remember the dead. And no one will ever know how we died."

With the house full of men straining to hear how their king would react, a heavy and strained silence settled, that of the space between two armies a moment before the first battle cry.

Slumped on the throne, the dying king took a few moments to respond. Slowly, a wide grin spread over his face until Brei could see the yellow of his teeth. His eyes were stone cold though. It was no smile, more the snarl of a wolf. "Such passion in the chest of one so small," he growled. "And so these are the lies you have been spreading through my land when my back was safely turned?"

Still no cough... and he'd let her expose herself. Her heart sank and she saw Helig's shoulder's sag. With such an easy dismissal of such an obvious truth, she wondered how it could be that the gods granted power to those who lived in such ignorance of how the world turned.

"Well?" Bleddyn asked.

Brei thought quickly. If she was allowed to simply walk out, then too much of his precious authority would leave with her, and so she braced herself for the crushing reprimand. She looked up at the inside of the roof, at the cross beams and the long oak poles of the supports, all leading up to a single point at the top. In her near panic, it somehow seemed full of symbolism. Just like the thirty poles rising up from the circular wall to the apex, so had all the years of her life led to this moment.

They could also represent the strong men of the Ordo-wiki, the clan chiefs and war band leaders. Stood together as one, they could bear a great weight, but pull a few away and the whole thing would collapse.

She thought of Gwain and with what power and passion he had wielded Gordd-ap-Duwia. Every swing was meant to smash a head open or cave in a chest. With enough space, he could knock three Dogs clean off their feet in one go. Brei wondered if she was about to meet him again, or if the gods would leave her spirit forever in the shadows of the Otherworld for the crime of showing such disrespect to a king.

In her mind, she held the sacred hammer and the hundred-year-old head decorated with age-faded motifs. It felt as light as the seed of a dandelion. In her hands it swung as fast as a swooping hawk.

She'd learned a lot in her time on Mona, but Gwain had taught her the Ordo-wik way of fighting, which was never to step back in the face of the enemy, but always to make the gods proud. Even if it meant death.

"What would I have you do?" Brei asked, aware that not only her life but possibly the existence of the whole tribe had all come to rest on just these words. She cast a glance at the fire and hoped the flames would be reflecting off the torc fists while she spoke. "I want you to die."

Two dozen hands grabbed hilts of swords and shafts of hammers. Helig, as with the line of other men on the benches, sat but was coiled to leap up at a moment's notice. It seemed that no one else in the house dared even breathe.

"I called you sister..." Bleddyn began as his face reddened.

"And once I was your queen," Brei retorted. Bleddyn looked shocked... yet was breathing without issue. "Times change. What would I have you do? My answer is this: go with a druid to the waters and let him perform the three-fold ritual so that in your sacrifice, you die a hero's death. The gods cannot help but favour the tribe when their king offers himself in such a way."

"Counsellor," he growled, shaking his head. "You sadden me, but you leave me no choice. For the good of the gods, and the way that things need to be done, such words of sacrilege cannot be spoken in my house."

"You can't banish me," she warned. "I entered the Laws and Ways."

"Yet you are no druid," he nodded, clutching the head of Gordd-ap-Duwia. "For such words, I will cut out your tongue and then banish you from these lands with no tribe, no clan, no family and no name."

She had no time to move before one of the guards clasped her arms at her sides, as strong as though she was held in a set of iron manacles. In the hand of another, she saw the knife flash in the firelight.

"No!" Helig roared, but it only took a wave of Bleddyn's finger for the guards to grab him too. He struggled, but they wrestled him down to the bench and pinned his arms behind his back.

"Anyone else wish to offend the gods and join my counsellor in speechless banishment?!" Bleddyn shouted, a strength in his voice instead of the blood in his throat she'd wished for. Once again the gods had ignored her.

One guard held both Brei's arms in one of his hands and with a fist in her hair yanked her head back. The other tried to force her teeth apart with his dirty fingers. She fought desperately but he shoved the knife between her teeth and twisted it to pry her mouth open. With a wedge of wood forced towards her back teeth, she was helpless. She felt the scream rise up, could feel the cold metal press against her tongue...

"STOP!" came a commanding voice that rose clearly above the din.

The guard's knife fell at her feet and suddenly released, she fell to her knees. Coughing and spluttering, she spat the wooden wedge out and she felt with her fingers to make sure her tongue was still attached. With a flood of relief she saw there wasn't even blood.

She looked up.

A couple of men had jumped back so fast they'd sprawled flat on their backs and weren't sure if they should stand back up again. Bleddyn was still on the throne but had recoiled so far across it he'd almost fallen off over the far arm. In his panic, he'd knocked over Gordd-ap-Duwia. Another terrible omen.

It wasn't the gods that had saved her though. Standing next to the throne, face deathly ashen, eyes dark and sunken, was Tegin the Druid.

Her brother.

Hands were on her arms again, but it was Helig helping her to her feet.

The white on Tegin's skin was simply a paste of chalk or ash and the dark around his eyes just smeared charcoal dust, but with his shaved head and face, he looked half dead, like a man who stood in the shadowy lands between men and gods. His voice too. So loud and clear, it was as though it wasn't a normal man talking. It came from training, just as a bard learns to sing over the voices of other men so his songs would seem to have an otherworldly power. The effect though was striking enough to make a king cower on his own throne.

"Are you real?" Bleddyn gasped.

"You think I just appeared next to you from out of thin air?" Tegin grinned. "You mistake magic for true power. Your guards are loyal to you and would stand against everyone in your house, even your counsellor. But when a druid asks them to sneak him in without saying a word, perhaps then you can see the limit of your power?"

Brei smiled. Appearing out of nowhere, as spectacular as it seemed, was incomprehensible to people with no idea that he'd simply slipped in unseen earlier in the day. But explaining the power he had over even Bleddyn's personal guard was a tangible superiority that every man understood.

Slowly, Tegin approached the throne, filling Bleddyn with obvious dread, but only to lift Gordd-ap-Duwia back up. It was an act of symbolism that, despite the shock of his appearance, couldn't be lost on anyone.

"Why are you here?" Bleddyn stammered, trying to regain his composure. Without taking his eyes off the druid, his hands fumbled for the cold metal head of the sacred hammer. He grasped onto it like a man with a broken leg holds a crutch.

"The heir to the Oak Throne died. On an ominous day. With the news that our most feared and hated enemy is waking from the sleep of a generation, you respond by trying to cut out the tongue of your most valued advisor. It seems it was good that I came!"

"She was plotting behind my back! She deserves..."

"No! I listened to the same words as you, and I heard her speak ones of *truth*. As you must know, truth is one of the highest attributes of the gods." He turned to Brei and asked. "Do you swear that it was no lie you spoke?"

She stood up straighter and hoped that her voice wasn't about to fail. "I do."

"She will not be harmed," Tegin announced.

"I am *king*!" Bleddyn said, finding some courage from somewhere.

"Speaking *false* words is cause for banishment. That is the law," Tegin agreed. "But I declare her words are true."

"But *where* is her truth? I hear of a fortress being built but I see no armies crossing our borders. No envoys come to see if we accept terms for surrender."

"So we wait for the scouts to return?"

"Yes!" Bleddyn sighed.

"Very well," Tegin said, seemingly satisfied with the answer. "Now rescind the banishment."

"Brei is no longer welcome here!"

"She's Gwain's wife!" Helig protested.

"*Third* wife!" Bleddyn almost did her the dishonour of spitting. "And not the mother of any of his heirs either."

Already emotionally charged, Brei choked at the sudden memories of the tiny pyres she stacked for her stillborn babies. Her hate for the old bastard burned as bright as those sad fires. She was close to picking the knife up and burying it in his chest. That would make him cough up blood.

"Will you come with me to the water's edge for the sacrifice of a king?" Tegin asked calmly, as though he was suggesting a stroll around the ramparts.

"No! I will not!" Bleddyn snapped indignantly.

"Very well," Tegin said. "For the greatest of sacrifices, a king must go willingly."

Still reeling from the shock of feeling the knife in her mouth, Brei wasn't quite finished yet. There was no time to worry about the repercussions now. Besides, anything Bleddyn could do to her wouldn't be worse than what to expect from the Romans. "Why not?" she shouted. "You are dying anyway."

A raw hate burned in his ratty eyes now. "On your life, you swore..."

"The cough you try to hide, the one you tell me doesn't mean anything. In a couple of moons, maybe the rest of the summer if the gods favour you, is all that you have left to live. You will drown in your own blood and there is nothing I or any other healers in this whole land can do to stop it."

Nervous murmurs rippled through the crowd.

And then he coughed.

It seemed nothing more than clearing his throat and in another context it would have hardly been noticed. In the painfully silent atmosphere, the strain of not allowing a second one to burst out wrote itself on his face. Just a single drop of blood on his hand would be enough to change the world.

But he didn't cough again. In a harsh rasp, he said, "She will not be banished, as even a king bows before a druid. But she disrespected my name and the sanctity of the king and for that there will be a punishment!"

Huge hands once again clamped around Brei's upper arms.

SIX

CADWAL LAY IN a muddy meadow surrounded by chaos. Battle cries and the clashes of hammers and swords smashing into shields came from every direction at once. Somehow, through the desperate melee of men half-maddened with a burning need to kill each other, he saw Gwen. In the midst of strikes and parries, grunts and cries, she waved for him to come to her. Urgently. There was blood on her clothes. She was hurt! He crawled towards her but was buffeted away by men wielding huge hammers in sweeping death blows. Others fell screaming in agony across his path and he lost sight of her. He called her name, but in the din of the fighting, she didn't hear his voice.

The fighters parted, and he saw her again. She was crumpled on the ground, covered in gore. Suddenly, the only thing that existed was the sound of his scream. It filled the ruin of the world like a never-ending roll of thunder echoing through the mountains. The sound of a grief so overwhelming it consumed the spirit as a pyre burns a body.

He woke with the sounds of the savage battle still raging and had no idea where he was. The warrior in him was instantly alert and he fumbled for anything he could use as a weapon. But as his surroundings slowly came into focus, he saw that somehow he was on the floor of a smithy's workshop. His ears rang from hammers pounding hot metal into shape.

He was still alive then. But from the pain in his ribs when he tried to draw a breath, it seemed he was on the cusp. He wouldn't be surprised if Arawn was lurking patiently in the corner like a crow ready to spread a pitch black wing over him.

At the memory of striking the little bastards' faces in the arena, Cadwal smiled and wondered what lies they'd tell each other about the bruises they'd be wearing for the next few days. Hitting some boys with a toy sword was the most pathetic victory to be proud of, but it was all he had to give the pain some meaning and so he cherished it.

He flexed the fingers on the hand hit by the guard's staff. He wouldn't have been surprised if it was broken but it seemed that Ordo-wik bones were stronger than Roman wood. Still, the lads in the arena must have spent quite a while stomping and kicking him after he'd blacked out. It would be many long days before his body was healed enough to walk, never mind fight.

But then he remembered that Owyn and Arwel had been taken by the Dogs. The pain of the beating forgotten, he imagined them frightened, bound, listening to the terrified screams of the others captured from Crow Hill. He saw again the last words on Owyn's lips. "I'm sorry." Heart rendered in two, he imagined how racked with guilt the poor boy must be, believing that because he followed his father out of the house to help fight, he'd brought about the defeat of the clan.

And Gwen. His promise to her lay as broken as his body.

Beside him was a beaker of water. Unthinkingly, he grabbed it. His hand wouldn't work as he wanted it to and he spilled most of it before managing to down a few sips. He looked around for more but became aware of someone standing over him.

He flinched in anticipation, but no kick came.

"They did a good job on you," the man said in the familiar tongue. "I've seen men die from less."

Stiffly, Cadwal looked up. From his prone position, the man towered over him with the same overbearing presence as Gwain. He held a hammer, had the poise of a warrior, but was clean shaven like a Roman. Square shoulders, square jaw, he resembled the anvil Cadwal lay next to. "Drink," he said as he leaned over to pour some more water. "Soon you will need all of your strength."

Cadwal swigged another glorious mouthful. "Thank you," he croaked. "My house is your house, my mead is your mead," he added in the traditional greeting.

It was met with a hearty laugh. "Actually, my smithy is your smithy, to be exact."

"You have my gratitude," Cadwal croaked. "I would like to know your name."

"Would you now?" came the surprised response.

"Yes," Cadwal said, a little confused. "I would."

"You can call me Master."

Cadwal waited for the rest, but it didn't come. "And who is your father?"

"It matters not who my father was," the man scoffed. "Master is all you will call me."

"Why?"

"*Why?*" he asked, incredulous. "Because I just *bought* you!"

"I am Cadwal ap..."

"No," the smith cut him off. "You are not. You are a slave. *My* slave. And until I decide what to call you, you have no name."

The idea that someone could just take his name away didn't mean much to Cadwal. It was intrinsically his as much as the blood in his veins. "Slave?" he asked and checked if the collar was still around his neck. It was. "Why did you buy me?"

The smith threw his hands up in despair and shook his head. "You have a lot to learn about your new life! One of those lads you attacked is some important man's son. You almost took his eye out. And you're alive now because someone decided that instead of killing you straight away, they'd let you live out your days serving men of Rome. I've never heard of that before, but you were cheap, so why not? They thought it would be worse than killing you."

Cadwal thought that if he'd have known who the boy was, maybe he'd have tried harder with the wooden sword. But about living being worse than death, with no way to get to the boys, he wondered ruefully if they might be right.

The smith motioned another man over and by the ankles he was swung up to an anvil, his bound feet over it. Instinctively, he tried to pull free as he wasn't sure he could take any more beating. But as the smith held him firm, Cadwal was surprised that they poured water over his feet and started to clean the wounds.

"You are a fool if you think you can fight Rome," the smith growled close to Cadwal's ear. "It's over for the tribes. It has been for a long time."

Through gritted teeth, Cadwal replied, "I was captured and brought here in chains. But it seems you *chose* your slavery."

The expected backhanded slap came, but the smith had large and strong hands and Cadwal had misjudged how weak he was. He swallowed the blood in his mouth rather than spit it out.

"I was Trinovanti!" the smith seethed. "I stood with Boudica before Paulinus' Twentieth Legion. Our army was more men than I'd ever seen in my life. Shoulder to shoulder we spread further than the eye could see… and they absolutely destroyed us. Not even in your worst dreams could you imagine so much inglorious death. The valley was covered in bodies like straw on the floor of a roundhouse! So don't tell me we didn't fight."

Cadwal knew the stories well, so had nothing to argue with. Besides, his attention was taken by the healer. Scouring the sand and dirt from the wounds in his feet was an agony Cadwal had never known before and he had no strength to resist as the smith pressed a gleaming blade against his face. He was helpless and steeled himself for the pain with a dull acceptance. With a shock, though, he realised it was his face he was cutting. Frightened it was a strange and drawn-out Roman execution he'd never heard of before, he instinctively tried to squirm.

"You're in a *smithy*!" the smith snarled. He pressed his knee onto the side of Cadwal's face, crushing his head into the packed earth. "You can't have long hair here."

Being shaved for his own safety meant nothing. Seeing the pile of discarded moustache hair was worse than if it was a puddle of his own life blood.

It was night, and with the smithy dormant, there was a sense of peace. Inside, at least. From beyond the thin walls, with the shouts of men and creaking wheels of carts trundling by, the fort still sounded busy.

A small earthenware pot had been set next to him. Struggling with his hurt wrist, Cadwal slowly pulled himself up and wolfed down the fishy stew. He didn't care how strange it tasted, he wanted more and scooped up the bits he'd dropped, not caring about crunching bits of charcoal. The water tasted like life itself, but the cup was empty long before he'd fully slaked his thirst.

With the food in him, he felt a bit better and forced himself up into a sitting position to get a better look at his surroundings. His head spun nauseatingly but he noted the bandages on his feet and a sweet smell of herbs which told him the healer had rubbed some salve on his back. Fed and cared for. It seemed he was going to live. But with the chain from his collar attached to the big anvil, he wasn't too sure how he felt about that. He pulled at it, but it was just as secure as the one from the back of the wagon had been.

Slowly, he became aware of a rhythmic sound coming from somewhere nearby. Ching, ching, ching. It was a small boy with skin so dark it looked as though he was covered from head to toe in charcoal dust. He was throwing and catching a small pouch of what Cadwal assumed were coins. Over and over.

He'd heard of such men that were blacker than the Picts were blue, and who came from a land so far away it was on the other side of Rome's vast empire. But far from being scared by such a stranger, Cadwal felt sorry for one so much further from his home than he was. A similar collar was locked around his neck, which was attached to an anvil, just as Cadwal's was.

"Greetings," Cadwal said. He got no reply, just a confused look from the big white eyes.

"More water?" he asked. There was no change in his companion's expression, so he turned the cup over to show it was empty. The boy nodded and dragged over a nearly full bucket. Cadwal nodded his thanks and practically dived in and drank so much so fast his neighbour chuckled. He held out some old bread and Cadwal scoffed that down too, trying to ignore how much his jaw hurt.

When he could drink no more, he sat back, but immediately the draw of the boys flared up. The urge to run to them burned hotter than the glowing charcoal of the forge. Crawling on his hands and knees through Dog lands, he wouldn't get very far. Even if he was in perfect health, it would be almost an impossible challenge to make it through a land where he'd be killed as soon as he was seen. And that was if he could get out of the gates of Deva. He tugged the chain around his neck. If he could even get out of the smithy.

He tried to stand. Wobbling on a knee, he tried to put a little weight on one foot and toppled over. Now fully aware of the pain from the beating, his mind flittered wildly between feet and shoulders, wrist and teeth, trying to settle on what hurt the most. Unable to think straight enough to work out what he could do, he gave up, and floated as helplessly as a leaf on the currents of an unrelenting panic.

Whoever thought that letting him live was more of a punishment than killing him, was right.

He poured some water over the hand he'd bitten but it was too dark to see the scar. He gnawed at the scab that had formed since he'd made the blood-oath to Gwen and he relished the taste of blood. The promise he'd made to her was the only thing that kept him alive.

Around dawn, he woke again and managed to shuffle around to squat over the night bucket. When the smith came in with more food, he looked surprised to see Cadwal sitting up. "I hope you're ready to work, not to fight," he said.

"I still live," Cadwal replied. "The Ordo-wiki still live, so we still fight."

The smith shook his head as he laughed. "Do you not even notice you're in chains?"

Cadwal reached up to test the band of metal around his still painfully chaffed neck. It seemed a good point. "Our gods still live, they still hold power over our land," he said, but was too weak to put much conviction in his voice.

"If that's so, maybe you should ask why they have plotted such a twisted fate for you, my friend!"

At the way the smith chuckled, Cadwal felt a cold shiver of warning. "What do you mean?"

"I'm not sure you want to know," the smith replied with a cruel smile. "Especially as there's nothing you can do about it."

"Tell me!"

The smith shrugged. "I bought you because there's a rush to make more weapons. The new governor of Britannia will arrive soon and the commander of the Legio Secunda Adiutrix, that's whose fortress you've found yourself in the middle of, wants to make a good impression. That's why he's done some deal with your friends, the Dogs, to take over your land, once you're all... gone."

"What deal?" Cadwal asked as he fought a panic strong enough to choke him.

"A deal with Rome. Something about it being a way for the tribal leaders to prove they can use tactics and discipline for fighting instead of just gallivanting off screaming like mad men."

"I don't believe you," Cadwal said, but reeled with the shock.

"Really? And what do you think that matters to me? Rome has been getting the tribes to fight among themselves since before Caesar set foot on these shores, so it's not unusual."

Knowing the Dogs had infiltrated Crow Hill with the help of Rome made Cadwal's heart sink of a depth he had never known before. "How do you know this?"

"I like to know what my craftsmanship will be used for," the smith shrugged as though it was no concern at all.

"We can still fight," Cadwal said, but even to his ears the words sounded hollow,

"Not for a *battle*," the smith smirked. "Your trade routes are already cut off, which you will feel this winter when your salt runs out. But *raids*... They're going to destroy your crops, kill the cattle, and burn the villages, so they don't even have to waste soldiers fighting you next year. You'll just conveniently starve to death, or die of plague. *Vastatio,* it's called. All dead. So, if you still believe in your gods, maybe you should ask them why they have you chained up here helping to make weapons to kill your own people. Seems they have a pretty twisted sense of humour, if you ask me."

"When?" Cadwal managed to ask quietly.

The smith laughed. "Even if I told you, there's not much you can do about it in your current situation, is there?"

"Why not?"

"Why not!?" he gasped, rolling his eyes. "Did they kick you in the head so hard it turned you into a fool? You're *my slave*! You have a collar around your neck! Why is that so hard to understand? Tomorrow, you are going to start working for me, and if you do exactly as I tell you, I will feed you. If you don't, I will beat you. It's very simple. There is nothing more than that in the world for you any more. Nothing! Do you understand?"

The healer began cleaning the cuts on Cadwal's back again. The scrubbing was much rougher than it needed to be. The absolute agony burned like he was standing too close to the Alban Hefin fire. It taught him in an instant why trained slaves fall to the knees of their masters begging to be spared from the lash of the whip.

He spent the rest of the day curled up on the floor, drifting in and out of restless sleep, with the same feeling of impotence as when he'd been dragged out of the fort gates behind the wagon.

At night, when the free workers had returned to wherever they slept, he was left alone with the dark-skinned slave, who, instead of falling fast asleep after a long day, sat rhythmically throwing and catching his purse of coins. Ching, ching, ching. In his pain and misery, Cadwal wondered how long it had taken to scrape them together, and how many years it would take before a slave had collected enough coins to afford his freedom.

He turned on his side to find a little comfort on his mattress of charcoal shards. The tears came, and he didn't care if the gods saw. Owyn and Arwel, and the women taken with them, needed to be freed and every last Dog bastard needed to die for what they'd done. And if the gods had any notion of justice, he'd be the one to do it.

He pulled at the chain again, wondering what he could do. Those captured had probably been taken to their huge main fort on Bastard's Hill as the raiders would want to proudly display their loot to Bellitius, their fat king. But if they were sent to labour on a farmstead somewhere, how would he find them? The Ordo-wiki needed to be warned of the death heading their way so they could organise a defence. With no warning, they would have no chance of fighting. It seemed the only hope for either was a man who couldn't stand up and had a chain around his neck.

For the next three days, amid the heat, sparks and chaos of the constant hammering of iron, Cadwal knelt by the forge, working the pair of bellows that fed the flames of the furnace.

Even knowing the horrific truth of what the smith was making, it was still mesmerising to see bent spears and arrowheads held in the white heat of the furnace, come out glowing and get beaten into perfectly shaped weapons. How the clan's metal workers could make tools and trinkets from rocks was a closely guarded secret that only smiths and druids ever witnessed. Being so close to the process felt a strangely privileged sensation.

But with every new batch of molten metal, the legion would have more gleaming weapons to kill his people with. And there was nothing he could do to stop it. On the first day, he'd pumped the bellows with less vigour than he'd been instructed, thinking the charcoal wouldn't be hot enough to properly soften the iron. A single lash from the smithy's whip on his badly bruised back was enough to convince him to keep pumping as hard as he could until he came up with a better idea.

At night, in utter exhaustion, every muscle from his thighs to his neck burning in protest, he wolfed down the strange tasting but nourishing food, then collapsed onto the pile of charcoal, arms and legs twitching. He didn't dream though, and every day, the supply of sharp pieces of metal, ready to be baptised in the blood of his countrymen, grew... along with the crushing desperation.

At the end of the long third day, he lay at the foot of the anvil, to have his meal. His fellow captive played with the bag of coins again, probably dreaming of the long distant day when it would be heavy enough to be worth his freedom.

Shouting came from outside. His body had healed enough to be able to move a little easier and so he shuffled forwards as much as the chain would allow and pulled aside the flap of the roughly stitched leather wall. He wondered how many of his tribe had ever peered out into the world of the Romans in the same way. And lived.

For days, his world had been reduced to just a forge and a set of bellows, but outside was a terrible sight. It was the dead of night, yet the activity was busier than any day a trading caravan had wound its way up the slopes of Crow Hill. Men worked with mule-led wagons, some coming to unload supplies, others loading up with finished goods. Another was having charcoal shovelled off it so the slaves could get the forges ready for when the skilled metal-working men arrived with the dawn.

It all felt so wrong and unnatural. At this time of night, the only eyes open should have been those of the guards patrolling the ramparts, and the only sounds those of the cockerels announcing the coming of the sunrise. And despite the sheer number of weapons the smith managed to make every day, his wasn't the only metal workshop. With the stack of finished spears ready to be taken somewhere, Cadwal guessed there must be a carpenter nearby as well.

A light moved above and with a horrible lurch of vertigo, he realised it was a guard walking on top of a wall. The tribes could dig deep ditches around the tops of hills, no matter how steep the slopes, and erect thick wooden palisades no enemy could climb. But looking up at the wall of Deva was like being on a beach staring up at the cliffs. Towering away in either distance, it stood higher than anything he'd ever seen made by a man's hand, and he could imagine an army of Ordo-wiki breaking against it as uselessly as waves at low tide. Pain could be fought, so could fear and panic, but against the hopelessness of seeing the sheer scale of what the tribe faced, he could find no defence.

He let the flap fall, crawled back to his bed of charcoal shards, and lay listening to his neighbour's bag of coins... ching, ching, ching... He wondered if, when the soldiers marched out to meet the Dogs, all joking and laughing about the slaughter to come he'd go completely mad. Being left to live was quickly turning into a punishment worse than death.

Ching, ching, ching...

In the Black Year, he hadn't been much older than Owyn was now, so all he remembered of the bloodbath that was the Battle of Mona was that almost nobody made it back home. Those that did, only survived because the legion had rushed back south to crush Boudica. But in the years since, from all the stories ever told, he'd always assumed that with enough men who had enough bravery in their hearts, the tribe could terrify any legion out of the mountains. Seeing that they were making weapons on the same scale as they were building the fortress, it was obvious that the fate of Crow Hill would be that of the whole of the Ordo-wiki. Unless a chained man could get a message to the king.

The smith was right; it was useless. There was nothing he could do.

Ching, ching, ching...

His mind, drifting on a river of pain, exhaustion and helplessness, floated back to Crow Hill. He thought about Tamm and the others toiling away in the darkness of the mines and couldn't decide if he was better off than them or not.

The mines. They were right next to the border of Ordo-wik land. On a clear day the hill they were digging in could be seen from the walls of Dinorwig.

Ching, ching, ching...

Twisting around, trying futilely to find a position to lie in that was slightly less painful, he wondered how long it would be until his body was healed enough to run for days over the hills to the fort of the White Walls, the closest safe place to Deva.

He felt the lock at his throat again and thought that although his fingers were useless for prising it off, all it needed was a tiny key.

Ching, ching, ching...

A key...

The idea came in a single heartbeat, like pulling the hide away from the round-house door to reveal a stunning dawn, the light spilling over the central hearth. So simple and beautiful, it could only be a gift from the gods. He allowed himself a few tears of relief and gratitude that he would have a chance to both rescue his sons and to warn the tribe of the Roman's terrible plan.

Sleep didn't come, and for the rest of the short night, he stayed restlessly awake running in his mind how the next few days could play out. In the half light before sunrise, when the smith came in, Cadwal got his still painful feet under him and stood up.

The smith's hand went reflexively to the hilt of the dagger at his hip. "Why am I ready for you to say something stupid?" he asked, looking level into Cadwal's eyes for the first time.

"I will go to the mines."

With a look as though someone had just hit him in the head with one of his hammers, the smith said, "That's a stupid idea, even for a fool."

"The gods spoke to me," Cadwal said. He had no idea if they had or not, but it seemed a better bargaining position than just a slave with a stupid idea.

"Did they now? And what did they say?" He clenched his fist, probably in readiness to pummel it into Cadwal's face.

"I can't walk to Dinorwig, you are right, so I'll take the boat to the mines and start from there."

"You'll *start* from there, will you? *Start*? Because the mines are normally where slaves *end*! But wait, wait," he laughed with a look of incredulity. "I think I missed an important part of your plan somewhere. How exactly do you think you are going to get there?"

"On a boat. One must dock here to take slaves along the coast."

"No, no. A bit before that. I mean, I've mentioned it once or twice before, although I'm not sure you have fully grasped the concept yet. But *you are my slave*!"

"You will let me go."

"Oh, will I now?" he scoffed with the start of another laugh. "Yes, because I often just let slaves I've just bought, fed and had healed, walk off and leave when they have an idea to..."

"For coins you will," Cadwal interrupted. "You bought me for not a lot. You said so yourself. But now I can stand and am stronger, so the mine owners will pay you more. You will make a profit."

"Maybe the gods did speak to you... Because no normal man would have an idea like that just come into his head. But you are serious, aren't you?"

"I am."

"If I sold you on," he mused. "I would get some extra coin, that may be true. But if you think you can just walk out of the mines whenever you want, you are very, very wrong. It's a one-way trip through those gates. Men go down, but only green rocks and empty chains come out again. No one escapes the mines. What special plan did your gods give you for that?"

"I won't go *into* the mines."

"No? How will you manage that?"

"I'll be the only one there with the key to their collar."

"Oh really?" the smith laughed and threw his hands up in exasperation. "And where exactly do you think you will get that from?"

"You will give it to me."

He scoffed again. "I wish my friends were here to listen to this because when I tell the story tonight no one will believe me... And why exactly would I give you the key?"

"Because you are of this land and should know what it looks like when the gods speak to a man."

The smith smiled again but this time it wasn't out of humour. "I know you don't wear that chain as a normal man would. You hardly even notice it. It might as well be a line of piss in the snow for all you care." He shook his head again, this time in disbelief. "I can see how much effort it will be to break you, so what do I care? You want to be a hero that men sing of... it's worth a couple of coins just for the story!"

Cadwal hadn't even worked up a sweat at the bellows before the smith came back. With him was a man who appraised Cadwal as coldly and as calculating as a trader inspects sheep. Being in the presence of someone whose job was to make coin out of the lives of men, he couldn't help but shiver with disgust.

Ordered to his feet, which thanks to the ointments and bandages of the healer, he could just about manage, the slaver looked appreciatively at Cadwal's forearms and handed over some coins to the smith. With elation swirling in his belly, he allowed himself to believe that the plan was working. He'd be seeing Ordo-wik lands soon.

"I don't know if it's your god is watching us, or mine," the smith grinned. "But whoever it is, I hope they have their amusement." He pressed a small key into Cadwal's hand.

Looking at it next to the scar of his blood-oath to Gwen, Cadwal wondered what plan the gods had for getting him off the ship and on the road to the king, then up the slopes of the Dog's main fort. He hoped it would be better than the one that had him beaten half to death and chained to the smith's anvil.

He would have to worry about that when he got there.

SEVEП

THE SHIP LURCHED and his stomach followed the motion. In the stench of what must have been many months' worth of slave's waste, Cadwal retched again. He was careful to spit the bile through clenched teeth, as the first time he'd thrown up, the key had come out of his mouth. He could only hope the others sharing the unpleasant journey had been too wrapped up in their own misery to notice him pulling it back with his foot, desperate beyond measure not to lose it between the floorboards.

Thin lines of light still made their way through the gaps in the deck planks above so the day hadn't yet ended. Yet it felt as though he'd endured the lamentations of those he was chained to for the whole turning of the moon. They'd been at sea so long, he was starting to worry that they were close to sailing off the end of the earth.

Another man wailed again, begging the sailors above for water, but not a drop had been offered since they'd left the harbour of Deva early that morning. His helpless pleadings soon faded to incoherent mumblings. Cadwal was as mindlessly thirsty as everyone else and drifted away with dreams of gulping the sea water he could hear slapping against the hull.

For a few of his hapless companions, it seemed their minds were as broken as their spirits. With their constant wailing and crying, he had to concentrate on an image of holding the boys in his arms to prevent their madness taking him as well.

A heavy thud resonated through the boat and along with most of the others, Cadwal cried out in fear. Hearing the men on deck shouting orders, he realised it was no sea monster about to devour them in giant jaws, just them bumping against the pier as they docked. Be it monster or Roman, the dread was much the same.

With the hatch open, the gloriously fresh, salt-tinged air that wafted in made Cadwal alert and ready to escape... although his most pressing need was for water. He followed the man ahead in the chain up the ladder and shuffled weakly into the bright light of a summer evening. On the pier, it still seemed as though the earth moved under his feet and he needed to dry retch again.

Through bleary eyes, he assessed what chance he had of getting free. A pair of rough-looking guards watched them intently. Even if he could unlock the collar without one noticing, or the others fighting him for the key, he wouldn't get more than a few steps before he was let out of the chain the same way as the dead Crows had been at the bridge.

Soiled at both ends, and with only scraps of rags over their cut and bruised bodies, the line of broken men must have been a sorry sight as they shuffled towards their deaths. Those at the front obviously knew what a lash of a whip felt like and only needed to have one waved threateningly for them to stagger along to a waiting mule-drawn wagon. Chained together, they moved as one.

Cadwal glanced up at the rounded back of the mountain that reared up from the shore, inside of which, it was said, no slave survived. Never mind being swallowed by a sea monster, if he couldn't get out of the chain soon, he was going to be consumed by a mountain! The key cut into the inside of his cheek so hard he could taste blood.

With the others, he climbed into the back of the wagon and as the doors were slammed shut, loud laughter from one of the mindless men filled his head and mocked his panic. As the mules were whipped into motion and the wagon creaked, it flared up bright and alive. It was only by searching for the place of calm that he managed not to spit the key out and try it in the collar.

Eventually, the bumping and crashing came to an end and the doors were opened again. Far from offering new hope for escape, the sight was one of such horror that it wasn't the chains or the deathly thirst that held him with useless legs on the floor, but terror and dread. Some men began to wail again, even more high-pitched and urgent than they had on the boat. Those who still had strength in their legs tried to push themselves back from what was before them.

Hewn deep into the rock was a giant pit over an area almost the size of Crow Hill. The cries of those who saw it was the lamentation of the gods that such a crime could be committed against nature. Fires ringed the edges and through the foul-smelling smoke, stick-thin waifs of men, dressed in nothing but strips of rags, laboured under heavy baskets and sacks of rocks. Others huddled around piles of green stones, pummelling them to dust.

Cadwal's attention was drawn inexorably beyond the landscape of human misery to the gaping maw at the bottom of the path. Its darkness was the absolute absence of human hope. Despite the stories everyone had heard, he couldn't have imagined such a place could be allowed to exist.

"Take a rock," a guard snapped as the first man in the chain was dragged out of the wagon. He didn't understand so got a whack on the side of the head with a sturdy stick. As he fell, the chain yanked on the necks of the men behind.

"No!" Cadwal gasped as he was pulled forwards, closer to the horror. "No! Wait!"

"Water, *please*," another begged and was also rewarded with a swing of the club. At least he managed to raise his arms so his hands took the brunt of the blow, not his head.

"There's all you can drink down inside," the guard laughed.

"Wait!" Cadwal pleaded. Dying in the darkness was the fate for the other men, not him. He was only here to escape!

Only green rocks and dead slaves ever came out again.

Nothing but a miserable death awaited him in the dark hole. Once inside, far from the light of the sun, Cadwal would never see his sons again... and the warning for the king would die on his lips. He'd still be in there as the Romans and Dogs joined up and raided the land.

The gods had given him the idea to come here, they'd freed him from the forge, and now they had to free him from the slave chain, but they were fast running out of time. He looked up at the sky, not understanding why he saw only clouds.

There was no reason he could imagine for why he needed to carry a rock but didn't want to get clubbed in the head, so took one and stumbled off in the line down towards the abyss, legs weak as though his bones had turned to water. Somebody's bowels had.

He braced himself for the chains to melt away, or for a band of brethren ready to leap out in an ambush at just the right moment... even for someone to suggest that he worked at one of the fires outside. But the gods did nothing.

A thick metal door bolted over the opening into the rock was pulled open as he was dragged into the hole the last hope of seeing his boys again, never mind saving them, faded to nothing. The darkness took him like death itself.

The path wound steeply down and, unable to see, he couldn't help but scuff his shoulders on the sides of the rough walls. The air was a mixture of barely breathable dust and filth. But the noise was worse. Echoing off the passageway walls was the din of hundreds of men hammering at the rock from far, far below, mixed with wails of torment and cries to the gods. Gripped with a suffocating panic, as though a thick blanket was being pressed over his face, he was close to crying out with them.

The only light came from tiny oil lamps set in little recesses in the wall, but the rock seemed to absorb it. He couldn't even see the man right in front.

Down and down they were led, through twisting passages of low rock, through the bowels of the mountain, the cloying air getting hotter and hotter. From close by came the sound of flesh being striped with a whip and the related cries of agony, and then Cadwal noticed a pair of tiny feet wiggling in a small hole. The thought that children were in the mine, suffering along with the men, was the worst realisation of all and he almost dropped his rock.

The incessant pull of the chain forced him onwards and, hunched over with his head bumping into the back of the man before him, Cadwal trudged ever further down.

In an open space, lit with a dozen oil lamps, the chained slaves clustered around a bucket of water. Cadwal was dragged over and in a desperate free-for-all, they dropped their rocks and splashed their dirty hands, greedily drinking whatever they could.

"Like animals, aren't ya!" the guard cursed but Cadwal felt no insult and scooped up as much as he could with just as much appalling need as the others, until he was buffeted out of the way by the biggest man in the chain. He picked the bucket up and took a few long, long swigs, and, with a loud belch, simply poured the rest out onto the floor. For a moment, Cadwal thought the guard was about to bash the man's brains out with the nasty looking cudgel, but instead he threw his head back and laughed as though it was the funniest thing in the world. The few drops Cadwal had managed to dampen his tongue with did nothing to calm the raging terror.

When he'd finished laughing, the guard took the connecting chains from between a few of the men but left them attached in pairs. Cadwal was desperate to spit the key out and get the collar off but there were still too many men around for him to slip away.

A bucket was thrust at him. It contained a couple of rounded stones like the one he'd carried down and the man he was chained to was given one of the oil lamps. Then they were pushed down a small passage to the side. "Get in as far as you can go and follow the line of green in the wall. Ten buckets of green rocks is worth a bit of bread. Got it?" The guard showed them the piece of broken animal bone. "Hack the rock with this."

Arms out to stop from banging his head, Cadwal fumbled along behind his partner, but soon they were forced to drop to their knees and crawl, which was difficult as the chain was so short. They scrambled clumsily over a dead body. "We're never getting out of here," the man ahead moaned.

The passage got so narrow and the chain so short, the only way they could move ahead without choking each other was for the other man to shuffle backwards, feet first. Cadwal followed, struggling to keep the bucket out of the way, until they finally got to the end of the shaft. The small flame illuminated a seam of green rock in the wall.

The man's mumblings became louder, until he was openly sobbing. He hit his piece of bone against the vein of green, but it was such a cramped space that he couldn't get any strength behind it. Even with a half a dozen attempts, only a few crumbs of green rock fell out. Already giddy from hunger, and desperate to the point of madness for water, Cadwal knew they'd be half dead before they got their ten buckets for a piece of bread.

"I can't do it," the other man cried. He dropped the rock and began shuffling back up the narrow tunnel. There was no space for two bodies though, so he tried to force himself through the tiny gap between them.

"Calm down!" Cadwal snapped.

"I have to get out!"

"You won't get past the guards!"

Struggling to get out of Cadwal's grip, the man knocked the lamp over and the burning oil set his trousers alight. Screaming at the top of his voice right down Cadwal's ear, he frantically forced himself away from the pain.

Pressed as he was between the narrow walls, arms pinned to his sides, Cadwal couldn't reach to put the fire out, so he grabbed the chain and, with gritted teeth, pulled it tight so it dug into the other man's throat. Gasping and choking from the thick smoke, he twisted around and held on in a death grip... until the man stopped flailing his arms and went limp.

With a hand up between his chest and the man's legs, Cadwal patted out the flames, then in the suffocating darkness, coughing on a thick mix of dust and smoke, he managed to shuffle back up the passage a little way from the body. Finally, he took the key out of his mouth and felt for the slot in the front of the collar. With a dizzying sense of triumph, he put the key in.

It wouldn't turn.

The weight of the whole mountain above crushed the air out of his chest.

He forced the key one way and another, put it in the other way up, but no matter what he did, it wouldn't work. He tried it in the dead man's collar, but again, it refused to turn.

With little lights dancing in his eyes like the sparks from the smith's forge, he inched himself and the body back down the tunnel until there was space enough to at least sit up.

Gagging with fear, he tried the key again, turning it different ways, pushing it in harder and pulling it out a little... until he sat listening to his pounding heart and realised the smith had betrayed him.

It was hard to breathe, as though his lungs had turned to the rock he was trapped under and his head spun so much that, blinded in the total dark, he had the horrible sensation of not knowing which way was up and which was down. To find his balance, he rested his hands on the ground.

If he worked hard to fill ten buckets for a piece of bread, maybe he could do thirty buckets and get a proper handful to eat and he'd have more strength. But those were the thoughts of a slave... and Cadwal was an Ordo-wik. He found a loose rock on the floor, felt for where the man's face was and lifted it as high as the roof of the tunnel would allow. With a sickening crunch, the second blow smashed the skull, and it didn't take many more hits before he could slip the collar over what was left of the head. With the stench of blood and brains and the feeling of the wet stuff over his hands, Cadwal couldn't help but throw up the handful of water he'd managed to scoop from the bucket. With the empty collar clinking on the floor between his knees, he began crawling back the way they'd come in.

Sounds of hammering and shouting seemed to come from every direction, but there was no light to head to, so with one hand out in front he dragged himself forwards, until the rock above got so low he couldn't even crawl and was forced to shimmy along on his belly. Soon, even that got hard. It wasn't the way he'd come in, but the air seemed fresher, less filled with dust, and so he shuffled on. With the floor pushing into his chest and the top of the passage pressing down on his back, he breathed out and pushed himself forwards a tiny bit... but then couldn't breathe back in again. He tried to edge back a little, but couldn't move at all. He tried to call out for help so the guard would come and pull him out by his feet, but the only noise he could make sounded like a dying man's whisper.

The panic rose to burst like the scream of a mad man in his head.

He saw the boys, huddled together in the dark, dirty faces, tired after a long day's work, wondering if every time a dog barked, or the warning horn was blown, it was their father coming to get them... while his body was rotting in a tiny hole deep underground. No spear shafts being hit on shields to send his spirit off, just the sounds of hundreds of hammers in the hands of slaves chiselling out rocks for Roman metal.

The pressure in his head began to build.

Memories and imaginations mixed into flickering reminisces of life. Taking Gwen's hand for the first time, watching the long line of the maimed being dragged back from Mona, the boy's first cries in the world... and Gwain.

Gwain the Great.

The former king had been a merciless instructor, brutal, and Cadwal had hated him with a passion... until the day they fought a group of Dog raiders who fancied taking a few Ordo-wik heads to adorn their fort with. Impetuously chasing a man away from the fight so he'd be praised for bravery, Cadwal had found himself surrounded, and although the swords weren't sticks, he'd managed to stay alive, until Gwain came to his rescue and the others scarpered. Gwain let him have the heads of the two he'd felled and Gwen watched proudly as he mounted the skulls on stakes outside the fort.

"You didn't panic," Gwain smiled and the young Cadwal had never felt so happy... but then got beaten bloody for running off and leaving the fray.

Don't panic.

Warrior calm. He'd learned what those words meant that day.

The fast but tiny gasps he could just about manage to drag into his chest weren't enough to calm him completely, but the throbbing pressure of the rocks on his chest was a little less every time he breathed out. The burning sensation in his lungs was just about to burst his head, but he blew all the air out and at the same time scraped against the ground with his feet and pushed back with his one free hand. He moved back a finger's width.

Don't panic.

Again, he lay for a while concentrating on breathing and waiting for his heart beat to slow. The lights stopped dancing in front of his eyes. With his feet finding a little purchase, he pushed back again. This time, the pressure of the rock was a little less and he could breathe a little more air. He kept going until he could turn on his side and breathe almost fully, coughing on the dust he'd stirred up.

He lay shaking, but felt a glorious relief flow into him, and despite everything, smiled at another image of Gwain. Looking up from the mud he'd just been kicked into, eye quickly swelling up, Gwain had said, "You'll thank me for this one day."

Shuffling back all the way until he got to a space big enough to turn around in, he then crawled back the way he'd come... until he put his hand in something warm and wet. He turned away from the headless corpse and this time, feeling against the walls instead of just the floor, soon found the passage to the side he'd missed before. With the chain still clinking behind, he fumbled along until he saw the first traces of light and, able to see the walls, he could focus. Only the druids could fight unseen enemies, but if he could see the guard, he could kill him... although his weapon arm was still weak and his whole body shook like a man racked with the worst fever.

He crawled over the other body that had been left to decay in the tunnel, unseen by the gods, and the passage came out at the open part where the guard paced back and forth in the light of the little lamps. Cadwal almost ran straight to the bucket of water. In that moment, he wanted a drink more than he did fresh air. But with an act of hard earned will, he forced himself to sit and wait. And watch.

A few moments later, a pair of men, chained together by the necks came and emptied their bucket of rocks into a big basket at the guard's feet. Cadwal supposed someone would come and carry that basket up to the pit out in the open air and wondered if he could sneak out that way. But then there were a dozen guards outside and as he didn't go willingly back into the hole, they would either beat him or kill him. What he needed was an army of Ordo-wiki behind him... and with a shiver of excitement, realised that half of his clan were in here. He had to clamp a hand over his mouth to stop laughing out loud.

He'd been so maddened with thirst he hadn't been able to think properly. He'd thought it was indifference that the sailors hadn't given the slaves anything to drink in the boat, but he had to admit that making the prisoners half insane before forcing them underground was a great way of control. Romans really understood how to utilise human suffering to their advantage.

First, though, the guard needed to die. And for that, Cadwal needed a weapon.

A rock to the side of the head might work, but the space was well lit and if the guard saw him coming without a bucket, there was plenty of room for him to swing the long club he held. He had a better idea though, and shuffled quietly back down the passage to get the snapped cow bone, figuring that if the end was hard enough for chiselling rocks, it would be good for stabbing into flesh. The joint fitted perfectly in his hand. His wrist still hurt, but he could grip it properly.

Crawling back, he felt like a warrior. The thrill of the coming kill filled him with strength.

He put some normal rocks in the bucket and with his head down as though he was a terrified slave, hobbled over to the guard.

"What's this!? *Green* rocks..." the guard managed to say before the cow bone was slammed into his throat.

As the guard slumped to the floor, spraying blood, Cadwal was surprised to see that he was also wearing a collar.

After dragging the body away from the light of the oil lamps, it was with a feeling of utter elation that he went back for the water. Sitting in the darkness, slaking his thirst, he downed handful after handful, and knowing his brethren were near, life began to flow back into him.

Once he'd drunk his fill, he patted the guard's body for the keys. A little pouch, hard to open as his hands were shaking so much, and there they were! He put the first into his collar, but the elation soon faded. He jiggled it every way he could think of... and then the next one. But none worked.

Another pair of chained together men came with a bucket into the open space and didn't look too alarmed that it was Cadwal who came up to them.

Gwain had taught a long-lasting lesson about not fighting alone, so he tried the keys in their collars. With a wave of confused relief, he unlocked both.

"Wait here," he said. "I'm going to unlock more men. Then we'll escape together."

"I am of the Cornovii," the first said, voice full of pride.

"Ordo-wik," Cadwal replied.

"Silures," said the other.

The first picked up the club the guard didn't need any more and for the Silure, Cadwal pulled the broken bone out of the guard's throat. They both crouched down out of sight of the main passage way and Cadwal was gladdened to know that they also understood it was always better to fight with a man at your side.

With a flickering lamp in one hand, and the bunch of keys in the other, Cadwal followed the sounds of the tools chipping against the rock down one of the other passages. At the end, he found another pair of men urgently hacking the wall. Freed of their collars, they ran back up the passage much happier with the thought of fighting for their freedom than bashing rocks for bread.

He was about to follow them but was stopped by a big hand on his chest. It was the man who'd drunk all the water. After what he'd done, Cadwal didn't think he'd be the best fighter to have at his back, but he was blocking the passage, so reluctantly, he put a key in the lock of his collar. It wouldn't turn though and the man's expression turned suspicious. Cadwal tried with the other keys, but none worked and when the big man's patience ran out, he grabbed the keys and tried it himself. One of them turned, and like a flame in the darkness, Cadwal's hope flared... but it was the key that had bent. The big man shrugged and turned away, pulling his chain partner along behind.

"Wait!" Cadwal called as he followed. "Give me back the keys!"

The big man wasn't too bothered about fighting with the others, and snatching the club from the first man Cadwal had freed, he stormed back up the way they'd come in. His hapless partner cried out as he was dragged behind.

With a sad certainty, Cadwal knew that as soon as a handful of unarmed and shieldless men ran through the opening into daylight, they'd be cut to pieces by the guards. As much as he wanted to run up to the light and feel the sun on his face, he couldn't follow them to slaughter. When he saw the sun again, it would be with the men of Crow Hill. And for that he'd have to go the opposite way, further down into the dark, towards where the terrible noise was coming from.

The dead guard was slumped over a stash of cow bones. Crouching down, Cadwal took a moment to decide if it was better to have one weapon and an oil lamp in the other hand, or two weapons, but be blind. The utterly lifeless darkness filled him with more dread than any man could, so he took a lamp and made an unsteady way down some roughly hewn steps.

Trying in vain not to scrape his shoulders and head on the uneven rock, he followed the winding passage down, chain clinking behind him, to a ledge that looked out over a large cavern. On scuffed knees, he crept nervously to the edge and looked down. As his eyes adjusted he saw that the firmament of little lights were dozens of oil lamps far below. And the awful roar, like the sound of a storm tide dragging pebbles down a beach, was from all the men toiling away with bones and stones hacking away for green rocks. The din was interspersed with voices of command and cries of pain echoing off the irregular walls. Somewhere in that dusty chaos of terror were men he'd grown up with. As he pushed himself up onto uncertain feet, he knew they were the only way he was getting out.

Down the last steps into midst of the horror, the dust was so thick that many had cloths tied over their mouths.

"Ordo-wik?" he hissed to a pair chained together. "Tamm?" But they ignored him and carried on their race to fill buckets for some scraps of bread.

Tripping over rubble, slipping on the uneven floor, Cadwal held the lamp up to sweaty, sunken-cheeked faces with the hope that the men of Crow Hill were here and not down one of the countless pitch-dark tunnels. But higher up, working on his own, he caught sight of the familiar and unmistakable outline of his brother's back. Heart leaping, he scrambled up and slapped a hand on a sweaty shoulder. Tamm flinched away, but then recognition spread across his face.

"My brother. You came for me!" he sighed, but with a voice that sounded worryingly weak and distant.

Like Cadwal's, his chain ended in an empty collar dangling in front of his legs. Whoever he'd been paired with hadn't made it. There would be time for mourning later. In the light.

"We have to get out of here," Cadwal said. "Fast!"

Framed by dust-matted hair, Tamm's eyes were wide and wild, but had no fire in them. He dropped his cow bone and sighed, "No gods will see the death of a man down here, but so be it. I am ready."

"Come on then!" Cadwal shouted, but Tamm seemed docile, as though the Dog's poisoned ale was still addling him. "Let's *go*!"

"What happened to your face, brother?" Tamm asked idly and reached up with a filthy hand to touch Cadwal's smooth upper lip.

"They shaved it. But it doesn't matter. We need to get out!"

Tamm laughed. "I can see you're the father of your youngest. Without moustaches, you look just like him! But a naked face is no way to greet the gods!"

From somewhere above came the piercing shriek of a horn. No warrior could fail to stand to attention at such a sound and Tamm was suddenly more alert. "Is that something to do with you?" he asked, voice a little deeper.

"I freed some men. I guess they're at the entrance already," Cadwal said... but didn't mention that they were probably being cut down by the guards.

Tamm's big hand slapped him in the face. "This is really you? You're alive? Really?"

"Of *course* I am!"

"Not some familiar looking spirit come to guide me to the Otherlands?"

Cadwal couldn't tell if he was joking or not... which was probably a good indication that Tamm was coming back to himself again.

Gwil and Bryn, chained together, called out Cadwal's name with joy, and so he shouted the terrible news to them as well. "The Romans are supporting the Dogs and are about to raid our cattle and harvest. They want to kill every last one of us. We need to warn the king!"

Serious again, Tamm seethed. "So, what's the plan?"

"Plan?" Cadwal stuttered.

"Where are the others? Did you already secure the entrance?"

"No... I."

Tamm grabbed the collar around Cadwal's neck and gasped, "You came alone?" He could only shrug apologetically.

"Right!" Tamm shouted to the others. "Time for fresh air, you bastards!"

"You know a way out?" Cadwal gasped.

"You think we were lying here after work just feeling sorry for ourselves? Of course we found a way. Just not an easy one."

"Gwil! Bryn!" Tamm called. "Get everyone together. Let's get to the other door we found."

"It's locked!" Bryn protested.

"Aye. But it won't take too much to budge! Come *on*!" With that, Tamm led them through the large cavern and into another tiny passage. Not big enough to stand up in, the floor was covered in loose rocks that made climbing difficult, but it was free of guards.

Gasping for breath from the effort and choking on the dust, Cadwal scrambled over a large pile of rubble, turned one more corner and saw light ahead. Daylight. His heart leapt with hope, and as he helped the others following behind over the loose stones, he shouted their enemy's plan of the raids. If everyone knew the message that had to be taken to Dinorwig, anyone could take it... and in the sun and fresh air he'd be free to go to the Dog's fort.

But a latticed metal gate barred their way.

Tamm tested the lock but there was no handle on it to pull. "It's almost as if they didn't want us to get out," he shrugged as he selected a large wedge-shaped rock from the floor. He and Bryn lifted it together, aimed it at the lock, and swung it into the metal. The noise it made in the small tunnel was deafening... and soon they heard urgent voices shouting orders from outside.

"You've got a long..."

The second swing cracked the metal open and the door shifted a little bit forward.

"...story to tell us when we get out," Tamm smiled.

The next time they hit the lock, it smashed. But as Tamm set his shoulder to it to force the rusty hinges open, a guard from the other side, metal-tipped cudgel brandished before him, shouted at them to stop.

Tamm pushed his way between the partially opened door and the wall, then charged. In the tight confines of the passage, the guard couldn't swing his weapon, and Tamm grappled him to the floor.

Cadwal squeezed through the gap and jumped into the fight. Something flashed in the light. A knife. A knee set on the guard's arm and Cadwal managed to prise it free... and plunged it into the guard's exposed neck.

"I guess we can share that kill," Tamm quipped.

Heart racing, Cadwal looked ahead. They were so close to the light, but like a nightmare it quickly dimmed to darkness again. Another burly guard was charging down the passage.

Knife or cudgel, Cadwal had to think fast. He didn't trust his injured wrist, so handed the bloodied blade back to Tamm and crouched down ready for the attack, cudgel held in both hands. The guard came around the corner, and expecting the slaves to be behind the gate, didn't see what drove the breath out of him. Bent over, he practically presented the back of his neck for the second blow of the cudgel. Cadwal accepted the invite. The sound of bones smashing was similar to that of a rock being hit against a cave wall.

"That works out at about one each," Tamm gasped, sounding winded.

Cadwal led the men to the entrance and the fresh air and the blinding daylight were the most blissful sensations he'd ever experienced. He was either going to escape or die trying, but no one was taking him down into the tunnels again.

Crouched down, he inched out of the entrance, eyes watering in the brightness. He couldn't see any more guards.

"We're almost there!" Bryn grinned, pointing at the wall of the cliff out of the chasm. Hunched over and silent, apart from the clinking of chains, they ran out into the sun and scrambled up the rough wall of the pit to the soft grass on top.

Tamm was doubled over and had trouble finding a foothold, so Cadwal reached back and helped pull him up. They rolled together over the top, slid down the grass on the other side and lay out of sight while Tamm caught his breath. Cadwal crawled back up on his belly to make sure no one was following but saw the bodies of all those he'd free hacked to death in front of the entrance. None had made it more than a few steps.

Cadwal slipped back down the grass.

"We're free," Tamm sighed as though he couldn't believe it.

The other Ordo-wiki, some chained by the neck to a partner, some on their own, were running as fast as they could down the steep hill, but Tamm still lay on the grass as though it was a lazy summer afternoon. And then Cadwal saw his brother's blood-covered hands. He ripped away the remains of Tamm's tattered shirt and gaped in horror at the hole under his ribs, oozing dark red blood. The guard had stabbed him. It was obviously a mortal wound. Tamm wouldn't make it off the mountain. And part of Cadwal never would either.

"*Go!*" Tamm smiled, waving him away with a weak flick of the wrist. "To the king!" He took a couple of laboured breaths and said, "I thought I was going to die... listening to the sound of slaves breaking rocks." He coughed and globs blood splattered over his dirty chin. "I was going mad down there, but thanks to you I have the sun on my face and can hear the sounds of battle. That's a fine gift you give me, brother."

He pressed the guard's knife in Cadwals's hand. "Go!"

"No..." Cadwal sighed and tried to brush some of the dirt out of Tamm's hair. The shine of his red locks were dimmed to grey by the dust, and that was no way for a man to die. There was so much to say, so many things to thank Tamm for, the least of which was all the laughter that had given warmth to so many winter nights. All that came out though was, "I will speak your name."

"*Speak* it?" Tamm spat. "*Shout* it in battle, you bastard!"

Through the tears, Cadwal laughed.

"I will be at your back... with my hammer when... the last fight comes. And bring the boys up to be great men."

"I will," Cadwal nodded. "And tell the gods that there will be a few of us coming over as heroes when we meet the Romans."

"*Go!*" Tamm snapped.

One last longing grasp of Tamm's shoulder was supposed to convey a lifetime of love and gratitude.

Cadwal grasped the knife and staggered off down the hill. As he ran, the aching sense of loss stabbed his chest so hard it felt as though the knife was buried in it.

The others who'd go to Dinorwig with the warning were so far ahead, he couldn't see them, but there were trails in the grass where they'd run. He followed, but from either grief or relief, his legs were too weak and when it suddenly became steep, he lost his footing and sprawled on his face. As he pushed himself back up, he saw he'd ended up right on the edge of a high cliff. Another few steps and he would have gone right over.

He crawled forward and peered down. Far below were the mangled bodies of all the others, bright red blood mixing with the white froth of the waves.

Fighting the need to throw up, he only just found the strength to grab some clumps of grass and pull himself back to safety. Knife clutched in a shaking hand, he crawled into a hollow against the cliff, a shelter that sheep had worn away to keep out of the wind and rain. Flopping to his side, he dragged some air into his painful chest and tried to think.

The gods had given him the idea of how to get here, he'd told everyone the news, so he'd increased the chances of the warning getting to the king. And they'd escaped the mines, which no one had ever done. Yet instead of being impressed by such bravery, they had seen fit to dash his brethren on the rocks at the foot of the cliff. It made no sense at all.

As he turned his head, the chain clinked. To the west, in the foothills of the majestic mountains, misty in the late afternoon sun, his people lived, unaware that their two bitterest mortal enemies had joined forces. If he didn't get to Dinorwig, they'd have no chance to stop the raids.

He stared up at the clouds and wondered if he was supposed to be dead on the rocks below with the others? Did the gods *want* the raids to happen?

The other way, in the land of the Dogs, Owyn and Arwel were waiting for their father to come to them. The need to hold his boys close to him burned almost as hard as a lash of a whip. He couldn't simply hobble into the Dog's fort alone, he'd stand no chance. But after the king had been warned, maybe there would be men with loved ones taken from Crow Hill who could go with him. Or he could get to Gavo's fort of the White Walls. There would be men to help. That seemed the best chance.

The king first.

Decision made, he began to push himself up, every muscle shaking, but shouts from above snapped him back to attention and he rolled back under the overhanging tufts of grass. Two guards crept close to the edge and peered over. When they saw the bodies of the Ordo-wiki below, they burst out laughing.

The rage was fierce, but Cadwal was in no state to fight. However, as soon as they turned around, they'd see him lying helplessly there. He had no choice.

And they were Dogs.

Cadwal had no idea where the strength came from, but suddenly he was leaping at them. In one ungraceful but effective motion, he kicked one in the back of the leg and sunk the knife into the back of the other's knee. Both went down, the first man's scream trailing off as he fell, but before he went over, the stabbed one managed to twist around and grab Cadwal's arm. Faces close together, he watched the sheer panic in the Dog's eyes turn to a desperate pleading. "I am Ordo-wik," Cadwal grinned and watched as the man's expression changed from hatred to acceptance. With no mercy to be begged for, rather than giving Cadwal the satisfaction of killing him, he let go.

It was such a long way down that there was no sound of his body breaking onto the rocks.

As Cadwal lay listening to the wind in the grass, he felt no sense of triumph. Trying to catch his breath and willing his heart to slow down, he knew he had to move. Legs about as strong as roofing reeds, he crawled along some winding sheep trails down the curve of the hill, which eventually led him down to the beach below. The soft sand felt good under his feet. Holding the other collar so it wouldn't slap against his legs, he tried to jog along on the firm part close to the waves. If anyone was looking down the coast for an escaped slave, he was out in the open, but he made much more ground than hugging the dunes and bushes a little inland.

But despite the exhilaration of freedom, it didn't take too long for his energy to fade and it quickly got hard to walk, never mind run. Even if he'd started fresh and strong at dawn, by foot, Dinorwig was a full day away. With the sun getting low in the sky, it began to seem impossibly far.

A little further down the headland, he came to the mouth of the river and when he saw how wide it was, the last of his strength evaporated. On any day, it would be a hard swim to get across, but barely able to pull his feet out of the soft silty mud, and with the chain around his neck, it would be foolish to even try.

On the other side was Ordo-wik lands... So close. The ford crossing was a long way upstream through Dog territory, and besides Roma had built a cavalry fort there now.

All he had was the knife. He looked back up the beach and resolved that if anyone was chasing, he would drag it across his throat before they caught him. He wouldn't be going back to the mines alive. To make sure it was sharp enough, he pressed the tip against his palm. It drew a drop of blood... and gave him an idea.

Above the high tide line stood a lone weeping willow. The pebbles crunched together under foot as he made his way up. He might be too weak to swim across and defeat the will of the gods, but maybe he was a little cleverer, and the message would get to the king after all. The gods might not care enough about the people for that, but Cadwal did.

He sliced off a few branches, stripped the leaves off, then set about pulling together the largest pieces of sun-whitened driftwood a storm had left at the top of the beach. When the bundle was big enough, he dragged it down to the water. Facing the direction of the mines, so no one could come up behind him unawares, knife at the ready, he began lashing the sticks together with the supple strands of willow.

The end result couldn't honestly be called a raft, but it floated. Still checking no one was coming, he waded out into the cold water, draped chain over the wood and clamped the blade between his teeth. With the bundle tight under his arms, he struck off from shore, but before he even started kicking properly it tipped over, and the chain, with the other collar at the end of it, fell in and acted as an anchor. Coughing and spluttering, only just able to keep his head above the water, he swam... but only to spite the gods.

Muscles burning, he wiped water from his eyes to see how close he was to the other bank, and was dismayed that he wasn't even halfway. The current was also much stronger than he'd thought and he was being swept out to sea. He could almost hear the laughter of the gods and it was only with a heart full of hate that he struggled on kicking and paddling. If they had been paying any attention when his feet finally touched the bank of the opposite side, they'd have seen the curse he directed up at the sky.

Getting to his knees took a warrior's effort but staying on his feet was even harder. Every now and then on the strength-sapping sand, his legs folded under him, like a new-born foal struggling on muscles that had never been used. Pushing himself back up got more and more of a challenge and with sand in the collar, his neck felt like a ring of fire.

The beach ahead was cut off with a rocky headland jutting into the surf, so he was forced inland to find a way through the gorse and brambles around the back of it. With Gwain's gruff voice in the back of his mind goading him on, he made it and rolled clumsily down the other side. When he came onto a track, he knew he could just follow it all the way to Dinorwig without having to think too much. The relief didn't last long though as after just a few more steps, he found himself lying with his face in the mud, helpless.

He managed to roll onto his side and looked at the bright dandelion flowers and the blue sky above. He'd done well to escape the clutches of Rome, as well as the mines, and get himself back to the land of the ancestors, but to die in a ditch halfway to the king was a job only half done. There was no bard who could make that sound like a heroic victory instead of the tragic failure it was.

Darkness seemed to close in around the edges of his vision and his eyes wouldn't focus, the white of the clouds above seeming to meld into the cow parsley flowers.

A silent apology left his lips, to boys who would grow up waiting for a rescue that would never come. With his head in the cool mud of the lane, a few bright dandelion crowns close by looking like tiny and distant suns, he was gone.

EIGHT

BREI STOOD BAREFOOT in the field, staying safely in the shade of the hawthorn and hazel. She listened to the gentle breeze rustling through the tall grasses. In the full bloom of summer, with birds singing their songs and trees in full leaf, everyone should be looking forward to the bounty of autumn's harvest. Pricking at her attention like a thorn in a sandal, she couldn't help the uncomfortable sensation that the land on which every ancestor she could name had been born, buried or burned, wasn't her own.

She let her gaze drift over Heulwen, to the mountains in the south. Rolling heather-sloped hills at first, then the higher jagged and exposed rocks towards the peaks of the high mountains. Nothing about that had changed since the days of the Old Ones. Only barrows and standing stones were left of those people now. Not even the names of their gods. Legend said the Ordo-wiki's forbearers had come to this land later and replaced them, but that was so long ago not even the Elders truly knew when. Hundreds of years? A thousand? More generations than even an Elder could count. And a man in Rome scratching a quill over a parchment was all it took to bring an end to it all. A border redrawn, a legion mobilised, a people wiped off the earth... And once the screams had quietened and their blood had soaked into the soil, the Dogs would simply come and build their farmsteads right where she was standing. And the same land would offer *them* a sustenance to bring up their children and welcome their dead.

It was a curious feeling of impermanence, that of the dandelion seed before a gathering storm. And again came the debilitating thought that some ill fate had befallen the gods. If Gavo's outrageous comment had some merit, and Mars had led the pantheon of Rome to win a war in the Otherworld, the tribe would have no hope against what was coming. It would be pointless to even try.

She chased away that thought by insisting to herself that the gods were immortal, elemental. They could no more be defeated in battle as the wind could be stopped from blowing, or the rain from falling... And yet there was still a stubborn seed of doubt.

"What are you thinking?" Heulwen asked. Brei snapped from her thoughts, returning to the agonising burn in her back. She'd kept her tongue, so was still free speak ill of the king, but Bleddyn had saved his pride by ordering a hard flogging. The strips of leather wielded by a man's hand had left bruises from her neck to her hips so deep that three days later it was still hard to breathe properly, never mind squatting down to pick herbs from hedgerows.

The young teryn, holding a woven wicker basket that was far too big for her, bent down to pick the leaves and flowers to restock the herb supply.

Forcing her attention to the soft, scented breeze and the butterflies flitting over the field, Brei smiled. "Just about how beautiful this land of ours is. And how one day I wish it could all be yours."

"It *is* very pretty," Heulwen mused. "At least *now* it is. I wish it was summer all the time. Then we wouldn't be cold and hungry and dark in the winter. Why can't it be like that?"

Brei smiled. Seeing her seventh summer, Heulwen was well over half way to being a woman. Another handful of years, and the straw doll sat up in the basket on a bed of fresh leaves, would be her own first child. But with a sudden flush of rage, she remembered that Rome had appointed a new governor to the land they called Britannia, and he was on his way to Deva. With both the purest love and the bitterest sorrow, she watched as Heulwen foraged among the grasses for useful leaves and stems. Children are forever the future, but Brei wasn't sure there would be one after just one more turning of the moon. At least not one worth living. "That's just not the way of it," she said, trying to keep the pain out of her voice. "Everything in life, in the world, is a cycle. Everything lives for its time, but then someday, it will come time to die."

"I don't want to die."

"Everyone and everything dies," Brei sighed. Even peoples and cultures, she thought. And gods? "But you shouldn't be sad because what follows is rebirth."

"Yes, I know. That's why men are so brave in battle. So the gods will notice them and they'll be reborn as warriors again." Heulwen looked up with a quizzical expression on her face. "When I get reborn next time, will I remember who I am? Or was? Have I been alive before in someone else's body?"

It was a joke of the druids that it was always children who asked the hardest questions. Brei was far from being in the best frame of mind to come up with a satisfactory answer, so she changed the subject and nudged a plant with her foot. "What do we have here then?"

"Feverfew and woundwort," Heulwen said proudly. Looking around in the shade of a row of ancient hawthorn trees, she added, "And this is coltsfoot, to help stop coughing. And this one with the pretty little flower is motherwort." Delicately, she bent the tall stem over the basket and held it close to her little straw doll so it could see.

"That's right. And what do we use motherwort for?"

"If we boil the root, it helps you sleep."

"Well done," Brei smiled.

It also helped calm tremors, and if Bleddyn wanted her to make him an infusion, it would be better to have some of it drying in the roof beams. What they needed most, though, was sage. Maidoc's pyre had taken all of her supply.

They both heard the sound at the same moment. Brei turned around, gasping at how much the sudden movement hurt, while Heulwen instinctively squatted down among the wild wheat, clutching her doll protectively. They were a long way from any good shelter, so she pulled Heulwen over to a thick clump of burdock at the hedge over the sunken track. She gently dropped to her knees and lay on her belly, head just above the top of the bank, and parted a clump of dandelions to get a better view.

"What if they have dogs?" Heulwen asked urgently. "They'll smell us!"

"Just be quiet," Brei whispered as she felt for the knife at her hip.

Heulwen squeezed her eyes shut.

The sounds drew closer. Brei heard the clinking of metal and hoped it was a harness on a horse rather than a weapon against armour. And what had happened to the world when noises on the track could be a band of enemies as easily as a simple trader?

A few moments later, she breathed a sigh of relief at the unmistakable clip clop of slow-going horse's hooves. No Romans or Dog raiding band would lead with a wagon. Soon, two men, bare chested in the day's heat, came into view. They led a pair of very tired looking horses, ribs clearly visible under the skin.

"It's just traders." Brei breathed a sigh of relief and reached over to stroke Heulwen's hair soothingly. "You stay here."

Pushing herself to her feet took a lot of effort, but no matter what Bleddyn ordered done to her back, it wasn't as bad as what had happened to the unmoving man on top of the reeds on the cart. From head to toe, his near naked body was covered in cuts and bruises.

"Good men, halt," she said.

They both cried out in shock and as their dogs began barking, Heulwen couldn't help a muffled scream as she held her doll protectively.

"The gods!" the first man gasped.

"I am no god," Brei smiled as she eased herself through the gap in the hawthorn. Trying not to gasp too loudly at the pain, she dropped down between the gnarled roots lining the banks. The men held the dogs back by their collars but seemed reluctant to resheath their knives. Over the barking, she laughed. "Fear not. If I had meant you harm, you would already be dead."

"Brei ap Kelwyn! The healer herself! We are on our way to see you," the older one said.

"What happened?"

"Don't know," he shrugged, finally putting his knife away. "We found him in the middle of the road. Left out for wolves to gnaw at your bones ain't no way to die, so we put him on the wagon."

"You did the right thing," she smiled.

Wrists bruised from where she'd hung in the ropes, it was difficult to pull herself up, so she used the spokes of the wheel as a ladder. Her back hurt so much she couldn't help calling out a curse, one she directed at Bleddyn. Looking at the cuts and bruises covering the man's body, she judged that both of them understood the same pain. She tried to look beyond the dried mud that caked his face to imagine what he'd look like with long hair and moustaches and wondered if she recognised him.

Fingers on his neck beside the collar, she felt for a pulse. "He lives, but his heart is not strong." With a dangling foot, she felt for a spoke of the wheel. If she was any other woman, the men would be eager to help her, but neither of the grizzled traders dared put a hand on one close to the druids. "We'll go on ahead and send some men down to help you up to the fort," she told them.

Basket of herbs in one hand, Heulwen's sweaty palm in the other, they began to jog back up the track, but didn't get too far before the bruises hurt so much she could hardly breathe. She couldn't go much faster than the half-starved horses.

As soon as they came out of the trees, the gate guards saw them coming and Brei waved to let them know something was wrong. Two quick toots on the horn alerted everyone inside and a few moments later, four riders burst around the tight turn at the end of the ramparts. At the pounding of their hooves on the ground, Heulwen hid behind Brei's back and squealed at the clumps of turf kicked up as the first rider reined in.

"What trouble?" he asked, long sword already drawn.

"A badly wounded man. He's being brought up in a cart."

"One of ours?"

"I can't tell," she shrugged. "But we'll treat him as one until we know anything different. Bring him to me and I will prepare my herbs."

The men kicked their horses and galloped off down the track.

At the top of the hill the men on duty were understandably nervous.

"Just a wounded man," Brei called up, breathless. "Nothing to worry about." She hoped the women and children would be spared the ominous sight of men on the ramparts unwinding slingshot cords from their wrists and readying spears.

In the open space between the cluster of houses, some shirtless boys were laying down branches of coppiced hazel so the ground wouldn't be so muddy the next time it rained. Behind, a younger one was hanging out of a grain store with a handful of smoking reeds to kill bugs in the thatch. They paused, watching her, wondering if they needed to get ready to fight. She gave them what she hoped was a dismissive wave so they'd continue with their tasks unconcerned.

Ducking to go through the doorway, it took a moment for her eyes to adjust to the dark, but inside was a scene of timeless domestic bliss. Lyss sat in the light near the entrance, busy at the huge loom with the beginnings of a new shawl. Afric, heavy with child, knelt at the quern rocking the heel stone back and forth. Her surviving daughter fed in the grain at the top and scooped the flour from underneath. Riana, two husbands gone and too old for a third, sat at the wheel spinning thin lengths of flax into threads.

Brei thought that the world had probably been just like this when the Old Ones were heaving their monoliths across the landscape. And if Rome hadn't sent her legions and new gods to their border, maybe it always would.

She wondered if the shawl Lyss was working on, full of the yellows and blues of Bleddyn's line, could be the last ever made by the Ordo-wiki. It was the saddest thought she'd ever had.

"Everything all right?" Lyss asked, shuttle paused in her hand. "Thought I heard the horn."

The world was as far from all right as it had ever been, but the hearts of old women or pregnant girls needn't be burdened with matters they could do nothing about. "Just found an injured man," Brei said, making an effort to sound relaxed. "They're bringing him back so I can tend to him here."

"So *we* can," Heulwen corrected.

"Don't mind us then," Lyss said and carried on with the weaving.

The hearth fire had burned down to smouldering ashes. Without being told, Heulwen set her doll safely aside, knelt to blow on some kindling, and packed the stones for boiling in a tight circle around the flames.

Brei rummaged through the basket of herbs. Thankfully, they'd got plenty of fresh woundwort before being disturbed. She began ripping the leaves, concentrating on the familiar process to try and subdue the rising scream in her chest. That was until she gasped from the sting of the nettle Heulwen had accidentally picked. To an untrained eye, the two leaves looked much alike so it was an easy mistake to make.

She was about to point it out so the young healer could learn the difference when Lyss announced, "He's here," as the man from the wagon was carried in. Brei cringed at the sight of the horrible collar that, with a click of a lock, turns a man into a commodity.

"Put him down on the bed, on his side. Gently!" she chided the men. "He's hurt, not drunk."

Dabbing at the caked mud on his face with a damp cloth, she didn't need to reach behind his head to feel the scar tissue of the wound left by the slingshot stone. A few months ago, that injury had almost killed him, but now he seemed even closer to the Otherworld. Even though Bleddyn's scouts hadn't yet come back, she knew everyone from Crow Hill was either dead or a slave in Roman chains.

Apart from one.

How that came to be, she couldn't begin to imagine, but until he woke up, she'd have to make do with reading what tales his wounds could tell. The heavy whip marks on his back, much harsher than her own, along with the cuts and sores on his neck under the collar, showed he'd fought hard against his slavery. It was the deep scrapes on his shoulders that were the most curious though, like he'd tried to tame some viciously wild lover. Or a nymph from a bard's song who'd turned into a she-bear. Along with the patches of missing skin on his knees, elbows and palms, the scratches told a story she could hardly believe.

"Will he wake up?" Heulwen asked.

"That's up to him. But if he does, he'll be in a lot of pain, so we'll make some willow bark powder. Really strong."

"What about honey for the cuts?"

Brei smiled at how much the teryn was learning. "Yes, but first we'll need to clean all the places where the skin is broken."

"I'll boil the water for the woundwort!" Heulwen said and Brei watched how with a pair of tongs, the young girl took the pebbles from close by the fire, and dropped them in the jug until they stopped bubbling. Scooped back out, she set them close to the flames again, repeating the process until the water was hot enough to sprinkle in the leaves.

"You will be a great healer for the tribe one day," Brei said.

"Just like you?"

"Just like me," she said and gave a brief smile.

By the time she'd cleaned the man's wounds, the sheepskins on the bed were soaked in the greenish water. He had so many cuts that by the time she got to the scabbed mess that were his feet, she needed a third jug. Once done, she allowed Heulwen to dab the worst ones with honey.

"What's this?" a gruff voice called from the doorway and Brei's heart sank at the sight of Bleddyn, the first she'd seen of him since he'd watched her strung half naked from the rafters, being lashed.

Helig followed behind and wagged his finger at the teryn to stop her from running over and greeting him. Almost unnoticed, Derog slunk in behind.

The king leaned over Brei's bed to look down at the man. "Who is he?" he asked, expression devoid of any sympathy.

"I don't know," Brei replied in the most neutral tone she could muster. "The traders said they found him lying in the road."

"Is that a Roman collar?"

"Yes, it is."

"An escaped slave!" he spat and took a step back. "This is no place for a slave of Rome."

"I have never heard of a Roman slave escaping," Brei said.

"Me neither. But people keep telling me that these are changing times. Maybe he's an infiltrator."

"A *infiltrator*!?" she gasped, shocked that he could imagine something so utterly unfounded. "He's not sneaking around the fort trying to find out our secrets, he's half dead."

"He could be a Dog," Derog offered with a weasel-eyed smile.

Brei was uneasy that he was standing so close to where she slept. "Maybe, but we won't find out until he wakes up."

"If..." Bleddyn dismissed with a wave of his hand. "If he's not one of us, then I want him dead. And if he asks any strange questions, just slit his throat where he lies. Understood?"

Brei gave a non-committal nod.

"And don't waste any honey on him," he snapped at Heulwen. "Our supply is getting low, and I want mead for Beltane."

Before he turned away, Brei asked, "Would you like another brew of mother-wort?"

"You want me dead, so what's the point?"

"I want you to die a noble death, not to choke on your own blood in front of all your men. There is a difference."

There was a soft thud as Lyss dropped the weaving shuttle on her way out of the door. The others had already left. The crackling of the fire and the clacking of the stone weights under the loom were the only sounds in the house.

"You say that in front of my daughter!" the king seethed.

"I said it in front of the entire clan in your house, if you remember."

"And I had you whipped for it... *if you remember.*"

There was another strained silence as they stared at each other like tom cats ready to claw at each other's eyes.

Brei caught the look of ecstatic joy on Derog's face. Maybe at the thought of seeing her stripped to the waist and flogged again.

"Bring me news if he wakes and tells you anything," Bleddyn said and turned to leave.

"But..." Helig protested. "Something's obviously happened out in the country. Wouldn't it be best to...?"

The knife was out of Bleddyn's cloak in a flash, its edge pressed up against Helig's neck before he could offer a defence. "You question me, boy!? I am the king! THE KING!" he roared, eyes mad wide and teeth bared. "If he's got a collar on his neck, he is not one of ours anymore, is he? And now I've changed my mind. If he doesn't wake up soon and tell you anything useful, I want his head on a spike. Do you understand?"

"Yes," Helig said. "My king," he added with the slightest hint of reluctance.

"And if either of you defy me in *any* way again, I will banish you from these lands. Then, if I see you again, it will be with *your* heads on a spike! Do you understand?"

Bleddyn stared into his nephew's eyes for a long moment before pushing him away. Helig, already off balance, dropped to a knee, where with deference, he stayed.

Derog, not trusting himself not to cry out in joy at his elder brother being treated in such a way, had to put a hand over his mouth.

"And what's this?" Bleddyn asked.

Brei wondered what more he could say to his already cowed nephew, but it was Heulwen's doll he'd found. "I told you about this," he said, holding it by a leg. "You're too old for such toys."

"Nooo..." Heulwen screamed as he dropped it into the fire. Braving the heat, she snatched it out, but once she'd patted out the flames there wasn't much left apart from the smouldering straw knot of its head. "I made him. I gave him *life*!" she cried, scrunching what was left in her hands.

"My whole family finds such delight in finding ways to torment me," Bleddyn grumbled as he ducked under the doorway. Derog scurried after him, a hungry dog hoping for scraps.

Helig stood up and straightened his shirt.

"Are you all right?" Brei asked.

"I am. But what about you? Don't you fear another whipping?"

"He can see he didn't break me with the first, what would be different with another?"

Delicately, Helig took her wrists and in his big hands turned them over, looking at the marks the ropes had left when her legs had given way. He grinned with admiration. "If the gods wish it, I will be king of the Ordo-wiki. But I will never have such courage in my heart as you do in yours." Nodding at the unconscious man on her bed, he asked, "Did he tell you anything?"

"He did," Brei nodded. "But none of it is good."

"No he *didn't*!" Heulwen said indignantly. "He's been sleeping all the time!"

"He's woken up then?"

"No," Brei smiled, waving her fingers in front of her face. "I was using my druidic magic!"

Helig's eyes widened in shock.

"No!" she scoffed. "I was joking. But don't you recognise him?"

"No."

"He is Cadwal ap Madog of Crow Hill."

"What?" Helig asked. "Are you sure?"

"His hair and moustaches have been cut off."

Helig moved closer to the foot of the bed to look him straighter in the face. "The gods..." he gasped. "What happened to him?"

"The marks on his body tell many things, but look at the cuts on his shoulders and knees."

Helig lifted the man's limp arm. "Like someone pulled him through a hedge. Many hedges."

"Not a hedge," Brei smiled. "Small passages. I think he was crawling through tunnels."

"What tunnels?"

"I think he escaped from the mines."

"Then he must be a hero!" Helig whistled.

"What's a hero?" Heulwen asked.

"If men believed he was a hero," Helig mused, "one come right at the exact moment we need him... If he was to lead an army, there would be nothing Bleddyn could do about it."

"Bleddyn wants him dead," Brei reminded him.

"That's how a *coward* treats a hero!"

Brei punched Helig's arm as hard as she could. "What if someone hears you say that?"

"I'll tell it to my uncle's face myself. A man who managed to escape the mines is worth more to the tribe than Bleddyn has done in all of his years on the Oak Throne."

"*Helig!*"

"I speak the truth," he protested.

"Sometimes, this world has no place for the truth! I spoke it in the great house and almost lost my tongue, remember?"

"I care not what the old man..." he started before she hit him again, although with the pain that flared in her back, the effort probably hurt her more than it did him.

"You're talking in front of his daughter!" Brei hissed.

They both looked at Heulwen, but she'd never had any affection for the man she thought was her father. Brei had brought her up as her own and it was her she was fiercely loyal to and as Helig lived, no one suspected he was actually her father.

"What does a hero do?" Heulwen asked.

"He gives hope," Helig said. "And you can do an awful lot with a bit of hope." To Brei, he said, "We need him *healed*. Quickly. When can he walk?"

"Walk?" Brei exclaimed. "He's barely alive."

Helig looked unconvinced. "We should send for a smith to get that iron off. A hero needs a torc around his neck, not a slave's collar."

"We don't need a smith for that."

"You have some other druid skills?" Helig asked nervously.

"Heulwen, could you get me the special box under my bed?"

She brought it back and shook it, listening to the sounds of the jewellery rattling inside. "I am a trader come from lands afar," she said. "Can I sell you some beads and trinkets?"

It was no time for playing and it wasn't some decoration to pin to her shawl she wanted. Sifting through jewelled arm bands, woven gold bracelets and necklaces, she found the large gold brooch. Many years had passed since an Ordo-wik smith had fashioned anything so beautiful. It had been repaired and the pin at the back was now iron. She sprang it open, laid it over one of the boiling stones by the fire and hit it with another until it bent. Pushed into the collar's lock, she tried turning it.

"What are you doing?" Helig asked.

"Romans have some amazing devices. But if you know it's not some strange and awful magic, just a mechanism that needs the right amount of pressure in the right place..." With a scratching sound, the lock turned, and she pulled the collar from the man's neck. "It also helps if it's not full of sand and rusted from sea water."

"By the gods!," Helig said, and then winced at the wound underneath.

"Gwen?" the man croaked and Heulwen squealed in alarm.

"Lift him up into a sitting position," Brei commanded as she reached for the cup.

Helig pulled Cadwal up and sat behind him, resting his head against his chest.

"Gwen?" he asked again, his head lolling to the side as he tried to sit up.

"You're safe," Brei said. "Try and be calm."

"Water!" he gasped, and she lifted the cup to his lips.

"I'll go and tell father," Heulwen said.

"No!" Brei and Helig snapped together. "No. Go and find Tegin."

In a heartbeat the little teryn understood that she should disobey an order of the king and with nod turned to leave. But before she could take a step towards the door, she turned straight into the druid. Heulwen screamed and Helig gasped in shock. Brei only laughed though. While their attention had been taken with the collar, he'd simply slipped quietly in. But she understood how shocking such a seemingly insignificant thing would look to the uninitiated.

Heulwen, deciding that the king's mead supply was less important than treating the wounded man, dipped her finger in her father's precious honey, licked it, and then set to work on spreading it over Cadwal's knees.

Some of the water went down the wrong way. Cadwal coughed, but he was so desperate he didn't really care if he drowned. Any longer before those precious drops had passed his lips, and he'd have turned as solid as a stone.

"Cadwal," the girl's voice came again, and his heart leapt so high it took flight and soared with outstretched wings on the warm winds of hope. The craving to grasp Gwen's hand in his own was almost enough to make him weep.

Crusty eyes cracked open. After a few worryingly blurry moments, he managed to focus on the girl kneeling next to him. The second most beautiful woman the world had ever known was offering a cup to his lips with two hands as though he was the king of the Ordo-wiki. The shadows under her eyes told of more than just sleepless nights, but the summers that had passed since he'd first seen her, the day she married Gwain, had taken nothing away from that beauty.

And finding himself next to her was more of a surprise than if she'd been Gwen.

The apex of soot-blackened beams and thatch above looked nothing like any abode of the gods he'd ever imagined, and the little girl with Gwain's eyes looking at him from by the hearth wasn't Arawn welcoming a warrior to the Otherworld. But as long as he wasn't back in the mines, he didn't care too much where some kind person had dragged his broken body.

"Dinorwig?" he croaked, voice sounding more like a toad than a man's.

"Yes," Brei said. "And you are free now."

He lifted a heavy arm to touch his throat. The collar was gone. "How?" he asked in disbelief. It was nearly a full day's walk from where he'd fallen in the mud to the king's fort, and he remembered not a single step. Maybe the gods had helped? But with a heave of his stomach that threatened to bring the water back up, he recalled the broken bodies of his clan at the bottom of the cliff and doubted it was the work of the gods.

His fingers unfurled into a curse for any of them who would lead his brethren to such a death.

But however it had happened, he'd made it to the king. All the way from the forge in Deva he'd managed to bring the message that had a chance to save the tribe. Once he'd spoken it and men were called to the defence, he'd be free to go for his sons. "I have terrible news," he said.

"We know," said a new voice.

The pain as he twisted his neck to see who spoke with such authority from the other side of the bed, made him grimace. If Brei was here with him, maybe he lay before the king himself. The sight of a druid looming over him, a deathly spectre of whitened skin and darkened eyes, made him press back into the bed. The last place in the world for a man who'd just cursed the gods was under the gaze of a priest.

"It's all right," Brei said, a delicate hand on his arm. "This is Tegin, my brother. You can talk to him. He's one of us."

"The fort of Crow Hill is gone," the druid said with a slight nod.

Most who found themselves face to face with such a man were discussing how they were about to die and Cadwal found that summoning the words past his lips was far from easy. "The Romans are coming."

"Are they?" Tegin said with disdain, as though Cadwal had said something childish. "Do you think we didn't notice five thousand soldiers building a fortress so close to our border? They will march to Mona again. This is not news."

"Not when the fortress is finished," Cadwal gasped. "*Now*! Soon. The smiths are making weapons as fast as they can."

But what Tegin had said didn't quite sit right, and when he remembered why, the full terrible truth flooded back in a wave of nausea. "Not marching," he continued. "They've made a deal with the Dogs. They're going to attack us *together*. To raid our settlements and crops. They want to destroy the harvest and starve us."

"The bastards!" a voice thundered so close to his head he jumped in shock. It was no god though, just a man holding him up into a sitting position.

"Troubling..." Tegin mused.

Despite being under the gaze of a man with powers greater than Cadwal could imagine, he scoffed. Every man, woman and child in the whole land was going to share the fate of Crow Hill and 'troubling' was all he could say. Only his terribly parched throat saved him from shouting an insult. "The men who took Crow Hill," he gasped. "They pretended to be enemies of Rome and their own tribe. The teryn took them in."

"Bleddyn's blood," the man he was leaning against sighed. "It seems the daughter is the same as the father when it comes to seeing who the enemy is."

"Helig!" Brei hissed.

Helig? So he was lying in the arms of a son of Gwain the Great.

Brei hit the king's nephew so hard Cadwal felt the thud through his back. Then she asked, "What does it mean?"

"Well..." the druid sighed. "With a band of Dogs running around the countryside, protected by Roman cavalry... They could fire their burning arrows and torch every settlement of ours, destroy the grain stores and kill the cattle before we've even thought about bringing enough men together."

"Why would they fight like that?" Helig asked.

"If we lose the harvest and animals," Brei said sadly, "by next spring, we'll be so weak they won't need a legion to fight us."

"Starved!?" Helig cursed. "Where is the honour in that?"

Cadwal knew exactly how much honour the Dogs had. "They killed druids at Crow Hill."

There were a few moments of silence as the weight of such an unbelievable act settled on them.

"You saw this?" Tegin asked.

"I saw their heads tied to a horse."

The druid spat a curse more usually heard from common men, and Helig snapped, "We're fighting *monsters*! But, if this is proof the Romans have no intention of making any kind of peace, do you think Bleddyn will finally get off his arse and pick up Gordd-ap-Duwia?"

His question was answered by another hard thump from Brei.

"No," Tegin said slowly. "The king will not be burdened with this news."

"But..." Cadwal started, mind reeling with what possible reason they wouldn't want the king to know their enemy's plan.

With a gentle pat on his arm that was meant to be reassuring, Helig said, "I'll explain later,"

"The king is ill?" Cadwal asked.

Brei shook her head. "He doesn't believe the Romans mean us harm."

"As a battle leader, we can consider that the king is lost to us," the druid said. "But not *all* is lost, as long as we know when they will attack, we can be ready for them. I am sure you are about to tell us."

Chained to the anvil in the smithy, just hoping for escape, Cadwal hadn't pressed the smith for every detail. "I don't know," he had to admit.

"What about *where*?"

Burning with shame, again he had no answer.

"So what *do* you know?" the druid snapped, and in such few words all it had taken to get from the forge to Dinorwig, all the lives it had cost, maybe even Owyn and Arwel's, was dismissed. With no more reasonable words left, Cadwal spat, "I know the gods are against us."

"Do you now?" Tegin growled, voice ominously deep and slow, and Cadwal immediately regretted blurting out such stupid words. An eyebrow, raised on the unnaturally pale face was more threatening than a raised sword. "And what would make you say such a thing to one such as I?"

Like a scolded dog, Cadwal turned his head away, hoping the druid's sister would offer some mercy. More worrying than the priest questioning him was the look in Brei's wide eyes though. It looked like an invisible fist had just punched her in the belly and she was trying to coax a breath back into her chest.

If Cadwal had enough strength left when the opportunity arose, he would ask her why his words had so terrified her. He drew in another painful breath. "We got out of the mines. But all the others fell over the cliff to the rocks below."

"You really got out of the *mines*?" Helig asked, incredulous.

"I told you so," Brei said.

Cadwal was about to ask how she could possibly know, but Tegin snapped, "And how did you manage to do that?"

"I was supposed to have the key to the collar," he said and wanted to weep at how the brief moment of freedom for the men of Crow Hill had ended. And found out that as well as the gods being against him, the king was as well.

"I think you've missed a few important details out of your story," Tegin said. He nudged the chain with his foot. Cadwal flinched at the sound of it.

"He needs to rest," Brei cautioned.

"He has a few more things to divulge before taking another nap," he taunted. To Cadwal, he ordered, "Carry on."

"A boat to the mines was easier than getting through Dog lands on foot."

"A boat?" Helig exclaimed. "By the gods!"

The druid was less impressed. "You just waved one over to the shore and jumped aboard, did you? How about you start your story from the *beginning*? You were taken from Crow Hill..."

Cadwal sighed, not entirely sure if he could keep his eyes open long enough to tell the whole sorry tale. "A smith bought me as a slave because he needed help to make more weapons..."

"So before you got on a boat and escaped the mines, you escaped Roman slavery in the middle of the fortress?" Tegin asked, tone laden with scepticism.

"I told you he's a hero," Helig said from behind.

"He is nothing of the sort," Tegin scoffed. "What did he say that will help us?"

"Was it the smith who told you of this plan?" Brei asked softly. She was trying to sooth him, but the rough edge of fear in her voice pricked like a thorn under the skin and he couldn't decide if it made him more nervous than disappointing a druid.

"And why did this smith let you get on the boat?" Tegin asked.

Cadwal hadn't noticed the staff before, but now, with feathers and dangling bones strung to the top, it was leaning over him. If he was supposed to be intimidated, it was working. The battle against the exhaustion about to be lost, he said, "I thought the idea to go to the mines was god-sent and because the smith believed so too, he sold me to the mines. There was a profit in it for him."

"Well, we got there in the end," Tegin sighed. "God-sent ideas and profit."

Behind him Helig coughed. "Some song this will be one day."

"Let's see if there will be anyone left to sing it first," Tegin said ominously.

"Do you have a plan?" Helig asked.

Cadwal was amazed at how familiarly Helig could talk to one of the Laws and Ways. He'd never met a man who wasn't terrified of just the simple mention of one. He wondered if there was something special in Gwain's blood.

"As a warrior, a plan is *your* task," the druid said. "But not knowing where and when they plan to attack, leaves us almost helpless. We can't set patrols at all the passes and river crossings without Bleddyn knowing."

"Wait!" Cadwal said, trying to get them to stop talking long enough for him to catch up. "The king doesn't even want the borders guarded!?"

"That's something we'll remedy," Tegin assured. "But we still need to know more. And for *that* we need the most powerful weapon a man can wield."

In the expectant silence Helig asked, "What's that?"

"*Knowledge*," he said with a hint of a grin. It was the closest Cadwal had ever seen a druid come to smiling.

"And how do we get this *knowledge*?" Helig asked.

"You can't send him back!" Brei protested.

"What?" Helig and Cadwal asked in unison.

"God-sent and gold," Tegin smirked. "If the smith sees him again, after sending him off on a hopeless journey to the mines, he'll tell us what we need to know about the raids. Especially with a nice heavy pouch of gold as an offer to loosen his tongue."

Cadwal tried to follow the reasoning. The smith would take gold, he was sure enough of that. But the other part of the plan seemed a little confusing. "Sees me again?" he asked.

"Yes," Brei sighed and looked at her hands rather than in his eyes. "You'll have to go back."

Such casual words said with such import and weight, Cadwal felt the mountain crushing down on his chest again. And talking about him just casually strolling back into Roman slavery as if they were noting some mild change in the damn weather! A command of a druid or not, there was no way he'd be going back to Deva. He tried to get off the bed, but his arms and legs were so weak it felt as though the air was a thick as the sludge from a bog. As he lay helpless, he could find no reply for the death sentence that had just been pronounced. Nor knew what to say without getting a more immediate one for telling a druid what objects he could insert into a certain orifice.

The memory of the smith's betrayal and the panic of fumbling with the useless key in a dark tunnel came back in all its vivid awfulness. "He can't be trusted. He'll just keep the gold and keep me as a slave!"

"So, you take in half the gold and we'll have the rest waiting for when he brings you back outside," Helig said, dismissively.

But that wasn't the reason Cadwal wouldn't be going back to Deva. "I can't." he managed to say.

"*Can't?*" the druid boomed. "Gwain trained you as a warrior, didn't he?"

"I have to go for my boys," he said and was surprised that without the strength to get off the bed, somehow he'd found the courage to argue with a druid. "I delivered the message, I did my part."

"Your *boys?*" The druid's voice was like a rumble of thunder echoing through the mountains.

"I promised," he whispered.

"How touching," came the mocking response. "And what did you promise your teryn when she let you take Crow hill as your home? What did you promise Gwain on the day you became a warrior? Tell me where a promise to two boys sits with the ones you made to your clan, your king, and your tribe?"

Weakly, Cadwal held up his hand to show the mark on his palm from when he'd bitten it in the arena.

"What's this?" the druid asked.

"A blood-oath."

"Who to?"

"My wife."

"Well," Helig mused. "You can't break a blood-oath. It's *sacred.*"

The druid was quiet for a moment. "Where did you do it?"

"The arena in Deva," Cadwal answered before he understood why the druid had asked.

"In Roman territory. Then our gods wouldn't have witnessed it."

"A *blood*-oath!" Helig protested.

"No!" Cadwal snapped. At having such a promise to Gwen dismissed, his rage was about to erupt. "I care nothing at all for Roman gods," he seethed. "And our gods let the men of my clan die at the foot of the mountain, so I care even *less* for them!" At that moment he wasn't even worried about the warning rattling of bones above his head on the end of the staff. Neither the gods, nor a druid who spoke for them would stop him going for Owyn and Arwel.

Tegin was silent. Even the bones were quiet.

For a moment he thought Brei was rhythmically punching Helig, but it was his heart pounding.

Helig saved him from having to say anything else. "What if we raided a Dog settlement and kidnapped a few fighters? We could get some information out of them."

The druid's burning glare lingered on Cadwal for a few moments longer, but he finally answered. "You could. But just as it would be with us here, only the leaders would know the full details. And besides, in my experience, men will say anything you want them to so the pain will stop."

A shiver ran down Cadwal's spine at what the druid must have done to know that, but with the terrible attention diverted, at least he could breathe again.

"Maybe we can sneak into one of their forts, take a chief and bring him back for you?" Helig asked, enthusiastically.

"You sound like a boy with thirteen summers planning his manhood escapade," the druid chided, and lying against him, Cadwal could feel Gwain's son tense at being spoken to in such a way. It didn't cow him into silence, though. "Could you not look into the flames of a fire, or spill some entrails so we can see ahead a moon or two?"

"We do have powers beyond most men's wildest imaginings, it's true. But we can't do that."

"But, I've seen you do it..." Helig stammered.

"No. That's what you *think* you saw."

"Which is what you were supposed to see," Brei offered as an explanation. "If the Oak Throne is yours, I'll explain it to you one day. But never mind that now, I know how we can find out what we need to know. Heulwen," she called to the young girl crouched by the fire. "Can you bring me a woundwort leaf, and a nettle one?"

"But I didn't pick any nettles."

"Have a look again."

"Oh," the girl exclaimed when one in the basket sung her. "I didn't notice."

Brei smiled as Heulwen presented her with the similar looking leaves and she laid them on the bed next to Cadwal's leg. "What do you see here?" she asked Helig,

"Err... Leaves?"

"Go on."

"Stinging nettle leaves."

The young girl pointed down over Brei's shoulder and helpfully said, "That one isn't. It's woundwort."

"I don't understand," Helig mumbled.

"One nettle," Brei brushed one of the leaves over Helig's hand. "And one woundwort."

"It's just two leaves. They look the same. Why would I care?" Helig protested.

"Exactly my point!" she said as her brother chuckled knowingly.

"What is?!" Helig gasped, frustrated.

"One leaf heals, the other stings," she smiled. "They may look the same, but they are very different. And you can't tell the difference because they look enough the same you wouldn't even *think* they're different."

"What?"

"Appearance is everything," the druid said.

Helig scoffed. "I still don't understand what you're trying to explain with a couple of leaves!"

The effort of concentrating on what nonsense they were talking about was making the poles of the house swim before Cadwal's eyes.

"She means that a more subtle approach is needed," the druid explained.

"It can only be our eastern border the Dogs will attack," Brei continued. "If the Cornovii to the south know we've stripped fighters from the settlements to face the invasion, there'll surely be clans eager to expand north." She picked up the nettle leaf. "So what if we go to Deva..." Cadwal watched as she then put the harmless woundwort one over it. "Pretending to be from the Cornvii tribe with an offer of men to push north at the same time the Dogs attack?"

"You're not talking about going to find the smith with a bag of gold, are you?" Helig asked.

"No. We'll go to the commander himself and look him in the eye, with the torcs around our necks, gleaming with the light of Lleu."

"Appearance is everything," Helig said and Cadwal felt him chuckle.

"The Romans will think we're the healing one," Brei said, waving what Cadwal thought was the woundwort leaf.

"But we'll be the one that stings!" Helig finished.

Cadwal listened intently but couldn't believe how casually Brei was suggesting that she would simply walk straight into the heart of his worst nightmare. He wondered if the idea was god-sent, but the druid next to him gave no indication she'd said anything out of the ordinary. He didn't care though. With the relief of knowing he wouldn't have to go back to the smith, it felt as though he was floating above the bed. Brei and Helig could be the heroes for bards to write songs about and he was free to sleep and then work out how he could rescue the boys.

"When do we leave?" Helig asked.

"No," the druid rejected. "You are the last man there is to lead our warriors, so you are the key to what happens next. But if you disappear with the mysterious stranger and the king declares you banished, you can't call men to battle when it's a sentence of death simply for talking to you."

"If we don't find out their plans, I'll have nowhere to call men to battle to!" he pleaded.

"I can't travel alone through the lost lands," Brei said. "Romans have a poor regard for the status of women. I will need an escort."

"Very well," Tegin reluctantly growled.

"But," Helig said. "If we stop them raiding our lands… what then? There is still a full legion at Deva."

"First one battle," Brei sighed. "Then the next. If we protect our crops and animals for the winter, at least when the spring comes, we won't be half-starved and dropping from plague. And there's a lot more fertile land to the north of Deva that should be easier to take and more profitable than the grazing lands of our sheep. If the new governor is only interested in expansion, maybe he'll simply head north to the land of the Brigantes."

"So there's hope?" Helig asked, a little brighter.

"There's always hope," the druid said. "Without hope, there is nothing." But he then looked down at Cadwal again, eyes as dark and foreboding as tunnels leading underground. Before their awful scrutiny, all he could do was squirm. "And our hero here goes back to the smith." His words were punctuated with the staff banging on the floor.

"No!" Cadwal gasped as it thudded beside the bed again. His head spun so much he was worried he'd faint again before he could beg not to be sent back to the smithy.

"He is in no fit state to travel," Brei said. "He's hurt. He can't even get off the bed to stand up, never mind sneak into the fort again."

"His task is to go back as a slave, and that's exactly what he looks like."

"No…"

The staff loomed above him again, and he knew to fear it much more than a Roman's whip. Cadwal wondered if some magic was being performed over his bowels or if they were churning on their own volition.

"You *will*!" the druid said. It was as though it was a different man speaking from a few moments before. Deeper, stronger. Cadwal winced just from the sound of it, but the feeling of despair was worse when he caught up with what was being said. "If you don't go to Deva, you and I will go for a short walk to the wetlands to make a sacrifice, and only I will come back. And your boys will stay where they are. Forever."

"You'll *sacrifice* him!" Helig gasped. "He can't even get out of bed. Brei's plan is worthy of Gwain. We don't need him!"

The druid sighed heavily. "Before us we have *two* possibilities to find out the legion's plans. You are a warrior, so tell me this: facing your worst enemy for the final fight, would you keep half of your force back? No," he answered himself, "You would throw everything at him. Our guest shall go. If he comes back with what we need to know, *then* you can think about calling him a hero." He hit the staff on the floor again, shaking the bones.

"No..." Cadwal stammered, but no one was listening to him.

"How do we get him out of Dinorwig without Bleddyn knowing?" Helig asked.

"Leave that to me," the druid said. "Shave his face properly and get him ready to ride a horse out of the gate before dawn tomorrow."

"N..." was all Cadwal could manage before the staff thudded on the floor for the third and final time. The bones still rattled as the druid announced, "It's decided."

Cadwal was outraged they were talking about him like he was no more than a slave being bundled into a wagon. He wanted to shout his protest, but nothing intelligible came out of his mouth though. His mind ran over the threat again, in case he hadn't heard it properly... but the druid really had said that if he didn't offer himself as a slave back in Deva, he'd be dead. Cadwal didn't doubt it. The gods, he could curse, the king, no one seemed to care about, but the man standing over him with the staff had more power than either. He would have to go, out of helplessness, but the feeling was no different from when he'd been chained up in the smithy.

"Can I come too?" the young girl asked.

"Oh, no," Brei said.

"But I won't get in the way. I will do as you say."

"You might only be small," the druid smiled. He reached a bony hand out to stroke her hair in the most human gesture Cadwal had ever seen a man like him make. "But if you think you're brave enough, you'll have a big job here."

"What is it?" she asked.

"If someone asks where Brei is, you tell them that she went out picking herbs. And that Helig went hunting."

"But that's so easy. Why do I have to be brave for that?"

"Because the longer it takes people to find out that they've gone, the further away they will be before your father sends men after them."

"Oh," Heulwen nodded. "That *is* very important."

"A job for a teryn."

"Will I be as brave as Brei?

"You already are," Tegin smiled.

Something else Cadwal had never experienced before; he saw a flicker of human emotion cross the druid's painted face. He lifted a finger to the little girl, a gesture that would have disturbed the bowels of any man it was pointed at, but said softly, "But not a word of this to Bleddyn."

He got a serious nod back in return. "He burned my doll," she said with a pout.

"Did he? How terrible. Hmm..." Tegin mused and shook the staff a little so that the bones made their strange noises again. "Did you hear that?" he asked.

"Yes!" Heulwen gasped, eyes wide. "What does it mean?"

"That's the gods suggesting we call it a sacrifice. And a *noble* sacrifice as well, performed by the king in the fire. The gods are pleased."

"Really?" the girl asked in wonderment as Cadwal cringed in fear again.

The staff was tapped on the floor three more times. "Yes."

The sweet interaction reminded Cadwal of everything that had been taken away from him and his heart bled for the boys he couldn't go to. With gritted teeth and clenched fists, he lay in a speechless disbelief that the druid spoke kinder words about a straw doll than him.

Then the druid turned his attention back, all softness gone from his eyes. "*All* sacrifice is noble."

"We leave at dawn tomorrow," Brei said. "We'll get to Gavo at White Walls and the next day on to Deva."

"Very well." The bones at the top of the staff tinkled again. "I'll stay to watch Bleddyn. A man who sets a whip to his counsellor is obviously in need of some good counsel."

"And Derog too," Brei added.

Fear and dread clenched a cold fist around Cadwal's heart. There was so much he didn't understand, so many questions to ask.

Just a couple of days ago, he'd been chained to an anvil with a metal collar around his neck. But somehow, even though he was back with his tribe, he was even further away from his boys.

Yet even though his fate had been decided for him by the word of a druid, deep in his heart he still held his promise to Gwen even higher.

NINE

S HAKEN AWAKE BY a druid, the death-like face illuminated by the hearth fire, was no way to start the day. As he tried to spoon some cold stew into his mouth, Brei smeared a thin paste over his face, but it was only when she dabbed the ground charcoal around his eyes that he realised what Tegin's plan was. Of everything he'd done in the last few eventful days, nothing seemed as unbelievable as being painted like a druid.

Thick cloak around his shoulders, the hood pulled up, the disguise was complete.

"Kings cower in the presence of a druid," Tegin boomed. "Do you know why? Because of our *presence*. If you want to look like a beaten slave with a painted face, stay hunched over as you are. But if men are to see someone of the Laws and Ways…"

Cadwal gasped as his shoulders were roughly pulled back to jerk him upright.

"…Ride like *this*."

A command of a druid was not something to disobey, but he could barely put one foot in front of the other.

With a tut, Tegin shoved the gnarled staff of twisted hazel at him as though it was just a normal piece of wood he'd found on the forest floor. "Maybe this will help? Be very careful with it though," he warned, as the bones tied to the top made their creepy noises. "The Elders won't be too amused if you shake it the wrong way and burn down the whole fort."

Brei's little giggle hinted that it might not be the whole truth the druid spoke, but joke or not, Cadwal's palms were already sweaty. Instead of using it as a rod of power, he held onto it as a cripple did a crutch.

"If the guard at the gate stops you, look at him as though you have chosen him for the next sacrifice," the druid said calmly. "Power is magic, and magic is power, remember that."

Brei stifled another laugh at his words, and as she helped Cadwal duck down under the low hanging thatch over the door, she said softly, "You can't imagine how many years I studied on Mona before I heard such words."

If they were so important, Cadwal didn't know why the druid would say them to him, so off-handly. The thought was quickly lost, as outside, in the silence of the early

115

morning, the idea of spending a day on a horse seemed a lot worse than the threat of a king to kill him.

Helig helped him up into the saddle as though he was a little girl, and nervous with his clumsy attempt to mount, the horse moved before he'd set himself in the saddle. With weak hands, he couldn't hold onto the pommel properly.

"Careful," Helig said as he bundled him upright. "We need you alive, hero."

"Just act as Tegin would and you'll get straight out," Brei said. "And we'll catch up with you outside."

Cadwal had half a hope the guard would see through the obvious ruse and he wouldn't have to leave. Brei handed him back the staff and he rested it across his knees carefully so the bones wouldn't make any noise. He didn't know what terrible magics existed in the tinklings and didn't want to find out.

Helig slapped the horse's rump, and from trying to keep his balance with legs splayed over the saddle, many new pains accrued from the past days presented themselves to his awareness. As he neared the light of the flickering torches over the gate, he made sure the hood was pulled forwards to protect the white paste from the gentle rain, but not so much that the light of the guard's torch wouldn't illuminate the pale paint.

"Who's there?" one of the lads on duty shouted down.

"Tegin," Cadwal called in the same tone Gwain used when one of his charges had acted disappointingly stupidly. He hoped the tremor in his voice wouldn't sound suspicious.

"Where are you going at this time of the morning?" the lad on duty asked cheerily.

As he'd been told, he slowly raised an accusatory finger and snarled, "You question me?" He watched bemused as the young guard slipped down the steps on his heels and backside in his haste to get the gate open. "We're just supposed to ask, that's all!" he wailed.

What a man could do with such power, Cadwal thought.

He rode slowly along the muddy path that curved between the huge earthen ramparts of the ditches and banks, then out in the open made his way slowly down the hill, careful with the staff in case it was to send out a bolt of lightning. He had a flash of inspiration but was sure of what the answer would be if he asked about blasting a hole in the wall of the Dog's fort with it.

A few moments later, he heard the others trotting up behind.

"Any trouble?" the druid asked, chirpy, as though he was a lad about to join them out on patrol.

"No," Cadwal replied and handed back the sacred staff with what he hoped was due reverence. "The guard thought I was you."

"Appearance is everything," Tegin chuckled. "Where you're going, it will be good to remember that. But you should have seen his face the second time he saw me! I said I was practising some new magic to fool the Romans with, and if he told anyone about it, I'd turn his tongue to stone."

"We should hurry," Brei warned as she helped pull the hooded cloak from Cadwal's shoulders.

"No one will pass me," the druid said, his voice instantly full of foreboding again. He slammed the staff into the mud of the track and the tinkling of bones sent a shiver of alarm down Cadwal's spine.

Pleased to be free from the attentions of a druid, Cadwal nudged the horse forwards. It plodded slowly away in the dark and he allowed the animal to feel its uncertain way along the track, clopping through the mud at its own pace. He didn't get too far before realising how much of a challenge it was going to be to just stay on the saddle. Every lazy step the horse took rolled his hips from side to side and even at such a sedate pace, it felt like a fresh lash of the smith's whip. Despite the cold morning air, sweat was soon trickling between his shoulders and he wondered how long it would be before Brei made the next cup of willow bark. Yet, desperate for sleep, the lazy rhythm of the horse and the sound of the wind in the trees lulled him into a doze. When a cock crowed, he opened his eyes. In the gathering half-light, he was surprised to see they were at the lake... which they should have been nowhere near. "We're going over the *pass*?" he asked with fear.

"Did you forget they built a fort to block the ford across the river?" Helig said.

Cadwal groaned. It would be easier to sneak around a Roman fort in broad daylight as even in good weather, the sliver of a ledge between the cliff and the sheer drop was treacherous enough for those who had no trouble walking. He'd seen what the gods were capable of with the men outside of the mines, so up where only pack horses and sheep went, he could be swept off the edge as effortlessly as an ant flicked off a twig. He'd be completely at their mercy.

He thought again of the broken bodies in the surf. By his reckoning, surely the gods should be proud of men who'd just made it out of the mines, not angry enough to kill them after only a few moments of fresh air. Why they would allow such a thing to happen, or even cause it, made no sense at all... until he realised something so unsettling it was a struggle to stay in the saddle. If the gods had killed the men of his clan, just as the Dogs and Romans had done, didn't that make the gods themselves his enemies?

His chest clamped so tight for a moment he couldn't breathe. He was about to call out to Brei, but but thought better of uttering such words, especially so close to the lake.

"Are you all right?" Helig asked. "Your face has gone whiter than when it was painted."

Cadwal nodded but Helig's look of concern turned to one of scorn. "Still don't want to go to Deva?"

This time he shook his head.

"We'll talk about it once we're in White Walls," Helig said, dismissively. He nudged his horse a step or two ahead so no more could be said.

A little further the track narrowed and with the low branches of stunted oaks reaching over them, gnarled roots clutching mossy stones, it felt as though they'd entered the lost world of the Old Ones.

Staring at Helig's broad back, Cadwal's thoughts ran on unbridled until he came to a reasoning that made him sit bolt upright. If, for whatever unfathomable reason, the gods had set themselves against the Ordo-wiki... what then did the words of a druid who spoke for them count for? If they meant nothing, wasn't he free to ride off to the Dog's fort?

No longer chained to an anvil, nor to the command of a druid, a trickle of strength flowed back into his heart. Enough to give the idea that he could fight. He decided that if he survived crossing the pass, he'd tell Brei and Helig he wasn't going to Deva. Knowing he'd see his boys again soon was the first uplifting thought he'd had in what felt like an very long time.

Ahead, Helig swung out of his saddle and immersed in his deep thoughts, Cadwal watched bemused as he set about tying a length of leather cord between two lichen-covered trunks. "That will give us a few extra moments if anyone is chasing us," he beamed and twanged it with a finger to test its tautness. But the smile was wiped from his face by Brei's glare, as piercing as any druid's.

"I can take it down," he said, sulkily, like a chastised young boy.

"It's not that," she replied, rain dripping off the folds of her cowl. "It's a trap for the necks of our own tribe."

"Bleddyn's choice," Helig mumbled grumpily as he mounted again, and it was in a moody silence they carried on climbing up the narrow valley, mountaintops on either side lost in the low cloud.

Soon, the last of the trees thinned out into the grazing lands. On the rain-lashed slope, the gusts felt urgent. Blowing through the stunted bushes dotted among the wind-flattened grass, the wind sounded like the sighs of displeased gods and the higher they climbed, the closer Cadwal was to simply presenting his body for them to flick off the cliff.

Such contemplations were Brei's domain though. He lifted his head to see her hunched over in the saddle, waxed cloak drawn as tight around her as the wind would allow, the loose ends flapping against her horse's flanks. She seemed to be paying the storm no attention, so the only comfort he could take was that if she wasn't worried probably nothing too awful was about to happen.

Near the top, the thick mist wrapped around them, making it hard to see as they scrambled around the rocks that had fallen from the cliffs above. Some were as big as roundhouses. As the horses found a way between, a song came to mind, about how one day all of the majestic mountains would roll into the sea, rock by rock, until all the land was as flat as the estuary. It was one that men always laughed at with a scorn of disbelief.

Maybe Brei was thinking the same thing, as when the gusts lulled long enough his ear caught a few notes of song. Over the whipping of his cloak, he couldn't make out what ballad it was, but every note of her voice touched his heart. For a few precious moments, the absolute perfect beauty of it helped him forget he was drenched and freezing... and that the boys were prisoners of the Dog.

Hooves slipping on the sodden ground, the horses got them to the top and they pulled into the shelter of a bluff where the sheets of sideways rain blew above them rather than into their backs.

"That was the easy part," Helig shouted above the noise of the gale with a childish grin. He dismounted and passed up the water skin. With a hand blanched white from the cold and a long morning of gripping the saddle's pommel, Cadwal took it gratefully.

"Ready to see if the gods love us or not?" Helig laughed.

Wounds chafing painfully against his soaked clothes, unsure if it was water, sweat or blood running down his chest and back, Cadwal was in no mood to smile.

When Helig tied his horse's reins to the straps of Cadwal's saddle, the fear welled up with a vengeance. Confining holes underground, never seeing his children again, or a son of Gwain calling him a coward, were all one kind of fear. They were earthly worries, just as every farmer fretted about rain and weevils, and every mother hoped her child's cough would be better in the morning. But making enemies of the gods for simply bringing the warning of the raids to the king, was a fear like flailing in the air after running off a cliff.

He handed the skin back and let Helig lead the horse to the start of the pass and wondered if he was enjoying his last few heartbeats in the world. There was no relief though as, although they were out of the worst of the wind, the other side was shrouded in a fog so thick Cadwal could only just make out the shape of Brei's horse ahead. She was also walking. And had stopped singing.

Some said the blinding whiteness was the same as a cloud, the only difference being that it clung to the ground rather than float in the sky. But all said that whenever you can't see the world of man, you are close to that of the Otherworld.

The track hugged the side of the sheer cliff and soon narrowed to not much more than an arm's length. Keen to keep away from the edge, the horse scraped Cadwal's leg against the rough rock face. The drop was so far down, no man could survive the fall… and a puff of a god's breath, a flick of a god's finger, was all it would take to push him over. Thinking of what must have gone through his clansmen's minds as the elation of escaping the mines turned to terror as they fell, the anger and defiance in him rose. He'd delivered the message to the king despite them, and if they didn't want him to sneak into a fort to save a pair of grubby-faced boys from a life of misery and pain, then damn them, they could knock him off and be done with it.

In a silent dare, he loosened his grip on the saddle's pommel.

His horse was unsettled by the bitterly cold water splashing over the side of its neck from a little waterfall of storm water cascading down the cliff. It shook its mane, and planted its feet wider for balance and Cadwal was sure the time had come. Peering over, he saw that his horse's hooves were just a finger's width from the edge. One loose rock, one slip, or one little nudge, and he would disappear into the void and join his god-cursed clansmen.

Helig turned around with a mad grin. Yet, one unsure foot after the other, the horse plodded on, and where the track widened, he dared to let a little hope seep back into his heart, like a beam of sunlight making it through the fog.

When he saw there was space enough for clumps of grass to grow at the edge, and that the sheer cliff on the other side had softened into a sodden bank, he allowed himself a loud sigh of relief

As the track led further down, the fog began to thin and the lush green of the grass and pinks and purples of the heather, came back to his eyes. It was all dotted with yellow spires of agrimony and dappled in patches of fast-moving light where the sun was breaking through the clouds. It was the land of the living and no landscape had ever looked so beautiful.

With a cry of jubilation, Helig untied his horse, swung into the saddle and galloped ahead to the remote high valley, the summer grazing pasture for the tribe's precious flocks. Cadwal shared the sentiment. The gods had let him live and soon he would be cradling his boys in his arms.

Up where nothing but short grass and ferns grew, only a couple of rough houses stood, smoke and steam rising through the soot blackened thatch. Almost naked despite the weather, children ran out to greet them, squealing at the sight of the sullen and drenched strangers. Brei handed them a few strips of dried meat, which they thrust greedily into their mouths, before holding mucky hands out for more. A few followed and got braver with their cheeky insults, until Helig made his horse dance in a circle and roared a battle cry while reaching up for his war hammer. They shrieked off in delight.

Another pleasant thought was how easy the rest of the ride to White Walls would be compared to the pass, but that lasted all of a few heartbeats. As soon as Helig called out for the horses to speed up to a trot, it felt like all of his joints had popped out of their sockets. Balance lost, he slumped over the side of the saddle, and grabbing the reins, made the horse turn sharply. At least the wet bracken gave a soft landing.

Helig slipped off his mount and clasped Cadwal's hand, ready to help him back up.

"Go on without me," Cadwal said. "I can rest here and get to White Walls later." And maybe if they left, he wouldn't have to explain anything... and could just make his way to the Dog's fort without a confrontation.

"We're not leaving you!" Helig exclaimed. "The people up here are around nothing but sheep all their lives. Who knows what they'd do to a pretty naked-faced man they found lying on the grass?"

Despite himself, Cadwal laughed, but the stupid joke reminded him of Tamm. Helig's smile faded as well. Maybe he could see the hurt and fear on Cadwal's face.

Brei, a few locks of drenched hair matted over her face, began preparing a welcoming cup of willow bark, but it wasn't the pain in his body that kept him on the ground. He took a long breath of the damp and fresh air and said, "I'm not going back to Deva."

Helig moaned with disappointment. "You still want to go to the fort of the Dogs for your boys? Even after what Tegin decided?"

"I don't refuse a druid's command because I am *feeble*."

Helig's full-bellied laugh sounded so like his father's, and, for a moment, Cadwal was back in training at the foot of his terrifying teacher.

"You can't even stand!" Helig mocked "How do you think you can even *get* there? You'd get to live a few moments longer only because they'd be laughing at you so much it'd be hard to cut your head off! Come on, get up. Fight me. Imagine I'm a Dog guarding the gate." He clenched his fists and took a ready pose. "Show me how you will face their guards."

Cadwal looked at the bulging muscles of Helig's arms, the fluid way he moved and wondered what he would give to just spring up to his feet and embody such strength and prowess. He'd need half a moon at least to recover to the point he could run and swing a hammer properly. "My sons." He spoke through gritted teeth, willing Helig to understand. "If I go back to Deva, the smith probably won't let me leave again. I *cannot* go back there while my boys are slaves of the Dog."

Helig gasped in exasperation. "A man who freed himself from Roman chains and then was the only one anyone had ever heard of to get out of the mines. Can you imagine what a story it'll be around a fire, horns full of mead? We would all call out curses to the bard for trying to take us for fools, because no one would believe such a tale. My father was called Great, but he never escaped slave chains and got himself out of a Roman fortress! Can you imagine how easy it would be for a man like that to be able to gather men to fight? Never mind what the old king says, they would *flock* to him like crows to a battlefield!"

Helig was suggesting that Cadwal step into Gwain's heavy mantle, something more than any warrior could ever dream of, but it was the last thing Cadwal wanted. When he didn't move, Helig leaned over, to stand with his hands on his knees as though he was admonishing a toddler. "The smith thinks you're god-touched," he said, a hardness in his eyes. "That's *just* as important as Brei going to speak face to face with the commander in Deva. Maybe more so. Besides, it was *Tegin* who said you will go to the smith. A *druid's* plan!"

Cadwal still didn't move.

"You would put the lives of two boys above the whole tribe?"

Said in such a way, it sounded like an accusation of a great weakness. But the terror of going against a druid, the future king, and the gods themselves, was nothing compared to imagining the rest of his days without the Owyn and Arwel. The world was worthless without them. "You don't have children. You can't understand."

Helig stood up again and looked at Brei. "Can I tell him?"

She shrugged.

"You know Heulwen? The girl at your bed."

"The teryn? Minura's sister?" Cadwal asked.

"She's not the king's daughter." Helig grinned with a hint of pride. "Granddaughter of Gwain. *My* daughter. So don't tell me what I should or shouldn't feel about protecting a child. I am here with you to try to save her from what is coming."

"It's not the same at all," Cadwal croaked. "She is safe with the king of our people. Mine are with the king of our *enemy!*"

But then something snapped in Helig, and face reddening in much the same way his father's used to when one of his charges had failed at something simple, he yelled, "I'll take you back to my father's skull over the gate at Dinorwig so you can piss on it! Come on, on your feet! I *command* you!"

And just as Gwain would have done, Helig pulled a big foot back, ready to kick his legs. Unable to defend himself, Cadwal braced for the impact.

"Stop!" Brei shouted, her voice carrying near the same authority as her brother, and the kick never arrived.

She stepped between them and with one hand held up to Helig, warded him off. In the other, she offered Cadwal a cup of medicine. He only just had the strength to raise his arm to take it. As much as he was loathe to admit, Helig was right. Climbing over fort walls and running down a mountain with a pair of children was far beyond him. He concentrated on tipping the cup to his lips without spilling too much.

"Helig, son of Gwain," Brei said, eyes wide and a finger pointed. "I have been the king's counsellor for more years than I was married to your father, and now I offer words to the heir to the Oak Throne. Will you listen to me?"

The anger left him a beat of the heart. "As though the gods themselves were speaking to me."

She might not have had a shaved head, or a face painted to resemble a skull, but Cadwal noticed that her presence certainly put terror into the hearts of normal men. And future kings.

"Bleddyn has led us to where we are by not doing what needs to be done. Now the tribe is split into those who know what is right and what we must do, against those who wish to honour their king, and therefore the gods. Both sides are justified, but one will end in the death of us all. The only hope we have of stopping the Dogs and Romans destroying everything and everyone we love is knowing where and when they will attack. Is that a truth?"

"It is," Helig agreed.

"Cadwal," she said, and at the sound of authority in her voice, suddenly he had more fear of her words than he'd had for Gwain's boot. "I will ask you a question and you will answer me with truth on your tongue."

He nodded his agreement.

"What would you call a man who escaped Roman slavery and then the mines to bring a vital message to the king?"

"Say it!" Helig prompted.

Reluctantly, Cadwal spoke the words she wanted him to say. "A hero."

"A king, a hero and a druid," she said, finger tracing a circle between them. "The three of us can do what is needed for the tribe and our song will be sung around the fire for a thousand years. Or..." In turn, she looked at them both in the eye with a penetrating gaze. "*Or,* we can be a banished nephew, a coward, and a girl with a few years of teachings... who all die tomorrow."

Brei's accusatory finger had stopped tracing a circle and Cadwal looked at it pointing at his chest.

"Cadwal ap Madog, as counsellor to the king, I hold you to the pledge you made the day Gwain gave you your sword. You will go to Deva."

In her sweet feminine voice, the words sounded much worse than Helig's rough command.

"Thank you," Helig said. "Will you listen to *her*?" he mocked, but then the dreadful finger was aimed at his chest.

"And in exchange, Helig, you will go to the Dog's fort."

Cadwal was suddenly alert.

"What?" Helig gasped in surprise. "I'm not going anywhere for just for two boys! The war with Rome has started! As soon as we find out what their plans are, I need to get back to Dinorwig."

"For two boys," she nodded. "And *Minura*."

"Minura?" he asked, confused.

Swilling the medicine around at the bottom of the cup as though it was the last of the king's finest mead, Cadwal resolved that if he should ever stand face to face with the teryn again, he wouldn't mention he'd not given her a single thought since being pulled out of Crow Hill.

"Bleddyn's daughter will be enjoying the company of the Deceangli king, as well as Cadwal's boys. How well do you think it will serve us when we want him to call men to fight if we present her to Bleddyn?"

The deep furrow in Helig's brow had gone. "And not to be declared banished!" He looked at Brei in awe. "What magic is it that gives you such ideas?"

"No magic," she shrugged. "Simply from understanding men, their motivations, and what needs to be done."

Magic or not, it seemed to Cadwal that Helig was suitably impressed with the idea of saving Minura. "Can we attack with Gavo's men?" he asked eagerly.

"I think they can be persuaded," she nodded.

"It's a big risk though." Helig rubbed his chin as he thought. "But it's a huge fort, so maybe we could stage a fake assault at the main gate to create a diversion while a few of us sneak over the wall."

The father in Cadwal recoiled at the idea of someone else saving Owyn and Arwel. But although Helig's plan sounded a lot like the ones he'd come up with in Brei's house, when the druid had chastised him for making childish suggestions, the warrior in him knew Brei was right. He'd have trouble getting onto the horse again, never mind running to the top of a mountain. So, having Helig, son of Gwain the Great, scaling the wall, was a lot more than he'd wished for.

"Do you agree?" Brei asked.

Speaking the words that would make him a slave again, Cadwal said, "I do."

"And you?" she asked Helig.

"I agree," he nodded. "I'll go to the Dog's fort for Minura."

From the heights of being offered a real possibility of rescuing Owyn and Arwel, Cadwal's heart sunk again. Helig had only mentioned the teryn, the part of the plan that mattered to him.

In the same way that he gathered the warrior calm around him, Cadwal drew strength, and despite lying prone on the ground, tried to snap a command that sounded like a king or a druid rather than a broken man. "And the boys!"

"Yes, them too," Helig said with a wave of his hand.

But it wasn't enough, and Cadwal found himself doubting the words of a son of Gwain. He forced himself up to kneel at Helig's feet. "If I am to spend my days at the end of a short Roman chain," he said, flinching a little when raindrops fell close to his eyes. "At least I will *know* that my boys are free."

"They will be," Helig said and breathed out heavily. It was only the slightest sigh of impatience but was too much to ignore.

"Swear it," Cadwal demanded.

"Swear *what*? I just said I'll go to the Dog's fort!"

"Even if I don't get back out of Deva?" Cadwal said as he got a foot under him.

Helig took a deep breath. "How do you invoke the gods?" he asked Brei.

"No gods," Cadwal said. "Just you and me."

"Very well," Helig sighed. "If you go to the smith in Deva, I'll organise a raid to the Dog's fort. I spoke and my word is my bond. Is that enough for you?"

Infuriatingly there was still an unmistakable reluctance in his voice. Cadwal knew how Helig would react to what he had to say, but there was no way to temper the insult. "A blood-oath."

"*What*?" Helig gasped, outraged. "My *word* isn't good enough for you? What is worth more than the word of the heir to the Oak Throne and the son of Gwain?"

"An heir who is possibly banished," Cadwal pointed out. If he was already an enemy of the gods, making one of the coming king wasn't too much to worry about.

"Well..." Helig stammered. "That may be. But..."

"Or the story you want the bards to sing ends here, with the sheep and the wind."

Brei unsheathed her knife and offered it hilt first to Helig.

"Will you listen to *her*?" Cadwal asked and got a glare in return.

Still glowering, Helig pricked his left palm, then held it hilt down for Cadwal to take.

It took just about everything he had but he pushed himself up and like standing on hot embers and swaying as though he was being buffeted by a raging storm, he stood up. Helig was much taller, but at least being at chin height was better than at his feet. On the heel of his palm was the scab made a few days earlier for Gwen, when he'd been in the arena. Next to it, he made another cut and grasped Helig's open hand.

"I swear on my blood that I'll go and get your boys," Helig said.

Cadwal nodded his agreement. "And I will go to Deva and find the smith."

They both showed Brei the smudges of blood on their hands.

"It is witnessed," she said.

"Now let's *ride*!" Helig ordered impatiently.

As much as Cadwal wanted to get back on his horse by himself, he needed Helig to bunk him up into the saddle. As they began at a trot, he was too tired and hurt to move himself to the rhythm of the horse, so waves of pain shuddered through his body with the rhythm of the horse's gait. Thoughts about the boys, the betrayal of the gods, a blood-oath with the coming king, everything was forgotten as it took his full attention just to stay upright.

The long, silent ride through the mountains was interspersed with a couple of breaks for food and for the horses to catch their breath. It wasn't until just before dark that they finally stopped. Brei led them through a thicket of trees into a shallow hollow out of sight of the road.

"Why don't we carry on to White Walls?" Helig asked. "We're close."

"Because if anyone there thinks our plan is foolish, I don't want them trying to stop us."

"Gavo will beg us to allow him to come with us!" Helig laughed.

"Not Gavo. There's an Elder in the fort. Would you dare argue with Tegin, never mind an Elder?"

Helig was quiet.

"Exactly," she sighed.

"You think our plan is foolish?"

"No," she shrugged. "I would say it was mad, not foolish."

Cadwal felt a touch of jealousy as he watched how easily Helig swung out of his saddle. He could think of no way to get off his horse without cause for amusement, but thankfully, Helig made no comment at how he simply slipped into his arms. From where he sat, propped up against the trunk of a young oak, he tested some twigs to see if they were dry enough for kindling.

"No fire," Brei said.

"Is this Dog territory, or ours?" Helig asked.

Brei shrugged. The raids hadn't started yet and they didn't even know what land was theirs or not.

Cadwal resigned himself to spending a shivering night wrapped in a dark cloak, but his dark thoughts eventually led him to what might be in store tomorrow. "How will I get into Deva?" he asked eventually.

"Talking like a warrior at last," Helig grinned, but spoke in a hushed voice.

"How?"

From one of his saddle bags, he pulled out a bag. "My father would have been mad if he'd have found out, but when I was younger and Deva was just a small auxiliary fort on the estuary, we used to float down the river with sheep's stomachs filled with air under our arms." At that he blew into the bag a few times until it was inflated. "At the jetty, we'd pick up a box or an amphora and look busy, and no one noticed, because who cares about a slave? Then, when no one was watching, we'd set a fire, slit a throat or two, and in the confusion, jump back in the river and float away downstream. It kept them nice and frightened about what was waiting for them in the mountains."

He threw the stomach at Cadwal. He'd had heard similar stories but they were just escapades for boys trying to prove they were ready to be men. And a few who didn't get away, found that they didn't need to pretend to be slaves.

"Of course, that's before the full legion moved in," Helig added. "It'll be a bit harder now there's five thousand legionaries milling about. But if this works, your name will be remembered in these lands like Caradog himself."

"Caradog lost the battle to Scapula," Cadwal moaned. "Cartimandua of the Brigantes betrayed him and handed him over to the Romans in chains, remember?"

"They say he lives. And they call him Caractacus."

"Yes. In *Rome*," Cadwal said, exasperated. "With another name. Which is the same as dead."

It wasn't so dark that Cadwal couldn't see the change in Helig's expression. It went so quickly from jovial to sinister, eyes gleaming with malice, that a cold trickle of warning flowed through Cadwal's heart. Helig's hand, thumb pressing uncomfortably close to a bruise on his back, began to tighten until it felt like he was held in a metal worker's vice. Leaning in close, Helig growled, "I will not soon forget I had to give you my blood over my word. Fear me when I am king!"

Shocked speechless, all Cadwal could do was think how utterly unlike Gwain his son was.

But then Helig was all beaming smiles again. The moment was gone. Once the horses were unsaddled and secured, Brei unpacked the food and they all tore into the dried meat without another word.

TEП

THE NEXT AFTERNOON, after another agonisingly long day's ride, Brei tried to shift to a more comfortable position in the saddle. She'd struggled with the pain in her back from the moment she'd got on the horse before dawn, and it had got worse as the long day dragged on. It hurt more now than when it was freshly flogged. Enough to cloud her thoughts, right at the moment she needed them to be crystal clear. Cadwal's need for the last of the willow bark was greater than hers, so the only way of alleviating some of the discomfort was mouthing another curse for the king she hated.

Lingering on the horizon ahead, she could make out the pall of smoke and dust above the fortress. At least there wasn't too much further to go. They caught up with yet another cart. Pulled by lumbering oxen and loaded high with produce and belongings, the wooden wheels clattered noisily on the gravel of the unnaturally straight road. With the Silures subdued, the legion's southern fortress had been abandoned and so a long stream of families were on their way north to set up home in the shadow of Deva's walls. Ready to feed off the invading and murderous Romans like ticks on a horse's ear.

The noise drowned her words out for mortal ears, so to any god who cared to hear, she said, "For myself and all our people of the tribe, those that came before us and those who will come after, I curse you Bleddyn, in this life and beyond. Forever forgotten, may your name never be on any man's tongue!" Curse spoken aloud, she felt better, like emptying her belly after drinking a horn of bad ale.

At a point where the river wound closer to the road, they jumped the ditch and rode to the shelter of a stand of trees. Helig let Cadwal slump into his arms and set him carefully down on a dry patch of grass. She'd seen plenty of men fixed with an iron resolution as they prepared themselves for a fight, knowing some would fall to enemy swords that day and be left for the crows. The brutal fate she'd arranged for the last man of Crow Hill, riding back to his slaver, was nothing she'd known a warrior have to face. Her own suffering was almost nothing in comparison.

Helig helped him slide out of the saddle, and, before he could argue, she put the collar around his neck. She flinched in sympathy as it snapped shut. It was a horrible thing to do, but at least with it secured on him, she didn't need to worry about him giving up on the plan he believed was hopeless and trying to run to the Dog's fort instead.

"We will meet again soon," she said as she set down the last of the willow bark powder and a water skin. "In *this* world," she added hastily.

"If the smith lets me free for a second time," Cadwal sighed.

"If he sold you to the mines for a few coins, he should take you outside the walls for more gold," she said with a confidence she couldn't feel.

With the sheep stomachs inflated, Helig said, "Don't go until it's *full* dark."

Helig helped her back on the horse, and she turned back to see Cadwal slump backwards into the reeds. She hoped he'd manage to stay awake.

It was a rather unceremonious parting for one of the bravest men she'd ever met. He'd been trained by Gwain and it gave her a warm feeling to know that the great man's legacy lived on on some way.

With no herbs to lessen the tension crushing her temples, all Brei could do to calm herself as she approached the fortress, was to fill her chest with air and keep it there for a few heartbeats. The exercise lasted until they crested the last rise in the road, as seeing the overwhelming sense of cruel purpose in the high and straight walls, she forgot to breathe.

The horse carried on taking her closer as her muscles in her arms were too weak to pull on the reins to stop it.

Helig must have had the same thought. "Not even Vercingetorix's horde could get through those gates," he said with an uneasy awe.

To the south, in the rich lands of the southern tribes, she'd been in hillforts as big, but a native tribe's defences flowed in curves around the features of whatever hill it sat atop. What the Romans had built, with its brutally straight lines, was an imposition on the landscape and was clearly constructed by men who had no affinity whatsoever with the laws of nature.

The last of her hope turned to damp ashes in her mouth as they came to an open space for trading before the river. They pulled up next to a pair of slave wagons and when those inside, helpless and in chains, saw the plaid Brei wore, they cried out desperately for help, pushing hands through the bars as much as the shackles would allow. Brei had to draw deep to ignore such heartbreaking pleas but couldn't help a quick glance to see if she recognised any of the dirty faces.

Some men haggled over the prices of sacks of flour for the next day's bread, but the trading ceased abruptly when they noticed the new arrivals. A few stared with unbridled disgust, eyes gleaming with greed at the gold on her arms, but when Helig swung out of the saddle, they saw his size and wisely pretended they didn't exist.

Infinitely more unnerving than a few nosy traders were the four Roman auxiliaries guarding the bridge. Dressed in the same armour as the creatures of her nightmares, Brei's flesh crawled with revulsion. They were men from conquered tribes giving twenty-five years of their lives suppressing their own people for the distant reward of Roman citizenship, but were as foreign now as any other people consumed by the empire. Leaning on their spears, they stood with the nonchalant pose of very bored men, but watched everything with a mixture of hawkish attention and deep suspicion. Any threatening behaviour and in one quick, and well-practised, movement, the tips of the spears would be aimed at chests.

As Helig helped her dismount, they were accosted by a small group of beggars. Hunched, and afflicted with pus-leaking boils far beyond anything her herbs could help with, she couldn't deny them a few pieces of bread. But all equally hungry, they all wanted some and suddenly she was jostled by a desperate crowd trying to get into the saddlebags. Shouting a warning, a couple of guards came to push them away and mumbling curses, the hungry men shuffled off with whatever morsels they'd managed to grab.

One of the soldiers, almost the size of Helig, the broadness of his chest exaggerated by the strips of metal layered across his shoulders, looked them over and from the flashes of gold up Brei's arms decided they were worthy of attention. "What's your business?" he asked Helig gruffly.

Disgust rose up in the back of her throat so powerfully she had to fight the urge to retch. "We are of the Cornovii," she managed to say, giving Helig a squeeze on the arm as a reminder to stay calm. Helig's fists were clenched so tight his knuckles were white around the horse's reins.

It had been a long time since she'd spoken Latin, so slowly, and with obvious mistakes, she said, "We are friends of Rome and have come to speak with the commander."

"The commander?" he scoffed. He spoke in the native tongue with a thick accent. "About what?"

Back in the language of the land, she said politely, "I have warriors to add to his legion to help in the fight against the Ordo-wiki." Lifting her chin to show off the torc, she continued, "I have come to make a deal."

She moved her arm to adjust her shawl but only so the light of the evening sun would catch her arm bands and bracelets.

"Wait," he growled.

He'd probably been taken from his family as a young boy and, as an auxiliary of the legion, had been taught that anything not Roman was barbarian and beneath contempt. Yet wealth, it seemed, was a language known to many, and whoever it adorned was held in high esteem. Even a boy on guard duty knew high status when he saw it.

As he strode back to his post, his armour made the clinking noises that had haunted her dreams long after the Black Year. She worried that if her legs got any weaker, she'd need Helig to carry her across the bridge.

The most junior of the guards was sent jogging over to the other side to ask someone higher up if a pair of plaid wearing locals could cross. The wait did nothing for the tightening knot in her chest. Trying to bring down the sense of peace and clarity that fighting men called warrior calm, she patted the travel dust from her clothes and made an effort not to look at the massive wooden wall facing them on the other side of the river. A decade of learning on Mona, years as wife of the hero king and then counsellor to the next... nothing had prepared her for this.

She untied her rolled up cloak from behind the saddle.

"It's not going to rain," Helig said. "I'm no farmer, but even I can tell that."

"If there's a way to walk around inside the fortress and look for the smith, I don't think we'll last very long in plaid in a place full of soldiers trained to lust for our blood."

Despite being so close to men who would kill them in a heartbeat if they knew who they were, Helig laughed. She didn't stop him. It was good to show that he was relaxed, like a Cornovii would be.

Helig untied his cloak as well.

When the soldier jogged back, he gave an affirmative nod to his colleagues.

With another flutter of her heart, Brei took Helig's arm and was about to ask the guard what they should do with the horses, when one snapped at Helig, "You go alone."

"Actually, I am the one sent to negotiate," Brei said.

The guard looked at her questioningly. Conscripted from a tribe somewhere, she didn't think he needed to be educated on the elevated status of women in 'barbarian' society.

"Alone," he repeated.

She knew better than to argue.

Besides, she wondered if it was good fortune that Helig would be staying on the far side of the bridge. Inside the fortress, delicate skills learned at the feet of an Elder would be much more useful than those honed by the constant clashing of blades.

"I don't like the idea of you going in there by yourself," Helig whispered.

"Why?" Brei smiled. "Do you think you could protect me against five thousand Roman soldiers?"

"I could die trying."

"And then Derog would have no rival to the throne."

Helig mumbled in reluctant agreement.

"Keep the horses saddled," she said. "All night if need be."

The simple nod was all she needed to know that he'd be here waiting if they needed to leave in a hurry and she wondered if it was safe to allow herself to believe he could be the king the land needed. She'd watched his demeanour darken over the last few days, a change that had come to a head with his ugly words to Cadwal in the heather just beyond the pass.

The power inherent in the Oak Throne was an insatiable lure for a weak man, and could poison him as it had both Bleddyn and Derog. If it would effect Helig in the same way, it wasn't worth her crossing the bridge.

"Go and make songs for the bards to sing!" Helig grinned. "My father would be so proud to see you this day."

She tucked the cloak under an arm and smiled at the thought of the curses Gwain the Great would have bellowed at the idea of her going to talk face to face with the commander of the legion.

The soldiers parted for her and as she strode out onto the huge bridge she became aware of how the structure was symbolic of everything they were fighting. Everything about it, the complicated design, the sheer amount of manpower needed to build it and engineered with enough strength that even horses and carts could cross. It was utterly beyond what the tribe could imagine. To support uncertain legs, she rested a hand on the rail and felt the immense and almost inconceivable power of the enemy. Unbidden, awful memories of Mona flowed into her mind like the dark waters she stood over.

At the far end, six cavalrymen waited on the big horses and she saw the hunger of lust in their eyes, both for her body as a woman and her blood as an enemy. She was impressed at their discipline as none leered or even made a crude comment.

A foot soldier snapped, "Follow me." His Gaulish drawl marked him as another auxiliary. She smiled politely and fell into step to his side and about a pace behind.

As they'd seen on the road all afternoon, passing wagon after wagon, wherever an army went, its attendant traders and craftsmen followed, like summer flies behind a horse, and the settlement outside the fortress was already flourishing. Most of the houses had roofs on, although ones of rough thatch, not earth-coloured Roman tiles fired in kilns. Despite being so late in the evening, carpenters still worked on wood from roofing beams to wagon wheels, tanners stretched cow hides and sheepskins over frames, while what might have been the carcasses they came off were being chopped up by butchers behind the houses. Vegetable plots were already planted, and children ran around squealing with joy without the slightest care in the world.

Brei noted the discernible sense of expectation in the air, the assured belief that for as far into the future as they could see, in the shadow of the fortress they and their families would be perfectly safe. She couldn't imagine a life of such privilege.

Two women, sweet smiles on their soft faces, both soon ready to give birth, held bunches of flowers in their delicate hands, but when they noticed Brei's plaid and the thick twists of gold at her throat, their idle smiles snapped to frowns. The smallest children were pulled protectively behind skirts and tools in craftsmen's hands were held in a way that they could quickly become makeshift weapons.

The guard grunted with amusement, but the fact that it was Brei they were afraid of, not the Roman in full armour, felt like a slap in the face. Once she'd passed them, she cast a look back over her shoulder and saw that their frowns had changed to passive disinterest. Like the sheep up in the high pasturelands, as long as they got some fresh grass to munch, it mattered not who herded them. It seemed the Romans hadn't been content to just take the land of the people, they'd also claimed their spirits.

Then, with a wave of nausea, she caught sight of the curved walls of the amphitheatre. Death was the mirror of life, as natural as the dusk eventually following that morning's dawn. But the killing the men of Rome were known for enjoying was an aberration against everything she held dear. How they found pleasure and entertainment in such human suffering was one of the reasons they would always be such enemies.

The walls loomed up before her. Two huge and imposing square towers stood beside a pair of massive doors. The legion's banner fluttered between the arches, the red of fresh blood. Their motif was a horse with wings. It seemed somehow fitting, because if Brei couldn't find out the route of their march and the day they would leave, the Romans might as well fly straight over the mountains to Mona.

The smell of fresh cut clay and tree sap filled the air. The ditch was so deep that in the evening gloom she couldn't see the bottom. She peered down into its depth, wondering how far down they could dig before the earth started bleeding from such a wound. As the gatehouse rose up above, it reminded her of walking under the huge bows in the old sacred groves of Mona. Yet it stood over much more of a difference between the world of man and that of the gods. Passing under, Brei went from the land of the people, right into the heart of the purest enemy.

More guards waited just inside. These weren't common auxiliaries trading their heritage for a pension, but full legionaries, part of a cohort and century of the Second Legion. Men who looked at the same land but saw only what was foreign and to be conquered or killed. Their hardened faces showed deep suspicion and most regarded her as though she was something unpleasant they'd found on the underside of a shoe.

With her level of Latin, she just about understood the exchange as the guard explained her reason for coming inside, and once her shawl and cloak had been checked for concealed weapons, a straight-backed soldier waved her to follow him.

On the other side of the gate house, there was none of the chaos of the vicus, just an atmosphere of the ordered readiness of disciplined soldiers. A group of bare-chested men laughed together outside what she assumed, from their reddened skin and the smoke billowing above the roof, was a bathhouse. With a few elbows nudging their friends to attention, they all turned to stare silently as she walked by. A couple spat on the ground in her direction, but a few of them proudly puffing out their chests was the worst abuse she suffered. More terrifying than their cruelty though was their restraint. The training to turn them from normal farm boys and men into Roman soldiers who fed off brutality meant they more resembled the bolt firing machines they used rather than any man she knew. The thought did nothing to calm her heavily beating heart.

At the central crossroads stood the imposing principia. Its gatehouse, even inside the fortress, was a match in size for the main entrance at the fort of Dinorwig. Even after everything else she'd seen since crossing the bridge, it was this monumental difference that almost crushed her. Those inside needed to see confidence, so she couldn't allow her sense of desperation to show. Standing straight, she told herself she was a Cornovii chief with many men at her back.

Another set of guards protected this building and with a few short words, she was handed over to them. One turned around and marched up the steps so fast his blood red cloak billowed out behind him. Brei took it as her cue to follow. As the door thundered shut behind her, she wondered how many gates and guards stood between her and home.

A grunt and a finger pointing to a place against the wall was the guard's way of nicely asking if she wouldn't mind leaving her rolled up cloak there.

The doorway led into a huge and open yard covered with more small stones than there were stars in the whole sky. They crunched under her feet with the sound of walking on a riverbank. How they were all so perfectly uniform, she had no idea. She'd been happy for a few branches being laid down on the mud in Dinorwig. To the sides were open corridors with the rounded stone columns holding up the overhanging roof. There was a kind of harmony in the angles and proportions of the square buildings, but with all the unnatural uniformity it was the stillness of death. To Brei's eyes, every facet of nature, the interlacing rustling of tree branches, the meandering of a stream bed, even the life-giving movement of the air, was all subjugated. The straight lines and the crushing permanence of stone and tiles made it a stranger place for her at thirty years old than the druid's groves and rituals on Mona had been when she was five.

Over the stones to the far side of the open space, she was led to three men standing around a table of scrolls, illuminated by burning torches. The guard got their attention, and when they turned to look, three pairs of hard eyes suddenly opened wide in surprise to see a woman before them. One adorned with plaid and gold. On the face of the most senior, a mask of sincerity descended, and he took a measured step towards her.

The first dusting of grey coloured his stubble, which put him at about the right age to have been a young soldier at Mona, revelling in his first blood. Maybe they'd heard the same screams that day.

"I am Quintus Lucius Valerius, Praefectus Castrorum, third in command," he said in a voice that sounded like the gravel she'd walked over. "The Legate and Tribune have retired for the night. Perhaps I could help?"

He walked and breathed just as she did and had a heart beating in his chest, but while she was a healer, dedicated to caring for people and wanting nothing but a peaceful future for the children of the tribe, his life's purpose was nothing but the pursuit of power and death. He was her complete opposite.

And then Brei realised he was speaking the native tongue, almost as well as she did. He looked at her with predatory eyes and a cruel smile. "No, we don't need a translator."

"You speak very well," Brei replied, careful to lay the foundation of their engagement with a compliment.

"To beat your enemies, it's best to know all you can about them first."

She was both disgusted at such an offensive statement and relieved that it would be much easier to articulate her lie. "I am not here as an enemy," she said as graciously as she could.

"Really?" he asked.

"I am Brei, of the Cornovii," she said, head held high, torc proud over her throat despite the untruth. "I have travelled far to bring you an offer."

As an experienced soldier, used to judging the threat of potential enemies, he eyed her up. Assessing himself safe, he dismissed the guard. "An offer?" he asked, seemingly more amused than interested. Exchanging a few words with the other two, and some agreement made, they were dismissed. In unison, they thumped their chests and thrust their arms out in salute, palms down. One picked up a helmet with a plume of purple horsehair arched across the top of it. To the Romans, it marked him as a centurion, a man in charge of the discipline and lives of eighty soldiers. To Brei, it was like standing next to a monster that had crawled out of a crack between the world of men and the gods.

With a look of open contempt, yet giving her the same distance as a dog whose temperament wasn't trusted, the other two left, striding confidently over the stones with a sound like crushing the skulls of a thousand druids.

"So... this... offer of yours. Please tell me what brought you so far, so I can determine its merit."

On the table was a parchment with a map drawn on it, much more detailed than anything the Ordo-wiki scratched on the floor with sticks. At the way he rolled it up so quickly, she wondered if it depicted Ordo-wik lands. Could she have just come so close to finding out what she needed to know?

With another deep breath, Brei calmed herself down and hoped she could pro- nounce the Latin name for Dogs. "We wish to join the Deceangli in exchange for land to settle, once the Ordovices are conquered."

"Well..." Confusion wrote itself in the crinkles of Quintus' forehead. "I am sorry you've had a wasted journey, but that's a tribal issue, not something we'd bother to get involved with."

"Yes, but the Deceangli are not the power in the land. You are. A treaty with Rome would..."

"A *treaty*?" he scoffed. "You're a tribe leader, are you?"

"Just a clan, not a tribe."

"Still," he sneered. "After Boudica, the idea of women leading men seems to have lost its... popularity."

"Among our people, a cock isn't the main requirement for power, or good leader- ship," she said, and was glad to see him smile.

"And how many men follow you?" he asked.

"Nearly two hundred."

"Two hundred," he coughed, hardly able to contain his mirth. "You're brave just turning up here riding in your... traditional clothes. All the way to the gates of the legion with such an... offer." He picked up an ornate jug and slowly poured two glasses of wine. "You have a lot of gold on your... body, for a leader of two hundred men."

"I confess, I borrowed some so I might make a better impression."

"Ah, I see. That would explain it," he nodded. "Deceit, we call that. Not the best way to enter a discussion about a treaty."

There was a hint of mischief in his eyes though. Maybe he thought he was having some fun, like a cat toying a mouse. She hoped the exchange would prove to be a little more even than that.

"You must be weary after your travels," he said.

As he picked up the glasses, Brei wondered which of his companions had just drunk from the one he was about to offer her. "I apologise for all the dust. As you might have heard, the new governor will arrive soon and we'd like to welcome him to a finished fortress. Gnaeus Julius Agricola is his name. Probably the name means nothing to you, but the legion he fought with, you might have. The Twentieth..."

Her knees faltered. It was the Twentieth that had destroyed Mona when she was a girl. One of the butchers had risen through the ranks of murderers and was now in charge of the whole land.

His words struck her worse than a lash of a whip and she wondered if she could hear the sound of distant screaming. All her pretence crumbled as she tried to convince herself he couldn't possibly know her plan and her mind flailed helplessly.

"But perhaps you could do me the honour of telling me the *real* reason you are here?"

Accepting the glass with a shaking hand, the only thing she could think of was to present the whole lie to make it sound like a fuller truth. "We heard there is to be an invasion of Ordovice lands by both the Romans and the Deceangli. We would be happy to join their ranks, but it's with you we want to have a treaty with for the land."

She watched the thin smile fade from his face and the light of laughter in his eyes go out. He nodded slowly, weighing her words. "And where did you hear of such a plan?" he asked, his voice a little harder.

"A trader."

"A trader?" he asked, his eyes wider for a moment before narrowing to a squint.

Distrust, she read, and suddenly, in the look of an eye, it was a dance of death. Anyone watching them wouldn't have noticed a thing, but she'd made a mistake saying it was a trader who'd brought the news and all had changed. And another shocking thought; what if Romans had different facial expressions to the Ordo-wiki and she couldn't read him, just as she couldn't understand the Latin they spoke?

"I see," he mused. "Well, that is indeed something to discuss with the commander tomorrow."

The humour had completely gone from his eyes. What she saw there now was unmistakably predatory.

"A toast to such a partnership?" he suggested.

Brei turned her attention to the delicate glass. Pale blue and almost translucent, it was one of the most beautiful things she'd ever seen, and she barely stifled a groan at how delicious the wine tasted.

"Imported from Narbo... although I don't suppose you know where that is. One of the perks of... cooperation." He emptied his glass in one swig and picked up the flagon again. "The thing is, about your... treaty though. We already have one with the Ordovice."

In shock, some muscles in her back clenched and the pain flared up. She tried not to writhe before the Preafectus. "Oh..." she managed to squeak.

"So there won't be any resistance in those mountains. In fact, I hope you and your men aren't expecting any battle glory, as the whole tribe are as weak as their leader. Only yesterday I said that if ever a historian were to write about the coming campaign, they'd have to embellish most of it to make it seem like we actually had an enemy to fight!" He laughed at his own joke, but the hawkish look hadn't left his eyes.

Brei wanted to be ready with a witty reply, but the enormity of his words stilled her tongue. And suddenly Bleddyn's stubborn reluctance to stand against Rome made terrible sense.

She smiled with feigned politeness.

"So," he said, his glass refilled. "What was he trading?"

Mind swirling in a confused turmoil, she stammered, "Who? What?"

"You said a trader told you about the planned invasion. What had he carried all the way to your lands to trade?"

Her heart felt like it was being stretched out over an anvil being beaten with a large hammer. It was a detail she hadn't thought about. "Beads," she gasped with no idea why that popped into her head. Maybe some old memory of the sparkly baubles she used to fawn over whenever a trader made it to Mona before the Black Year. But realised how stupid it sounded. "And trinkets."

"Beads and trinkets," he nodded.

She tried to tell if his thin smile was now a mocking one.

The Praefectus stepped closer, and she could feel the cruelty pouring off him. It wasn't hard to imagine how much he enjoyed the spectacles of blood and deaths performed in the arena.

He took a deep breath through flared nostrils. "Show me your back."

"Sorry?" she stammered, caught completely off guard for the third time in as many moments.

"I've been a soldier all of my life, and in my station I have flogged enough recruits and men under me to know how they stand for the next week. Show me your back."

The words were polite but had an edge that implied there was no choice. She took a sweeping look around the room for anything she could use as a weapon. The only thing in reach was the short sword at his hip.

He cocked his head, a sign of impatience.

She set the wine down and numbly unpinned the brooch. Shawl pulled from her shoulders, she turned around and lifted the back of her shirt up to display the full extent of Bleddyn's displeasure.

Behind her, Quintus whistled. "Like a painting of a sunset with all the reds and blues."

"It's a harsh world we live in," she said, letting the shirt fall back down. Fighting down the panic, she tried to compose herself back into the role of a Cornovii on a diplomatic mission. "It's why my clan needs to move, and why we are happy to fight alongside, or even instead of, your Roman soldiers."

"Banished?"

"Yes. But that doesn't have to be a death sentence if you have new land to settle."

"Ah. I see," he nodded. "So, who did this to you? Husband? Father?"

"The brother of my dead husband," she said, and speaking the truth, the tone of dripping hatred came easily off her tongue. "But I don't need to bore you with family stories. Simply, it would have been death to stay with my tribe. And now those who left with me see an opportunity to make a new home for ourselves. In alliance with Rome."

"But the Cornovii *are* allied with Rome," he said, handing her back the glass.

"Ah..." she gasped. She'd slipped again, and mind racing like a noisy brook, she was incapable of making up a believable lie on the spot.

From the way his nostrils were flared after looking at her bare back, it was obvious what he wanted. But instead of working out how she could use his arousal to her advantage, it caused her to freeze.

"Let's get you some salve for those bruises," he said. "Our medici have some wonderful healing potions."

Brei forced a smile but the thought of him laying his hands on her made her want to scream.

He took her inactivity as an invitation and put a heavy hand on her shoulder.

Women who weren't whores or slaves, or officer's wives, would be rare creatures in a military fortress. She supposed those he was acquainted with didn't often say no.

Strong fingers drew her closer and she had to stop him... without fighting him.

She'd come so self-assured, believing an expression on her face would outsmart a brute who knew nothing but marching and how to wield a blade. But with a few words, he'd destroyed her as easily as Gwain teaching a new recruit not to be so cocky.

In a strange sense of slow motion, she dropped the glass and followed it down to the floor.

The Praefectus swooped down to help, and for a moment they were close enough that his short sword was just about in reach. For a fighting man, the steel was an extension of his body and there would be no way to wrest it from him. Instead, she pressed her hands in the broken shards of glass and pretended to hold onto him for support, smearing her blood on his tunic. Even that didn't stave him off though, so she concentrated on the thought of his calloused hands on her naked body and, as she hoped, it created such a surge of disgust so strong she hurled the wine up over his legs.

His cry of despair was glorious. In it, she heard his desire die.

Angrily, the Praefectus grabbed the end of her shawl to wipe himself and above his curses she heard the crunching of at least a couple of guards running over the yard. He snapped a command and with big hands around her arms, she was hastily led away over the little stones.

She managed to grab her cloak before being manhandled out into the street.

ELEVEN

C ADWAL SAT GROGGILY among the reeds. The breeze had dropped and, in the still air, the surface of the river perfectly reflected the dark outline of trees on the far bank. The outward calm was not reflected in his inner turmoil, though. After two days on the horse, there wasn't a part of his body that wasn't aching or throbbing.

He touched the collar again. The unnerving sensation of the cold weight of it locked shut around his neck. It pressed on the chafe marks and bruises it had left before, and no way of turning it made the discomfort any less.

For the vain need to feel a touch of fortitude in his pained heart, he rubbed the two scabs on his palm. One for Gwen, bitten under the slave wagon the day he'd been taken from Crow Hill and the other, fresher and straighter, for Helig. The fate of his boys, the most precious things in the whole world, sealed in such small cuts in the skin. Instead of instilling strength, he thought again of how Helig's face had changed as he'd made his threat the night before at their roadside camp. As he shuffled his backside in a vain attempt to find a more comfortable position to sit, he found himself not trusting the son of Gwain. Thoughts darker than the encroaching night gathered in his mind... and like a storm even the most powerful druid couldn't stop, they kept coming. Minura was Bleddyn's daughter, so with the king's blood, she was closer than Helig to the Oak Throne. If Helig wanted so much to sit on the Oak Throne then leaving her to her fate in the Dog's fort would make it easier for him to take charge. And if Cadwal wasn't able to get out of the smithy again... Ordo-wiki or not, no oath had to be kept for a slave.

He tossed the weighty pouch of gold a little in the air and caught it again. Enough trinkets and coins to buy the freedom of dozens of slaves. Enough to pay a small army to raid the walls of the Dog's fort... He put the thought away quickly. Whatever he suspected about the motives of another man, his *word* was bond, never mind his blood.

He looked across the river again and saw that the waters had become as dark as the night sky, too dark for anyone to notice him swimming downstream. It was time. He forced himself to his feet, glad at least that he wasn't having to walk to the fortress.

How long before I will be brave? Almost the last words he'd heard Arwel speak came back to him as clear in his head as though he'd spoken them out loud. The

143

answer was as brave as a little boy kept as a slave, hoping every moment that his father would come for him.

Forcing himself to his wounded feet, he tried to see the marks on his palm again, but it was too dark.

Sweat-stained tunic at his feet, he shivered in the evening cool. The pouch of gold he tucked into his loin cloth snugly at the top of his legs then waded into the silty bank at the water's edge. As the cold mud oozed over his ankles, he squeezed the inflated sheep's stomachs to make sure they were airtight. With one under each arm, the cord between them around his back, he lowered himself into the water, and gasped a curse at how bitterly cold it was. Sinking down to his shoulders, it was hard to breathe.

Kicking his legs to move a little faster than the lazy current, he drifted downstream a little quicker than walking pace, floating blindly towards an uncertain fate. But it only took a few moments to realise his beaten body was far from ready for this adventure. The piercing cold quickly gnawed into his core, and with muscles locked tight in shock, all he could do was concentrate on paddling with his feet, careful not to splash in case someone was on the bank. When he realised he couldn't see the banks, the panic was almost as consuming as when he'd been trapped in the tunnels. With no point of reference, he floated in an age of nothing but frigid cold and worried that he'd slipped unnoticed into the realm of the Otherworld. Or worse, he was somewhere in between, a place men with curses hanging over them were left, unnoticed by the gods.

The first light he saw was a deep relief, even though it must be Roman. An old feeling of elation, like when he'd taken part in raids against the Dogs, quickened in his heart. He was close to Deva, and whatever was going to happen, at least he'd be spared the ignominious death of freezing to death in the river in the dark.

Paddling with his hands, he turned to face the current and focused on the flaming torches at the sides of the bridge. He remembered it as the place he'd been separated from Tamm and the others and he saw again his brother's dusty face as he lay on the grass outside the mines... and slammed into one of the sturdy wooden legs. Before he could stop it, a cry of shock and pain escaped his throat. With the water lapping around his ears, he tried to listen for the tell-tale call of alarm from above. None came. At least none he could hear, and he was swept along in the swirling current without being spotted.

In the eddies on the other side of the bridge's legs, he began to struggle to keep his face above the water. Splashing noisily, he felt the bags. One had burst. He slipped under the surface and flailed around coughing and spluttering, but the true horror was something wrapping around his foot. Gripped by a terror that the gods were reaching out to drag him somewhere even worse than the Roman fortress, he was about to scream, but bumped into one of the pier posts. In his world of water, the solidness of it felt like a victory against the gods and he grabbed hold of it tighter than he'd ever held onto anything before.

After all it had taken to get here, pulling himself up the bank should have been the easiest task of all, but from so long in the water, his arms and legs were almost completely useless. Flopping around in the claggy mud, he tried to claw his way out, but wasn't as quiet as he needed to be. The pain around his throat was so blinding that the cry came out only as a weak croak.

As he gasped for breath on the boards of the pier, men gathered around with burning torches to see what strange fish they'd caught. He felt the sodden loin cloth beneath his leg. The gold had gone. Another one of Helig's great plans...

His whole body shaking uncontrollably, Cadwal peered up at the men but none made a move to help him. A soldier pushed through, his shirt of metal rings reflected more points of light off the torches than the whole hoard of the ancestors in the night sky. A few grunts and kicks and it was determined that Cadwal didn't speak the tongue of the invaders, so someone else was called over. "Who are you and who owns you?"

Cadwal almost spat his name in proud defiance but remembered how important Brei had said it was to act like a slave. "I have no name," he gasped with words that sounded pathetic to his ears. "I am owned by the smith."

His words were translated and then the expected question, "Which smith?"

Cadwal tried to remember the name but could only remember what he'd been told to call him. "Master."

A few laughed, but not the soldier who began uncoiling his whip. "What were you doing?"

Cadwal couldn't bare a lash. "I didn't look where I was going. I fell," he wailed, sounding convincingly like a pitiful slave. He wasn't pretending.

The soldier shrugged and Cadwal understood the kick was an invitation to stand up. He knew he had to get to his feet, but bone cold from being in the water so long, his legs refused to work.

The soldier scoffed impatiently and grabbed Cadwal's hand. In the light of a burning torch he could see the white and puckered ends of his fingers.

"If you just fell in, why are you so cold as though you just rose from the grave?"

Someone leaned over the edge of the jetty and called out when they found the sheep's stomachs.

The soldier cursed again and pointed towards the walls of the fortress. Cadwal's arms were grabbed and he was dragged through to the huge gate, hope as feeble as his legs.

Even though it was terrifying to have the soldier's hands around her arms, Brei was glad for their support. They led her to a building at the side of the principia on a smaller street and while the guards fumbled to get the door open, she tried to work out where they were. She wasn't going to get anything from the Praefectus, so now she'd need to find her way to the smithy instead.

By the time they'd found the right key, the Praefectus had composed himself and had come to join them.

"I will inform the Legate of your wish to meet him tomorrow," he said, a tone of cold formality in his voice.

"Thank you," Brei replied, with equally factitious politeness.

"I hope you won't mind me setting a guard at your door for the night. The men are well disciplined, but like with dogs, if you put a bitch among them, who knows what ideas they will get."

"Not at all," she said, careful not to show any offence at the insult.

But it wasn't any other man in the fortress she was worried about. If he was to get over his disgust and decided to join her, no guard would stand in his way.

As the door was opened, she noted how much the hinges creaked. The room inside was a tiny square space with a thin bed against the wall and a small opening near the top of the far wall, not much wider than the span of her hand. The guard lit an oil lamp on a small table. It was the only source of light.

Far harder than was necessary, the soldier slammed the door shut and locked it. The lock was much too big to be opened by the pin on the back of the brooch so she wouldn't be getting out until they decided to let her. She took it off her shawl anyway. A few unexpected jabs to the face with the sharp pin sticking out between her fingers wouldn't kill the Praefectus, but it might get his hands away from his sword long enough for her to grab it. The life of the third in command would be a very small consolation for a failed mission though.

Although she was temporarily free of his attention, his words still held her. She paced nervously back and forth in the small and unnaturally shaped room. A deal with the Ordo-wiki? She'd never understood why Bleddyn was always so reluctant about not rising to meet the Roman threat. Could he really have made some secret agreement with the legion that his heir and counsellor knew nothing about? It didn't seem possible. Whatever sordid deal Bleddyn had made, she couldn't understand how it could involve the Dogs and Romans freely raiding the land together. What king could allow that?

From a smooth clay cup, she took a sip of water but spat it straight out as it tasted like someone had relieved themselves upstream. It was good enough to wash the blood off her hands and holding palms up to the lamp, she checked that there weren't any pieces of glass under the skin.

What Bleddyn had done could be contemplated later, first she had to get out of the room.

Door locked and the window too small to climb through, the only hope was over the partition wall, which had only been completed to the height of the other walls, not to the vault of the roof. With the table on the bed, she could reach the central beam. First, she balanced her cloak on it, then with all sorts of pain flashing in her head from the cuts in her hands and bruises on her back, she managed to swing up.

Pushing the cloak first and then shuffling up to it, she made her way along over the three thankfully empty rooms. At the last one, she dropped the cloak down and then like a kid playing in the forest, hung from the beam with her feet as close to the bed below as possible. In the dark, she couldn't see that there wasn't one, so it was a painful landing and she had to wait a while to catch her breath and for the stars in her eyes to recede.

Fumbling around for the oil lamp and using her fingers to find the hinges of the door, she poured the oil in them. It wasn't locked and teasing it carefully ajar, it opened almost without a sound. She peered around and spent a few long moments watching the guard idly pace up and down at the other end of the building. He looked bored. Cloak wrapped tight around her shoulders, hood over her head, she waited until he turned away, then slipped away into the dark street.

A lone woman in a fortress full of soldiers would attract instant attention so she adopted a stiffer, more aggressive gait in the hope that anyone's first impression would be of a small, but determined lad heading somewhere on an errand. Like every road and building the Romans made, the street was dead straight and following the map in her head, she turned left and strode between the high walls along the back of the principia.

By the time she got to the huge perimeter wall, the percussive noises of the smiths were unmistakable. Footsteps plodded along the ramparts above, so she pushed herself back into a pitch dark nook just before the corner. As she waited for them to pass, the panic got the better of her and she couldn't help doubling over and heaving up the last of the wine.

At the third workshop in the row, she felt for the leather flap Cadwal had explained was where the charcoal gets delivered. She pulled it open, ducked down, and stepped into a morass of smoke, hot metal, and sweat. At the anvil stood the broad chested smith. Heavy arms sheened with perspiration, his muscles bulged as he worked. The image reminded her so strongly of Gwain that her heart caught in her mouth.

She dropped the cloak behind her so in the light of the forge, he could see her tartan and gold. Stepping over piles of charcoal and all sorts of unidentifiable tools, she got close enough for him to see.

In mid strike, he jumped as though he'd hit himself with the hammer. "What the...?" he cried out in shock as the bar he was beating clanged to the floor and hissed at his feet.

"A man called Cadwal of the Ordovices," Brei announced with a grandeur Tegin would be impressed with. "You bought him as a slave."

There was nothing but confusion in the smith's eyes.

"He lives. He escaped the mines. As he said he would."

"Madness..." the smith hissed and wiped his brow. When he looked again, he seemed a little surprised to see her still standing there.

She took a step forward and slipped a bracelet off her wrist. "He is god-touched."

"It can't..."

"He got out of the mines even though you gave him a false key. You know I speak the truth."

"What do you want?" he managed to ask.

"We would know the date of the attack on the Ordo-wiki and the plans of march," she said, holding the bracelet out.

Too dumbfounded to resist, the smith took the gold.

She unwound a band from her upper arm, the ruby set in the spirals glinting the colour of blood in the glow of the hot coals of the forge. "Just where and when," she said, offering it to him.

His mouth worked to form the words he didn't know how to say.

But then there was a commotion at the front of the workshop and he stared with the same gormless expression at the man the soldiers were holding. Cadwal. They'd both failed. It was all over.

The smith, suddenly realising that the handful of gold he held looked more than a little incriminating, he dropped it as though it was as hot as the metal he'd been working on.

Instinctively, Brei began to step back but bumped into something. Before she could scream, a heavy hand clamped over her mouth.

"You know what I think," the Praefectus growled into her ear. His other hand balled into a fist in her hair and she was stretched to tiptoes. "I think you are Ordovice and somehow you learnt about the plans we have for you." He shook her hard, her neck pulled painfully taut. "And you think you can come here and ask me to my face what they are? Whoever gave you that whipping is going to blush at how soft they were if they ever find out what I'm about to do to you. Then, if there's anything left, I'll show you how we treat Ordovice bitches here!"

A soldier picked up her jewellery and held it accusingly in front of her. More soldiers grabbed the bemused smith and the Praefectus snarled, "While I lock down the fortress in case there are more of you vermin inside, the torturer will start his work! We'll find out all you know and what you plan!"

With such parting words, two soldiers held her tight by the arms and marched her, the smith, and Cadwal away.

TWELVE

D UMPED FACE FIRST on the floor, Cadwal's immediate instinct was to pull and twist his hands behind his back, trying to get free of the metal manacles. He could just about reach the locking part with the ends of his fingers but didn't know how it worked, never mind how to get it undone. As helpless as any other slave in the whole empire from Deva to the sands of Judea, he still pulled against them for all he was worth.

Brei, her fine clothes ripped and torn open at the front, was flung in and landed clumsily with a cry and a curse. She writhed against her restraints with the same desperation.

The burly soldiers manhandled the smith into a heavy chair in the middle of the small room and wrapped a rope tight around his chest. As they slammed the heavy door behind them Cadwal saw how the gust of it closing fanned the glowing coals of a brazier set under a little chimney. He knew it was no forge and the instruments laid out on a small table next to it were for transforming men, not metal. A cold fear coursed through his blood as he suspected that the three of them were about to be very jealous of Old Drust's death.

"I swear to all the gods," the smith spat, "I shall tear your head off and use your skull for my night soil!" For a few moments, he twisted his shoulders against the ropes, but even with all the strength in his heavily muscled arms, nothing gave. "We're not getting out of here," he sighed, suddenly still. "We can pull at those manacles all night, but it won't do any good. I know how strong they are. I probably made them. You've *killed* me!"

"We're not dead until we're dead," Brei said through gritted teeth, still trying to get up.

"It doesn't *get* any more dead than this! They'll be taking us out of here in bits to feed the pigs!"

Working her way up into a sitting position, Brei shuffled around on her backside like a dog with worms. "When will the army gather and where will they march to?" she asked.

Cadwal couldn't believe that even at a moment like this she could still be focused on the plan.

151

The smith arched his head back in exasperation. "I told your idiot friend here before he left on his little boat trip, I *don't know*! I just hammer out spears and arrowheads from dawn to dusk. What do I care where they get used?"

Brei manoeuvred herself around to Cadwal's back and asked, "Can you get my brooch off?"

"Oh yes, a great time to make yourself look pretty!?" the smith scoffed. "Or do you think you can bribe the torturer not to stick a hot poker between your ribs?" Then he started to laugh. "That was your great plan? Walk in through the main gate, ask me when the legion will set out, and go back to get your army ready? Futuo! You got me killed for a plan like *that*?"

Despite the myriad of pains from different places as he strained to reach Brei's brooch, Cadwal fumbled around unsighted with the little clasp behind it. He had no idea about what she hoped to achieve but trusted her enough to do what she asked.

"This is what Rome is fighting against, huh?" the smith moaned. "You idiots! You really think you can fight against all of *this* with your slingshot stones? They've conquered the whole world, can't you understand that? Your stupid mountains are at the edge of one corner of their empire. It goes all the way from here to the pyramids in Egypt. Even beyond! Who, by all the gods, do you think you are to fight against that? *Who*?"

"The last," Brei said over her shoulder.

Finally, Cadwal got the brooch pin undone and it fell to the floor.

Gasping with the discomfort, Brei shuffled around to reach it, then began squirming with it under her back.

Suddenly, Cadwal realised what she was doing. "Like you did with the collar!"

"Hopefully," she grunted and Cadwal was momentarily jubilant that they could simply slip the metal off and run off into the night. That joy was short lived though as the door opened and a fat, mealy-faced man came in. Behind him followed a flame-haired young girl, and seeing the deep sadness on her face made something in Cadwal's chest clench. She knew what was about to happen to them.

While the fat man stirred the irons in the brazier, he chatted casually. "You barbarians can die quickly in the sun," she translated. "Or very slowly down here in the dark. The smith can go home to his own bed tonight. All you have to do is talk."

It seemed a very reasonable offer.

"Just tell him you went to the mines and escaped," the smith snarled. "I'm sure he'll believe that. And I let you go. Futuo!"

Brei still squirmed. The torturer grinned down at her, amused by what he must have thought was her terror. He seemed unconcerned by her movements. Cadwal could believe that most of those brought down here struggled with the same desperation.

"Tell him something," the translator said with a touch of panic. "I've been down here before and you don't want to find out what he does."

If the torturer didn't understand Brei's words, he did her tone and chuckled as he continued stirring the pokers.

The smith shouted out in Latin and pulled desperately at his bonds again. It was no use, though. The poker was drawn out of the glowing charcoal. It glowed at the tip, and Cadwal cowered away, as even from where he was sprawled, he could feel its heat.

"Please," the translator begged. "He can make it last hours."

"Tell him the story, you bastards!" the smith yelled, veins bulging in his temples and neck, sweat beading on his forehead. "Tell your stupid story!"

"Can you hold him back?" Brei asked the translator. "Just a few moments?"

"You have to tell him!" the smith cried.

Cadwal couldn't help pulling against the metal around his wrists again, a desperate instinct that ignored the pain it caused. "We are Ordo-wiki," he said. "We've come to find out where in our land the army will strike so we can meet them with a proper army."

The translator gasped, but she translated quickly. The poker was still pointed threateningly at the smith though. "Futuo!" he cried.

"And you just walked into the fortress?" the translator asked, then added her own words. "He doesn't believe you."

"*I* don't believe you!" the smith shouted. Then cried, "Nooo!" as the tip of the poker was angled down to point at his groin.

"*Please* tell him," the translator begged.

"We pretended to be ambassadors of the Cornvii, come to make a deal with the commander so we could find out the plan to raid our lands and have a chance to defend ourselves," Cadwal blurted.

"Don't tell him that!" Brei gasped, still furiously struggling with the brooch pin behind her back.

But Cadwal wasn't talking to the man with the poker. "We're Ordo-wiki!" he cried.

"Keep talking!" the smith wailed, voice getting higher as the red hot tip got closer.

"It was the last chance we had."

With her back arched and her feet scuffing on the floor, Brei looked as though she was suffering from some kind of spasm.

"Fuuuuu!" the smith screamed then began begging in Latin as the front of his leather trousers began to smoke.

Cadwal recognised the smell. A campfire with the meat of a freshly felled deer being turned on a spit. Some dirty river water churned in his stomach.

Over the cries of the smith's agony, the torturer listened calmly to the translator but shook his head in disbelief. With a mocking look of apology, he put the poker back into the brazier. Sparks flew up the chimney as he found the hottest charcoal at the bottom to settle it in.

Red-faced and eyes bulging, the smith squirmed as he cried, but beside Cadwal came a little gasp of relief as Brei freed herself. Still holding her hands behind her back, she rolled over and watched the torturer, poised like a cat ready to leap at a mouse.

Poker back in a fat hand, he had a terrible smile as he angled it at the smith's groin again, but it was wiped clean off as Brei sprang to her feet and using all of her strength, smashed the manacles into his face. The poker clanged to the floor and as the dazed man grasped his split lips, Brei jumped on him and with the brooch in her other hand, stabbed him in the face and neck with the pin. He was strong though and with a meaty hand in her hair, twisted her neck painfully around. Holding her like that, he had a hand free to reach for the poker handle. The translator snatched it out of his grasp though. Eyes burning, she asked Cadwal. "Is it true what you say?"

He nodded.

The torturer had his hand out for the poker, expecting the translator to give it back. He got it, but not in the way he was expecting. The thwack it made when it struck him in the side of the head echoed around the chamber.

Brei didn't waste a moment and held a hand out to take the poker to finish him off, but the translator held on to it. "We have to kill him!" Brei implored.

"I know!" the girl snapped.

The torturer whined for mercy, and in a desperate defence tried to grab the softly glowing metal. As his fingers sizzled, he shrieked like a trussed pig. The translator hit him hard again. Dazed and bleeding, he lay helpless as the girl sunk the poker through an eye. Cadwal watched as she stared in disbelief at what she'd done, but Brei was already cutting through the loops of ropes around the smith's chest. Freed, he fell forwards and slumped with his head against the wall, muscles straining with the pain.

Brei got the lock on Cadwal's manacles open, and with his arms free, he felt a surge of elation. But instead of grabbing a weapon and fighting a way out, his body was oddly hard to move, as though he was still swimming down the river. He flopped on the floor with arms and legs as useless as those of a straw doll. Using the chair for support, he only just managed to get to his knees.

The crotch of the smith's leather trousers were still smouldering and as the translator doused him with a bucket of water, his relief was enough to be able to curse everyone again. "And what do we do now?" he groaned.

"Think," Brei replied. She pulled open his legs to have a look at his wound. "You will live," she announced, then squatted behind him to start working on his manacles with the brooch pin.

"*Live*? How can I *live*?" he snarled through gritted teeth. "I can't just go back to my workshop and start work like nothing happened, can I? I'm a dead man! They'll have my head on a stick before the sun comes up!"

"Then you'll have to come with us."

"Where?" he scoffed. "Back to your mud huts?"

"Well, I would say more wood and straw, really."

"And do what?"

"Live?" she suggested.

"And we're just going to walk out of here, are we?"

"Where's Helig?" Cadwal asked.

"He wasn't allowed into the fortress," Brei explained, still intently working on the smith's bonds.

"So he's with the horses?"

"Ready and waiting on the other side of the bridge," she said with a grin.

"Horses?" the smith asked, interested. "How many?"

"Three."

"Rested?"

"No."

"Bah!" he scoffed. "Even with the fortress locked down there'll still be men guarding the bridge. Are you going to magic yourself past them?"

"Yes," Cadwal said. All they had to do was get over the bridge and they'd be free.

"How?" Brei and the smith asked together.

"Like how I got out of Dinorwig yesterday."

"There's no druid's robes here," Brei scoffed.

"Are the guards outside?"

"I don't think he'll be too willing to give you his uniform."

"He doesn't have to be willing," Cadwal said then turned to the translator. "Go and get one of them down to help. Tell him the torturer is having trouble with something."

"And then what?" Brei demanded.

Picking up the poker, he said, "And then we'll ask him for his clothes."

"Es stultior asino," the smith grumbled.

"What's that?" Cadwal asked.

"He says you are as dumb as an ass," the girl said.

The torturer was a fat slob of a man and they needed the smith's help to drag his body into the corner.

Brei pushed the smith back into the chair and looped the ropes loosely back around his chest and Cadwal pulled the poker out of the torturer's face. With the steaming length of solid metal in hand, he took position behind the door. As the guard's heavy footsteps approached, Brei adjusted her torn shirt to better attract his attention.

"What now?" the smith asked through gritted teeth.

"Magic," Brei grinned.

The soldier came in. The smith, still apparently tied to the chair where he'd left him, was obviously no cause for alarm and so his gaze lingered on Brei's alluringly exposed state. Cadwal had heard it said many a time that a face full of a nice pair of breasts would be a good way for a man to die. With every last ounce of strength left in his body, he swung the poker at the base of the soldier's skull. It struck hard enough to be a killing blow... if the soldier hadn't been wearing the helmet. The momentum of the swing pulled Cadwal around and he fell to the floor and lay face to face with the soldier, who, stunned, stared with confused and terrified eyes, his mouth opening and closing like a fish out of water. Before he could get any words out, the translator dropped to her knees, and with one of the torturer's knives, stabbed the soldier in the side of the neck.

"A dead legionary," the smith groaned. "If we weren't dead before, we are now!" He shook the ropes off and doubled over again. "Now what do you suggest we do?"

"Now you put the uniform on," Brei said.

"What for?" he cried in exasperation.

Remembering how it felt to be trapped in the tiny tunnels of the mines with a key that didn't work in any of the collars, Cadwal said, "No! We can't trust him."

"You can hardly stand," Brei said. "Seeing you stagger along, they'll be suspicious long before we reach them."

"You are *mad*!" the smith gasped.

"Trust us," she said. "It's dark, the fortress is on alert for a horde of barbarians. You'll look like a soldier leading a couple of slaves somewhere. It's our only chance."

"And then what?"

"And then we try to stay alive."

"Not much of a chance though, is it?"

"He escaped the mines, didn't he?" Brei snapped. "Some say he's a hero."

"He's an idiot! I knew I should have just beaten some sense into him instead of letting him go. I didn't even make that much of a profit!"

As Cadwal got himself to a knee, the girls pulled the shirt of chain mail over the dead soldier's lolling head.

Despite his obvious pain, the smith pulled his sweat-soaked shirt off and helped him slip the tunic on, cursing as it lay against his burn. "As a legionary trying to cross a bridge," he sighed. "I often wondered how I was going to die. But at least it's not going to be piece by piece in this stinking pit. That's a slight improvement." He sniffed the water in the bucket, scowled, lifted up the front of his tunic and poured it over his groin.

As Brei untied the boots from the soldier's feet, she said to the translator, "You did well, thank you. We can tie you up to make it look like we overpowered you."

"What?" the girl asked, alarmed. "Why? No, no! I am coming with you!"

"We're going back over the river to our lands. And there is a war coming," Cadwal said.

"The guards on the bridge are auxiliaries," the girl protested. "They'll know me. I work for them as some of the traders don't speak Latin. That will help us get across the bridge, right?"

"It's a good idea," Cadwal nodded.

Brei handed the metal manacles to Cadwal. "Hold them behind you. They can be a weapon." She pushed his chin up and threaded a rope through the collar to tether him like an animal. With one looped around her own neck she handed the loose ends to the smith.

"You really think this will work?" the smith asked.

"You can stay here if you like," Brei shrugged.

He thought for a moment. "Let's go." Limping out of the cell, holding onto the walls for support, he led them out.

Cadwal loped behind, his body acting as though he'd downed a whole skin of mead, feet flapping around like a fledgling fallen out of the nest. But the elation of escaping quickly withered to despair as the steps to outside turned into a sheer cliff face. He sagged helplessly down, legs turned to water, and the smith grunted as he tripped over him.

"Futou!" he cursed and Cadwal felt himself being lifted.

He looked down at the ground, totally at the mercy of a man who'd sold him to the horrors of the mines. But at least Brei was with him, and for what they were about to try and do, he'd choose no one else from the whole land of the Ordo-wiki to have at his side.

Even with Cadwal slung over his shoulder like a hunting kill, the smith strode so fast, Brei and had trouble keeping up.

The darkness around the perimeter of the fortress was held at bay by torches mounted high up along the top of the wall. Scurrying like rats below, nobody on patrol paid any attention.

The smith led them off the main road into the rough buildings of the *vicus* but when they came out on the road up from the bridge, he stopped so suddenly, she bumped awkwardly into his broad back. He growled a curse and, peering around, she saw at least half a dozen mounted soldiers guarding the bridge. Far too many to trick with their simple ruse. Her heart sank.

"This way," the smith said and lead them back among the houses. He laid Cadwal down outside one of them and slammed his heavy shoulder against a door. It didn't offer too much resistance.

"Is this your house?" the Latin speaking girl asked.

"It *was*!"

Summoning a level of determination Brei would be impressed to see in a well-trained soldier, the smith struck a strip of steel along a ridge of chert and got an oil lamp burning. In its weak light, Brei watched him stagger to the end of the room where he lifted a thin mattress. Underneath were a couple of short swords, about the same length as her forearm. He handed one to her and the other to the girl. Doubled over, a big hand resting on a thick thigh, he pulled Brei's out of its scabbard and showed it to her. "Use it to stab. No waving it over your head and trying to slash."

She tested the balance of it and how the grip felt in her hand. "You have a plan?" she asked.

"Surprise is what we need, so hide it in your clothes. In Rome women aren't supposed to carry weapons."

"What are we going to do?" the girl asked.

"Stay alive as long as possible," he smirked. "Anything more than that is a little too much to think about right now."

"Our horses are on the other side of the river," Brei said. "We just have to get across the bridge."

"Half a chance, then," he said. "Tell me again, how many horses?"

"Three."

The look of his face suddenly darkened. "Three. All tired. And your friend is already on one. Five on three horses won't work."

"Why not?"

"She has to stay here," he said, pointing at the girl.

"But... I..." she stammered.

"You're a *slave!*" he snapped at her.

"Not on the *other* side of the river!" she wailed. She turned to Brei. "Please don't leave me!" she begged. "I killed the guard!"

"She is Ordo-wik," Brei said. "Not a chance!" the smith growled. "I'm not going to lose my life for a slave!"

"I command it!" Brei shouted.

The smith scoffed, but was shocked by the slap across his face.

"She comes with us. Home," Brei said. Whether his stunned look was the slap itself or that it came from a women, she didn't care. "Do you have any wine or mead?" she asked.

"Mead?" he asked, shaking himself back to the moment. "Do I look like I want to make a toast to Fortuna?"

"Not for luck. For the pain of your burn."

"We don't have time for that!" He went to the bed again, poured the oil from the lamp over it, then set the wick to it. By the time he'd managed to hoist the barely conscious Cadwal back over his shoulder, the flames were licking up to the rafters. "Let's stay alive," he said as he led the way behind the buildings in the darkness. "We'll worry about everything else later." Stumbling through vegetable plots and tripping over piles of building materials, Brei followed with the girl close behind.

When they got within sight of the guards, they squatted down.

"What now?" the girl whispered.

"Now we hope Fortuna cares to smile on us," the smith grumbled.

Thankfully, it wasn't long before someone up the street shouted, "Ignius!" and they were close enough to hear the guards curse as they turned their horses around, discussing the merits of staying on duty against going to help put out the fire.

"Incendium! Incendium!" came another shout. Brei assumed it was a stronger word for 'fire' as, cursing, three of the guards kicked their horses into a run, leaving just another three at the bridge.

"Half a chance," the smith said under his breath.

"What should I say to the guards?" the girl asked.

"You're going to kill them, not exchange pleasantries!" he growled.

"*Kill* them?" she asked nervously.

"You already killed *two* men," he said. "Just a couple more and you can stop for a while."

"I don't know what to do!" she protested.

"Stab up under the mail shirt," the smith said. "Don't slash. Straight up to get it in his belly. And stab at the horse as well."

"The horse?"

"Have you ever tried to ride a horse that's got a sword stuck in its arse? Ready?"

"No."

"Good. Follow me. And you have to walk this bit," he said to Cadwal.

"I can't," Cadwal wheezed.

"You can if you want to live."

Brei felt the hilt of the sword under her shawl, then followed the smith.

"Appearance is everything," she said under her breath.

As they walked up into the lights of the guards' braziers, the girl waved a friendly greeting and the smith called out in Latin, "Aveh!"

"Stabit," two of them replied at once, clearly nervous, spears ready to thrust.

In a sweaty grip, Brei held the sword tight and looked back at the fire. They would make a toast to Fortuna one day as the smoke was billowing across the road obscuring the view of the bridge.

Whatever the smith said, it didn't relax the guards, but suddenly he pointed to the bridge and gasped, "Barbari!" in such real terror, she almost missed her moment with the sword.

As the three soldiers spun their mounts around, she did as the smith had said and jabbed it up under the shirt of mail of the nearest man. He didn't scream, and she worried that she'd missed, until in the light of the torches, she saw the dark blood flowing down the blade. Slow and uncoordinated, as though he was blind drunk, the soldier fumbled for the hilt of his sword. She hacked at his arm, and as he lurched in the saddle, the horse panicked. Stomping its hooves close to her feet, it reared up. Not moving quick enough to keep his balance, the guard was pitched backwards. She ran around, ready to throw herself on him, blade first, but saw the smith grappling with another soldier on the floor, gripping his head and kicking at his arm to stop him from reaching his sword. "Here!" he shouted at her and pulled the soldier's head back to expose the throat.

Brei stabbed the struggling man just under the chin strap of his helmet.

To the side, the girl was holding on to the third horse's reins, trying to dodge its shaking head and the spear the rider was trying to kill her with. The tip of Brei's sword went deep into his leg, and on the other side, the smith dragged him out of the saddle. In a pair of hands used to bending iron from dawn to dusk, he snapped the soldier's neck.

The first man was still writhing on the ground, clutching his side. She knew how deep her sword had gone into him so wasn't worried about him getting up, so helped the smith bundle Cadwal over a saddle. As the smith hoisted the translator onto the back of another horse Brei looked back up the road to the fortress and saw a couple of the other soldiers coming back. Hopefully, with eyes full of smoke, it would take a few moments for them to see what was going on.

The smith helped Brei up behind the girl, and thrust the reins of the horse Cadwal was lying across, into her hands. "*Run!*" he shouted. From the slap he gave to its rump, the horse broke into a gallop.

Holding tightly onto the translator's waist, Brei turned around. The fool hadn't got on his horse and for some reason was wasting time collecting the soldier's spears. The other soldiers were about to run him down. Even more confusingly, she was sure he was laying the spears on the bridge, lodging them in the railings at the side.

A moment later, the hooves of the galloping calvary roared on the wood. But in a melee of screams and horse's shrieks, the lead horse tripped over the first spear and the smith was stabbing and hacking the fallen riders with his short sword. There was a splash in the water below. Man or horse she couldn't tell.

The girl urged their mount on, but suddenly someone grabbed the reins and the frightened horse spun around. Brei screamed, but with giddying relief, realised it was Helig.

"I thought the horns and the fire had something to do with you," he laughed. The thundering sound of hooves came from behind. A panting smith was on the third horse. "Can you ride?" she asked.

"Easier to do when my cock isn't on fire, but I'll give it a go."

He and Helig got Cadwal turned around so he was in the saddle rather than lying over it, and Helig called, "Hold on for your life!" as he kicked his horse into a gallop.

THIRTEEN

R IDING AT FULL gallop in the pitch dark, crushed in the saddle behind the translator, the girl's hair blowing into Brei's eyes, was a terror she'd never experienced before. It took her a few long moments to overcome the blind panic, but when she realised that no Roman was about to overtake them, and that Cadwal wasn't about to slip off his mount, she tried to think about what they could do to stay alive long enough to see the next dawn.

Above the sounds of the hooves on the stone-capped surface, she shouted over the girl's shoulder, "We need to hide!"

"Why?" Helig asked.

"Their horses are fresh. They'll catch us easily."

"At night?"

From beside her the smith called, "Who did you anger?"

"Valerius."

"Ah futuo..." he spat. "Best keep running."

Helig's horse snorted and shook its head in what seemed like indignation. "Are you sure they'll chase us in the middle of the night?"

"We killed five men back there. Five *Romans*!" the smith said. "Believe me, Valerius is a mean bastard, cruel too. He'll threaten a whole cohort with a good flogging if they don't find us before the legatus Terentius wakes up. Who, by the way, is an even meaner bastard."

What the Praefectus would enjoy doing to her if she was taken, was bad enough to contemplate... but if his superior was worse then they were really in trouble. All she wanted to do was run, but for any hope of surviving the night and not running the horses to death, they needed cover. "We have to hide in the forest," she shouted. "We can work out where we are and what we can do at first light."

"In Dog's land?" Helig called disparagingly.

"There is nothing else we can do!"

"What weapons do we have?" the smith asked.

"I couldn't carry the sword," the girl said from behind him. "I had to drop it. Sorry."

"I dropped mine on the bridge," Brei admitted.

163

"One sword for the five of us? Half a chance?"

They slowed down a couple of times to try and find a smaller road. In the faint starlight of the horde of the ancestors showing them the way, Brei could just about make out a track leading off and told the girl to push the horse to a run again, trusting it could see much better than its human rider. But already ridden all the way from White Walls, it flagged almost straight away, and she had to let it slow to a canter.

Ahead, she could just about make out the jet-black outlines of the rolling hills below the stars. In enemy land, not much safety lay in the forests of their slopes, but she was sure it was the only hope they had. It was an imperceptible change at first, but eventually the uneven silhouettes of the trees on either side began to loom up until only a thin strip of stars was visible above. The air too was a little cooler and smelt fresher.

She patted Cadwal on the back with a sigh of relief. He'd managed to cling on.

Helig led them off the track and, ducking down as they pressed through the undergrowth, they came to a small stream. She heard the smith get clumsily off his horse and with a flurry of curses and snapping twigs, splashed noisily in the water, where curses were interspersed with loud groans of relief.

As Helig helped Cadwal out of the saddle, Brei felt around with her hand on the ground for a clear place for him to lie. He slumped straight to the floor and stayed where they left him. His skin felt deathly cold.

"If they're coming, we can't let them get ahead of us," Helig said in a hushed voice. "They'll be waiting for us in the morning, and we'll have no chance in a fight."

She'd been horrified at seeing him string the cord between the trees at the foot of the pass, but tied for the throats of Romans, she had no objection. "Give them a necklace," she suggested.

Helig chuckled. "Ah... But we don't have any rope."

"What if we tied all the reins together?"

She lay Helig's cloak over Cadwal then took her old dagger from the saddlebag. Another gift from Gwain. For what was coming, it would probably be no help to fight with, but at least it felt reassuring not to be unarmed.

For the few precious moments it took to cut blindly but carefully, through the leather harnesses, feeling with her fingers as the blade slid close to the horse's hide, she felt hope rather than the gnawing terror of being stranded in the pitch dark in enemy land. Then, in the absolute darkness, she felt around with Helig, until the lengths of reins were knotted together.

She crawled towards the sounds of the smith's moans until she could rest a hand on his clammy shoulder. "You saved us back there," she said.

"I was saving *myself*. You just followed," he grumbled above sounds of splashing water from the handfuls he was scooping up to pour on his crotch.

Despite everything, she laughed. "I would like to know your name."

"Why? So you can tell your gods about me?"

"So I can treat you as a friend."

He took a moment to answer. "They call me Maximilian."

"Your *name*, not what the Romans call you."

There was a longer silence and a pause of the water pouring as old memories were stirred. "Togman," he said eventually.

Helig came back crashing through the undergrowth. "How many does the necklace have to hold?"

"Valerius would probably send out a full contubernium," Togman replied. "Eight riders. Hopefully they split up to cover more ground, so if Fortuna is smiling on us, maybe four."

"Riding out in enemy land, in the dark?" Helig asked.

"You're nowhere near home. This is *conquered* land. A barbarian here would hardly dare raise his eye to a Roman on a horse, never mind a sword. And they're chasing a couple of girls and a slave, so they have nothing to fear."

Helig sighed, but his despondency only lasted a moment. "They'll have to be in single file along here, so if they're going fast enough, they'll trip over each other. The necklace only has to pull one off."

"And then we swing about in the dark, as blind as newborn mice, one sword between us, hoping we don't kill each other, while trying not to get trampled by the horses?" Togman asked.

"That's about it," Helig said.

"Sounds great."

"I have a question as well," Brei said.

"And what's that?"

"Where will the legion head?"

Togman cursed under his breath. "I just had a glowing hot poker on my cock! You think I was keeping quiet to protect you? Futuo! I. Don't. Know. I just make things out of metal. No one tells someone like me about military plans. Why don't you understand that?"

"So there's going to be two thousand of us camped in the mountains with no idea when or where they're going to start raiding," Helig asked.

"Two thousand," Togman coughed. "Is that all you've got? Two thousand sheep herders against a whole legion? And you almost got me killed for *that*? Half a chance, my sweaty arse!"

"There will be more when they know the battle is coming," Brei said, but couldn't feel the confidence she spoke with.

There was a loud splash as the smith turned around quickly. "And that won't matter at all!" he snapped, angrily. "I saw a hundred thousand stand with Boudica against just ten thousand Romans, and they absolutely slaughtered us. If you're lucky, *very* lucky, you can catch them out if they're marching through the woods, but it doesn't matter if you have every man in the land standing with you, you *cannot* fight a legion!"

"Ssh," Brei gasped, as over the sound of the stream, she sensed the low rumbling of approaching horses. "They're coming!" She was answered with cursing and breaking branches as Helig scrambled to the track. Head down, hands up to protect against the twigs pulling her clothes and hair, she followed, dagger held tight. She felt the pounding hooves as much as heard them, and the noise quickly became a roar that got louder and louder until her heart was beating as fast as they were running. Suddenly, there were wild shadows dancing around the trees and she was ready for Arawn to step out from behind a trunk and pull her into the deep folds of his cloak. Then, with a stab of fear to her heart, the light of the first rider's torch came around the corner.

Too bright to look at, she had to shield her eyes and in the disorientating cacophony of the charging horses that seemed to come from every direction at once, she lost all orientation. A scream rose in her throat, but from right in front of her, the first rider caught the necklace. Torch flung from his hand, it spun away in a shower of sparks and the loud gasp as the air was violently expelled from his chest ended when the horse following trampled over him. Torch extinguished, the world turned into a roiling blind chaos of horse's high-pitched shrieks and the panicked cries of men.

A body slammed into the mud so close, it splashed her.

She leapt forward and with her left hand, felt for the man's head. Hurt, he gasped for breath, arms flailing around, trying to fight what he couldn't see. She felt the smooth, cold helmet, then the disgusting warmth and wetness of his sweaty face. With the tip of her dagger, it didn't take much to open his throat. The hot blood spurted over her face.

Hands out in front, she tried to orient herself, but a horse slammed her to the ground. Air knocked out of her chest, her head reeled, and she wasn't sure which way was up or down. Panting like a creature from a nightmare, the horse thrashed around furiously, hooves stomping close to her hands. Something swooshed close to her head, and she heard the soldier grunt with the effort of blindly swinging his sword.

She felt in the mud for the knife. It could have been right in front of her or have been flung into the stream.

Another furious stroke and the soldier's sword thudded into the tree behind her head. Without thinking, she aimed at the sound and grabbed his arm. Already extended and off balance, he fell from the saddle and before he could get to his feet, Brei fumbled for his sword. She found it blade-first and cursed, but the cuts weren't bad enough that she couldn't grab the hilt. Blindly, she swung it at the soldier. Sparks flew from where it connected with his mail shirt but she focused on his desperate cries to aim at his face. The sound of the sharp metal striking flesh was different. His screams told her she had slashed him in the right place and she kept wildly stabbing and slashing until he was quiet.

Heart pounding like the hooves of a charging horse, ears ringing from the dead man's cries, she still feared he was about to rear up and grab her. Desperately trying to control her ragged breathing, she found a part of him not protected by the armour, put the tip of the sword there and put her weight on the hilt. It sank satisfyingly into his body. She was pretty sure he was dead now and rolled into the safety of the foliage at the side of the track where she lay panting until she heard her name being called. "Over here," she managed to gasp, chest burning.

"Two down," Helig said in a guarded voice. "There's two more somewhere."

"Here," she wheezed.

"Where?" Togman asked but tripped over the body. He started hacking at it before he realised the man was already dead. "By the gods!" he exclaimed. "You got *two*! A *woman*!"

It had all happened so quickly there was still a light rain of leaves and twigs falling from the trees they'd been knocking into.

Helig began a howl of triumph, full of the power of victory, but was quickly muffled.

"Shut up, you fool!" Togman seethed. "There'll be scouts in the woods. If any are close enough to hear, we'll be dead before sunrise!"

Chastened, Helig reached down to help Brei to her feet and she manically patted his body to make sure he was unharmed. While she could barely gulp in air, somehow his thick arms were as still as the trees they'd tied the reins between.

Togman though, despite the ride and fight, was as cold as though he'd just stepped out of a winter lake.

"Your body is in shock," she said, concerned.

"That's not too surprising, is it?" he dismissed. "I was earning my bread at the forge this evening and now I am killing Romans in the dark."

"I've seen men like this after a fight," she protested. "I've seen them die."

"She's a healer," Helig said. "It would do you well to listen to her."

He huffed dismissively.

"Where's Cadwal?" Helig asked, concerned.

As loudly as she dared, Brei called his name, but there was no answer.

Helig cursed as he stumbled forwards, pushing branches out of the way.

"He's here!" the girl said gently and Brei felt her hands grasp her shirt; the poor thing held on as though she was drowning. She squatted down and felt around Cadwal's still body for wounds, hoping that he hadn't been trampled on by a horse in the medley. Her hands were shaking too much to tell if he was injured and were covered in the Roman's blood so she had no idea if he was bleeding.

Helig pulled her aside and was a little less subtle in determining what was wrong.

"Whaat?" Cadwal protested at having his face slapped so hard.

"He's *sleeping*!" Helig gasped in mock outrage.

"We're killing Romans in the dark," Togman said with scorn. "He's taking a nap!" Half laughing, half cursing, he crashed back over to the stream where they soon heard his moans of relief.

With a hand on his shoulder, Brei followed Helig back to the trail, and while he clicked his tongue and hushed soothingly to round up the spooked horses, she felt carefully around for where the dead men had ended up. She breathed in short, jerky gulps and the tremors had spread from her hands to her whole body. She had to stifle a scream every other heartbeat in fear that one of the Romans wasn't dead and was lurking in the undergrowth. How men could revel in such violence, she couldn't begin to imagine.

Not being able to see, and hands next to useless, she struggled to undo the clasps of their cloaks. How Helig could be calm enough to sooth the horses was a question for an Elder.

When the second cloak was undone, she stumbled around behind one of the horses Helig was leading back. At the stream, she was about to drape one of the cloaks over Togman's shoulders when the girl grabbed her. "I have to tell you something," she whispered urgently.

"What?" Brei asked, suddenly alert.

"I'm their translator. I mean, I *was*. I heard all of their plans with the Deceangli in our tongue and spoke them in Latin."

It took a moment for Brei to understand what she was babbling about, but with hope threatening to flow back into her heart like a river bursting its banks, she asked, "You know where they will meet?" she asked cautiously,

"Ow!" the girl cried out and Brei realised how hard she was gripping her arm. "At the cavalry at the fort at Canovium," she blurted.

"Where?" Helig snapped.

"The fort they've build on the Chief river," Brei said.

"When?" Helig asked.

From the way the girl sighed, Brei knew it was not going to be good news. "In two days."

She tried to fight the sensation of dissolving into the earth, like snow before a fierce sun, but before she could think of any words worth saying, Helig was stumbling over to the horses. "Let's go!" he called.

"Not in the dark," Brei hissed.

"We have no time!"

"We're in enemy lands! We don't know where we are or where this road leads. We could easily ride the wrong way."

"Two days!" Helig seethed. "*Dinorwig* is two days ride away! We're already too late. And in the daylight, the Dogs can see we're enemies!"

"It will be *one* day by the time the sun comes up again," Togman pointed out gloomily.

Brei was sure the answer for how they could ride through enemy lands without trouble lay with the dead soldiers scattered around under the trees. Despite her panic, she also knew that if Helig was anything like his father when his blood was racing, he'd be in no mood to be told what to do. "What did Tegin say about the two leaves?" she asked, hoping the little prompt was subtle enough for him to think he'd come to the idea himself.

"Appearance is everything?" he asked uncertainly, then clicked. "We'll strip the dead Romans and wear their clothes! And when we ride through the Dog's land, they'll think we're Roman soldiers and will let us pass!"

"That's a good plan," Brei agreed, happy it was so dark she didn't need to mask her smile.

"First light!" Helig announced. "And we ride hard to White Walls to get Gavo's men."

"Gavo?" the girl asked with a sharp intake of breath.

"Gavo?" Brei reached out to touch the girl's arm again. "Chief of White Walls? He's alive?"

"Why? Do you know him?"

"He's... my father."

"By the gods!" Brei gasped.

Helig laughed. "He's going to think we're heroes!"

"You're Rhian?" Brei asked as the girl's delicate fingers touched her face, probing for some familiarity. "You were at my wedding to Gwain. Little yellow flowers in your hair. Do you remember?"

"Brei!? The healer?" she cried and got a warning hiss from the smith to be quiet. "Buttercups," she whispered. "I picked them with my brothers."

"You were captured in a raid. But he never stopped believing he'd see you again."

"He lives?"

"Yes. And you'll see for yourself tomorrow."

Brei heard her sob again, but this time her tears came from happiness. "And my brothers?"

Brei was glad Rhian couldn't see how the smile left her face. "Sorry," she sighed, "No."

"Were they captured?"

"No. On the battlefield."

"Good. I wouldn't wish for them to be slaves of the Romans."

From what Brei had learned from her short meeting with the Preafectus, she could well believe that. "I have another question."

"Anything!" Rhian said eagerly.

"What do you know of a deal between Bleddyn and the legion?"

"Do you *never* give up?" Togman huffed.

"Bleddyn?" Rhian asked. "Oh yes! He's dying!"

"Not soon enough," Helig mumbled.

Brei's hand rose instinctively of its own accord to hit him to silence, but he was a little further than she thought and her fist found nothing but air.

"I know of no deal. Maybe someone else translated. Or he speaks good Latin and didn't need me?"

Confused, Brei tried to recall the Preafectus' words. She didn't think he'd meant any deceit about what he said about a deal with the Ordo-wiki.

"There *was* a deal. But it wasn't the king who came to Deva. It was a young man."

"Young?" Helig growled. "No, no. Don't say it!"

"Derog?" Brei asked, heart sinking.

"I think so, yes. Related to the king? But not his son."

"*Derog* made a deal with Rome?" Helig boomed so loud Togman had to warn him.

"Yes," Rhian said. "But no. They laughed at him."

At that, Helig howled with mirth and got a splash of water from Togman to keep him quiet.

"He's the youngest of the king's heirs," she continued. "So he was a long way from the throne. For him to become king, the commander gave him some poison."

Helig's laughter stopped.

"He went back to kill his two brothers so he'd be heir. And then he'd do the same with the king. But later, so no one would think it too suspicious."

Brei had known it as a truth when she'd seen his face in Bleddyn's house on the night of Maidoc's pyre, but hearing it confirmed offered no comfort.

"He only got one," Helig growled.

"Who needs the Romans when you have brethren like that?" Togman mused.

"I will rip his throat out with my bare hands!" Helig seethed. "I swear that to the gods!"

"Not if he is on the throne," Brei said.

"Why not? He killed Maidoc!"

"These might be strange times we live in, but you can't kill a king. Which is where he'll be if he poisons Bleddyn before we get back."

"He will die by my own hands," Helig cursed.

"But if the Dogs are going to raid," Brei asked, "what deal can he make if everyone in the land is starving or dead?"

"He's not going to be the king of the whole land," Rhian said.

"What's he going to be king of, then?" Helig asked, confused.

"The Deceangli will have the mainland, and he'll be king of the island of Mona."

"Mona..." Brei sighed, trying to comprehend the sheer breadth of the betrayal.

"He'll let his own people starve and be sold as slaves," Helig growled with disgust. "Just so those left will call him king," He sounded close to tears. "He killed Maidoc for *that*? We went off to face Rome by ourselves... while the real snake we've left to slither around the Oak Throne."

"That was always the tribes' trouble," the smith grumbled. "We always hated our neighbours with such vehemence, we never understood what a monster Rome is. If we'd have all stood together and not made any deals with Ceasar, Plautius could never have set foot in our lands a hundred years later."

"Never mind our neighbours," Helig growled. "It's my brother I swear to kill. Whatever happens, he is mine. I swear to the gods, I will see his life blood on my hands!"

Quietly, Brei said, "It is witnessed."

FOURTEEN

CADWAL WOKE IN the dark to the cacophony of birdsong. Elemental. A riot of life. Hearing it, he assumed he was more alive that dead. Despite his bed being no more than a damp nest of mulchy leaves and some clumps of moss, his sleep had been so deep he wasn't sure where he was. From a half remembered bad dream, he heard the echoes of panicked horses and men dying in the darkness. Jingling of tack nearby brought the unsettling sensation that maybe it hadn't all been just a nightmare.

Leaves crunching under footfalls brought him properly awake, and nervously, he tried to work out if the indistinct shapes moving quietly around in the pre-dawn gloom were friend or foe. A water skin dangling near his face suggested he was in the company of friends, but when he looked up, he saw it was his slaver.

"I don't expect you to forgive me," the smith said. "But for what it's worth, I'm sorry for sending you to the mines without a key."

"What are you doing here?" Cadwal croaked, still unsure of where 'here' was.

"I got you out of the fortress and over the bridge. Don't you remember? On my own shoulder. While I was stabbing the legion's cavalrymen."

"Why are you helping us now?"

"Don't misunderstand me, I am helping *myself*. And right now, to do that I need to help you too. My name is Togman, by the way," he added unexpectedly.

"That's better than Master," Cadwal quipped as he took a sip of water.

"And I am Rhian," the translator said softly. "Gavo's daughter."

"Gavo doesn't have a... Oh."

As she knelt to put Cadwal's hand on her head, he had to bite his lip to stop from shouting a curse at the gods. They hadn't knocked him off the pass or drowned him in the river, but it felt a special cruelty to have rescued somebody else's child and not his own.

Towering over him, Helig hissed, "Come on. We have to go. Now!"

Wanting to understand the urgency, Cadwal asked, "Why?"

"*Why?*" Helig gasped. "It's *tomorrow*."

"What is?"

"The start of the raids. We're too late."

The nightmare forgotten, what he'd woken up to was much worse. Swept away in the floodwaters of despair, the last semblance of hope flailed around one last time before being dragged underneath. All he'd done in the last few days for nothing. But somehow, the warrior part of him that Gwain had forged with long days of training, asked, "What's the plan?"

Helig spoke through gritted teeth. "No plan. We go to White Walls and get everyone to ride out to warn as many forts and farms as possible, we'll do what we can. And we go *now*!"

"No!" The smith tried to keep his voice down, but his vehemence was clear. "Last I heard, they were pulling most of the men from the auxiliary fort in the east to go back to help with the work in Deva. So if we happen to meet any coming the other way and if they see your long moustaches, they'll kill us first and ask questions later. If we ride through enemy land, we dress properly, and *really* look like Romans. It's the only way."

"We don't have time..." Helig started.

"We make time! We're only alive now because, thanks to Fortuna, no one was close enough to hear the noise we made last night. But now we have to help her. So, put on the armour off one of those dead bastards. And get shaved!"

"You want me to cut my *moustache* off?" Helig growled, outraged.

"Yes."

"How can I be king without them?"

"Right now, you should be thinking about how to stay alive. You can work out how to be a naked-faced king later."

Helig didn't have an answer to that.

Cadwal felt Togman nudge him with a foot in the small of his back. He tried to get to his knees, but his body felt as though it had been dumped in a cold bog for a few days after suffering a threefold death. Togman was in no mood for waiting though and simply hauled him to his feet as though he was a slave. Holding onto the trunk of the old hornbeam he'd slept under, Cadwal managed to stay standing as Togman bundled a large square of fabric over his head.

"This is your tunica," he said as he deftly folded it and tied a cinch around the waist.

"If they've gone to help with the work in Deva," Helig asked thoughtfully. "How many men are left in the fort?"

"No..." Togman scowled. "Don't even think about it!"

"Tell me."

Togman sighed. "At full quota, it will be a cohors quingenaria equitata, a mix of foot and horse soldiers. Five hundred in total, with a hundred and twenty of them cavalry."

"But it's not full? How many?" Helig pressed as Brei worked with a blade on his face.

"Most of the foot soldiers came back to Deva and most of the horsemen stayed," Rhian said helpfully.

"Makes sense," Togman added grimly. "Calvary soldiers are higher status than normal ones, so don't do so much menial work."

The weak light was enough for Cadwal to see the sad sight of Brei scattering Helig's long moustaches on the forest floor.

Against the morning chill, Cadwal welcomed the tunic, if he ignored the smell of the dead man's sweat. But the shirt of chain mail Togman dropped onto his shoulders was so heavy, he could feel his knees start to give. "This is your lorica hamata. A vital part of your kit. A single sword slash would kill you, but with this on, you could survive dozens of blows." A sword was fastened at his right hip, which Togman named a spatha.

"How many are at their fort *now*?" Helig asked, getting impatient. He held a handful of hair, reluctant to let it fall to the ground.

"Forget it!" Togman warned.

"I translated for a Deceangli wagon driver," Rhian said. "He was sent there to collect some rations back to Deva because so many men had left to work. He said there was hardly anyone there. They need to get it ready in time for the new governor who will arrive soon."

"Agricola," Brei said. "That's the new governor's name. He served in the Twentieth."

"When?" Helig asked cautiously.

Brei only nodded to confirm what Helig suspected. He'd been there in the Black Year.

"So less than a hundred cavalry and maybe twenty or thirty foot soldiers," Togman said. "But that's only a guess."

"A hundred and twenty men," Helig mused, iron in his voice.

"No..." Togman said, voice raised. "A hundred and twenty full time soldiers and horsemen who know absolutely nothing else in the world but warfare, men who drill every day, inside a fort that is the same design of the one you may have noticed yesterday. It's impossible."

"We have to fight. If they destroy the harvest..."

"Even a hundred thousand tribesmen against ten thousand legionaries is a battle that can't be won! Believe me, I know. Even with all of your two thousand men, you'd all be dead before a single one of you got over the wall."

"The Dogs, then," Helig said defiantly. "We can attack them before they get to the fort to meet up with the Romans. How many of them will there be?"

"I don't know," Rhian said. "Maybe two hundred."

"And how many fighting men can you get together by tomorrow?" Togman asked.

Cadwal knew that the thirty men of White Walls, the only sizeable fort they could get to in time, had no chance to stop their two worst enemies running around the land destroying everything they found.

"So what?" Helig snapped. "It's all hopeless? We just let it happen?"

"Yes!" Togman said in exasperation. "You *cannot* fight the Romans. Have you not been listening to me?"

Lastly, the polished metal helmet was slapped on Cadwal's head. At first, the cheek plates strapped under his chin felt strange and restricting, but after a few moments he felt a little stronger, ready to ride for his boys. He touched his throat, but the collar had been magicked away again.

Turning from her demasculising work on Helig's facial hair, Brei said, "It's by where you slept. Throw it as far as you can."

Again, Cadwal was shocked at her knack for knowing what men were thinking. Around his neck, it had made him feel a constant terror, but discarded on the floor, it didn't seem so threatening. As he bent down, the heavy helmet caused a strange dizzy feeling, and the weight of the mail made it hard to get back up again. But he managed to frighten a few birds as he flung it into the trees.

Naked and staring unseeing at the sky, the dead Roman soldiers didn't look so threatening. Like normal men. He'd ask what happened to them later. Now, all he cared about was that they stayed on the ground.

Helig helped Brei get her oversized chain shirt on. She tied one of the strange helmets under her chin but it was so big, the cheek guards touched at the bottom.

"You'll ride at the back," Togman said. He picked her up easily and sat her on one of the horses.

Helig squatted down to give Cadwal a bunk up. The strange protrusions on the sides of the saddle made it hard to get on, but he realised that with his thighs tucked under them they'd help keep him on the horse's back when he leaned over. Just another little detail for why the Romans were superior fighters.

He didn't have long to get comfortable though as the smith slung a shield over his shoulder and made sure it was secure on his back. "This is your clipeus. Hold it proudly!"

"Ready?" Helig growled.

"One last thing," Togman snapped. "To greet someone, you fully extend your arm, palm down and fingers touching. But keep your mouths shut! If they hear one word of your dirty tongue, we're all dead. Understand? Whatever happens, only let me and the girl talk."

The Roman horses were larger and stronger than those bred by the Ordo-wiki, so alternatively walking, trotting, and cantering, the five of them covered good ground. Heart in mouth, scattering chickens and children, they rode straight through the middle of a couple of Dog settlements. One look at all the shining metal they wore and the settlers cowered away, terrified about causing even a minor inconvenience to a contubernium.

But when the thought of spilling Dogs' blood wasn't enough to sustain him, all Cadwal wanted to do was curl up under a tree and sleep. He was so tired that as the ride wore on, he began to lose grip on who exactly he was. He seemed to remember being a druid wielding a bone-adorned staff, but he was also sentenced to death on the sands of the arena. And wasn't he a slave in the inescapable mines? Swaying on the back of the horse, he could feel the dead weight of the metal armour he was wearing, so he was a Roman soldier. Nothing made much sense and he worried he was becoming delirious, like a man with festering wounds just before he died. The little scars on his palm brought him back to clarity and he knew that more than all the dreamlike snippets of different lives he recalled, he was something much more important. A father.

He looked at the low, brooding mountains to the west. On one would be the Dog's huge fort. So close. He could almost feel their soft hair as he ruffled their heads, hear their laughter and toy hammers clattering together as they play-fought. He imagined their cries as the Dogs beat them for not working hard enough, and felt the rumble of their bellies as they went to sleep hungry. And he was no closer to being with them than when he'd got out of the mines.

Ahead, he heard Helig grumbling that there was no time to get more men. So even after half a morning to think, the son of Gwain still didn't have any idea about how to stop the raids. And Cadwal was sure Helig wasn't wondering how to break two little boys out of their enemy's biggest fort.

Idly, with eye lids getting heavy again, he wondered if he could wait for the raiding party to head out into Ordo-wik lands so he could sneak into their empty fort.

Rhian cried out. With a hand fumbling for the hilt of the short sword, Cadwal looked up. It wasn't a detachment of Roman soldiers she'd seen but the stark white walls of White Walls. With the sun almost at its midday zenith, they looked as resplendent as a torc around the neck of a king. Knowing the ride was almost done, Cadwal groaned with relief. But as they got closer, he saw that some of the houses inside were ruined, the burned supporting poles pointing up at the sky like the skeleton of some black-boned creature. The crushing, yet now familiar, sense of something important being ripped from his grasp threatened to pull him from the saddle. "Are we too late?" he asked, worried a new nightmare was unfolding in front of them.

The sentry on the wall blew a warning. Even from so far away, the haunting sound of the horn cut through daily life to announce that blood and death were near, that the enemy was in sight, still sent a shiver down Cadwal's spine. A few moments later, he watched as four riders charged out of the lower gate down the hill. All screaming at the tops of their voices, they whirled loaded slingshots above their heads.

"They better be Gavo's men," Helig shouted. "These will be our last breaths if they're not."

"Erm... Maybe we've ridden a little too far in the Roman armour," Togman suggested.

When the riders were near enough, Helig raised his right hand, a sign they came in peace. But as they continued to charge, his hand twitched towards the hammer that should have been slung over his back.

Cadwal was so sure they were about to be cut down, he nudged his horse forwards. If they were Dogs and a couple were delayed in killing him, maybe Helig and Togman would have a few moments of a fairer fight. But at the very last moment, as they wheeled to the side, Cadwal saw the big scar on Bevan's face, as white as the walls of the fort. With all the strength he could muster, he called out his blood brother's name. Suddenly the war cries changed to raucous laughter.

"I am Helig ap Gwain. Next king of the Ordo-wiki!" Helig bellowed, but it was Cadwal they circled around. "Tell us you killed Romans!" Maccus, the mouthy brother of Tamm's first wife, cried with joy.

"Killed them and took their horses and weapons!" Helig announced proudly.

Abuccus edged his horse alongside Cadwal's and clasped his painful wrist in a strong hand. "Ill news of Crow Hill, cousin," he said,

"He knows," Helig said. "He was there!"

"They didn't capture you?" Abuccus looked confused.

"They did. He escaped the Romans!"

"And Tamm?" Maccus asked excitedly, edging in sideways on his nervous roan.

Cadwal shook his head and the sparkle left Maccus' eyes.

"He's a slave?" Abuccus asked.

"No. He died rescuing the men of Crow Hill. In the sun."

Maccus arched back in the saddle and the keen he cried to the sky brought a lump to Cadwal's throat. "I called him brother," he cried. "But if he can make the gods laugh as much as he could men, they will make him one of theirs. Tonight we shall drink and speak his name. And what of the others?"

"Which others?" Cadwal asked.

"You said Tamm rescued those of Crow Hill."

"We'll tell you all when we're with Gavo," Brei said, sparing Cadwal the need to put words to the sad truth.

"Aye," Maccus nodded. "Best not to be out here in the open too long. Got bands of Dogs running around like fleas on a rat." He wheeled his horse around and stuck a playful leg out to kick the rump of Abuccus' mount.

Ditches and wooden palisades were how every other high place in the land was protected. So, ringed by a stone wall the height of two men, White Walls was unlike any other fort. As a boy, Cadwal had easily believed the story that they lived in the foundations of a huge hall built by a clan of giants.

The blast of the horn should have brought everyone inside to see what was going on, either with weapons ready in case it was foe, or excited children running along the top if it was family and friends. The lack of either made the fort seem abandoned. Burned buildings and no people meant bad news and a deep unease began to gnaw at him again.

The main gate was at the top of the hill, wedged between two squat cylindrical towers of stacked stone. Cadwal was looking forward to at last being safe inside, until he saw the druid on the wall. With snow white hair cascading all the way down his back and robes billowing in the strong breeze, it was an Elder. He squirmed so much he had to catch his balance.

"What's he doing?" Helig quietly asked as they rode through the gate.

"Watching," Brei replied.

"Aye," Maccus agreed. "Stands up there all day and most of the night, so anyone with stupid ideas knows the fort is protected with magic."

The Elder's unknown powers didn't protect a thriving settlement though. Between the huts clustered around the entrance, the rough looking war band offered a subdued welcome. From what Cadwal could see, there were no women or children inside.

Gavo's cheeks were a bit ruddier and his big moustaches a little less vibrantly ginger than Cadwal remembered. The huge plaid cloak wrapped around his shoulders surely took many moons to weave, but now the magnificence was faded and frayed, well past its best, not unlike the rest of the fort. Gavo greeted Brei with a fist on his chest but his smile was only a quick flash, as their arrival in Roman armour and on Roman horses was as ominous as having an Elder stood on the wall.

"Welcome to White Walls, such as it is," he beamed. "Come and share my fire."

"What happened here?" Brei asked as the chief offered his hand to help her from her horse.

Gavo's smile had been a little forced and the question was enough to wipe it away. "After what the bastards did to Crow Hill, we guessed we'd be next for their attention, so I sent the children and most of the women to safer places."

"And then what will you do?"

"We were going to stay to protect the harvest as best we could, but with what you are wearing, I have a feeling you're going to suggest we do something different." But then he stared wide eyed at Rhian. "The gods..." he gasped, the Roman attire instantly forgotten.

"Father?" Rhian whispered.

Dropping to his knees, the chief let out the most heart rendering cry Cadwal had ever heard. The men stopped in their congratulations, and mocking of Helig's naked face, to look at the girl. A few more recognised her and with disbelief began beating their chests and echoing Gavo's cries to the sky.

Rhian slipped out of the saddle and cupped her father's aged face in her hands. The sight of the two of them embracing after so long apart was just about the most bittersweet thing Cadwal had ever seen.

Bevan helped Cadwal down, and thankful to be spared the ignominy of slumping to his knees before the other warriors, it was the protective embrace of his blood-brother's arms he slid into. "Safe now," Bevan smiled as he fumbled with cord binding the helmet's cheek guards. With it off, someone saw Cadwal's shaved face and laughed.

"He escaped the *mines*!" Helig snapped.

A couple of sneers at such an unbelievable tale were silenced when Brei added, "It's true!" Counsellor of the king was a high position, but Cadwal hadn't thought her word commanded more respect than that of the next king of the Ordo-wiki.

"Some story you're about to tell us," Gavo said as he took Cadwal's other arm over his wide shoulders.

The small but excited group made their way down the steep slope to the fire that was set before a natural wall of the bedrock separating the upper and lower parts of the fort. It was mercifully out of the wind and after the long ride, resting on the sheepskins arranged around it were a real luxury. He leaned closer towards the fire to take some chill off his bones. A rotund woman, the only one Cadwal could see left here, had some strips of chicken roasting and as she turned the spits his stomach growled in anticipation.

"If we had any mead left, you could drink from my horn," Gavo said apologetically. "But the last of the ale is all I can offer."

The warmth of the fire seeping into him felt like life itself and as soon as he realised just how soft and comfortable sheepskins were, sleep started creeping up on him. Over the crackling flames, he looked out over the rolling landscape. For a reason no one had an answer for, the great stone walls of White Walls didn't ring the top of the hill, but enclosed the slope down its eastern face he was able to see halfway across the land of the Ordo-wiki, even to the saddle shaped back of the highest mountain in the land on the horizon. From where he sat, it seemed the fort was a throne of a god.

To the north, he could just about make out the distant ramparts of the Dog's fort. Perched so high the slopes below the walls and ditches were carpeted in purple heather. He couldn't stand but had to stop himself from trying to walk there. No one in the land who'd held a sweetly mewling bundle of new life in their hands didn't also know the pain of loss. Such was the way of the harsh lives they led. Yet he wondered if other men had ever thought that two young boys could be worth as much as everything else in the world.

Bevan pressed a horn of ale into his shaking hands. The whole right side of his face was a scar where a Dog's axe had taken part of his cheek. A finger's width to the side and his skull would have been split open. If Cadwal hadn't fended the attackers off, as Bevan lay helpless on the ground, the next strike would have been his end. For that, Bevan had sworn himself a blood-brother, and in a heartbeat would agree to go to the Dogs' fort.

Two men against a whole fort were odds no god could help with, though.

The wind changed and wafted smoke from the fire into his eyes. As soon as he closed them against the sting, he was close to nodding off. He dreamily imagined himself trying what the Dogs had done in Crow Hill; crawling to their fort, claiming to be an escaped slave. The wounds on his body would certainly attest to that story and maybe they'd let him inside. All he'd have to do then was find the boys and break back out again. If he could twice escape Roman slavery, he could easily slip out of the clutches of the Dog.

And with a son in each arm, he'd never stop running.

Bevan shook him with enough urgency he snapped awake with a shock to see the Elder shuffling around to sit right next to him. If he'd had enough strength left in his legs, he'd have leapt up. The Elder chuckled at his discomfort. It sounded like autumn leaves rustling in the wind.

Gavo, his daughter wrapped protectively in his arms, looked at Brei and mouthed, 'Thank you.'

"We have come to give," she sighed sadly. "But, I'm afraid, also to take."

The chief kissed the crown of Rhian's head. "The time has come, then? We knew it was close. What do they plan to do with us?"

"The Dogs are joining the Romans and will raid our lands. With a lost harvest and our borders blocked, we'll be too weak to put up any fight next spring."

"Joining forces?" he spat.

"Apparently they hate us so much they've made some kind of arrangement that benefits them both."

"I'll send my best rider to the king!" Gavo gasped, but before he could give the command, Helig held up his hand. "Bleddyn might already be dead."

"What!"

"Derog poisoned me and Maidoc so he could become king."

"The little runt!" Gavo growled.

"It gets worse," Brei added. "King only of Mona."

"Oh... and who will have the rest of the land?"

"The Dogs."

Behind Gavo, half a dozen men spat their contempt and curses. Bevan jumped up and set off purposefully down the hill, shouting threats ahead of him. Cadwal saw he was heading to a man bound to a post in the frame of a ruined roundhouse.

"Leave him!" the Elder rasped in a voice that came from the dank depths of a tomb of the Old Ones and Bevan stopped dead still as though he'd run into a wall. It was a woman's voice Cadwal heard and he was so surprised he turned around, but wished he hadn't. He'd seen people so old the weight of the years had bent their backs and sun and wind had wizened their skin to look like an old leather saddle bag. The druid's face, though, had seen so many years the wrinkles seemed as deep as the furrows of a ploughed field. The time-marked skin was the texture and colour of the outsides of a cheese left for months in the rafters.

Brei indicated the bound man. "Who is he?"

"A neighbour," the chief spat.

Knowing he was looking at a Dog, Cadwal was suddenly more alert. If it was one of the four from Crow Hill, never mind what the Elder commanded, he'd bite the bastard's throat out.

"Came about a month ago, begging to honour the old gods with us," Gavo said. "Told us he was banished from a southern tribe. But on Alban Hefin he torched a couple of houses. And while everyone was trying to put out the flames, he tried to stab the lads on the gate. The bastard almost got one."

"So his friends could stream in and take the fort in the middle of the night?" Helig asked.

Gavo nodded. "Just as they did in Crow Hill, I guess. But our men blew the horn, and with us ready on the wall, they didn't dare come up."

"What are you going to do with him?" Cadwal asked, suddenly more eager for the blood of an enemy than the roasting chicken.

"A reading," Gavo said.

"We don't have time for that," Helig dismissed. "We have to stop the Dogs joining up with the Romans."

"Why?" Gavo asked. "When do they plan their attack?"

Brei and Helig looked at each other, both reluctant to be the one to tell him. Brei sighed. "Tomorrow."

The chief sagged forwards and seemed to wither like a plant in autumn. "The gods are cruel. After so many sorrowful summers, you bring my daughter back, then tell me I'm going to die the very next day."

"No one said anything about dying," Helig smiled.

A big grin spread over Gavo's face again. "You have a plan? From the gods?"

Helig shrugged and the chief's smile disappeared. "So how do we stop them?"

"You *can't* fight the Romans," Togman said scornfully. "Just run. That's all."

"Who is this?" Gavo asked, arm still so tight around Rhian he was almost crushing her.

Cadwal could think of no nicer introduction. "The man who sold me to the mines."

A few threatening mumbles spread through the close packed men and Helig had to put an arm out to hold a couple of them back.

"And how does he fit into our story?" Gavo asked.

"We wouldn't have got out of Deva without him," Brei interjected. "He saved us."

"Aye. For all the good that did me!" Togman spat.

"We'll have to attack the Roman fort," Helig said, albeit a little fatalistically.

Gavo rolled his eyes. "Attack their fort? And what song or story did you ever hear about a tribe doing that?"

Helig opened his mouth to answer but Gavo cut him off. "Successfully?"

"Boudica..."

Gavo waved his hand. "Boudica sacked civilian settlements, not forts. That's a big difference. *And* they were undefended. And why was that? Because the legion was here butchering *us*!"

Unperturbed, Helig continued. "Rhian says most of the men from the fort on the Chief river have gone to Deva. So there's only a hundred or less, not five hundred."

Togman cut in this time. "That means nothing. I told you, twenty men could hold that fort against a thousand of you. You *can't* fight them."

"The Roman is right," Gavo said. "If we're on the outside of their fort and they're on the in, we cannot win. Not with every man in the land."

"We don't have to *fight*," Helig enthused. "Even if we just fake an attack, it will put them on the defensive and maybe they'll delay the raids."

"Delay them?" Gavo spat. "You said that the king is lost to us. If Half Seed has taken the throne, there will be no more men. So shall we go and we stand with our chests in range of their spears just so they'll raid our land a few days later?"

Cadwal tried to remember what Tegin had derisively accused Helig of back in Dinorwig when he was suggesting equally unrealistic ideas. A boy planning his manhood escapade? But with the Roman armour they were wearing, he knew they could get into the fort as easily as Brei had walked through the gates of Deva. And more than just getting the raids delayed, if the Romans were unprepared for a fight, the tribe would have a rare opportunity to inflict some real damage. Not simply delaying the raids for a few days, they'd be stopped before they'd begun.

Before he spoke though, thoughts of the boys stilled his tongue. Fighting Romans would get him no closer to them.

A flitter of movement down the hill caught his eye. For most men discussing a fight, a crow was an ill omen as it signified Arawn appearing to gather the dead from the battlefield. For a man from a fort called Crow Hill, it meant something much different. He wondered if it was the spirit of Tamm come to guide them to battle. "We're not going to try and crawl through the ditches and climb the wall," he heard himself say.

"No?" Helig huffed. "How else can we get in?"

"We will walk in through the gates."

"How, by the gods, will we do that?"

"Two leaves."

"What?" Gavo exclaimed.

"Oh, not that again," Helig cried and waved his arms in exasperation.

"Let him speak," Brei said forcibly.

"We are warriors!" Helig protested. "We need to fight with iron and blood and promises to the gods, not some strange words of the druids."

"Those strange words you speak of are what hold the tribe together," Brei said. "But where has that got us?" She swept a finger around what was left of White Walls. "No women, no children. No life."

Helig didn't have an answer for that.

"Just now, as we approached the walls, you thought we were Romans?" Cadwal asked those of the warband crowded around the fire.

"Aye," Maccus laughed. "Thought we were going to have some big-nosed heads on spikes for the wall!"

"The Roman soldiers are expecting a band of Dogs to arrive tomorrow."

"And...?" Gavo asked and looked around to see if anyone else understood.

"To make communication between them easier, maybe someone from Deva thought it would be a good idea to send a translator ahead. With a few of us wearing the Roman uniforms we have, they'll open the gates for us and welcome us in. And all we have to do is hold them open for the rest."

"To storm the fort," Helig finished.

"They won't even have their armour on," Gavo said, eyes sparkling with the thought.

"Or time to form a testudo," Helig added.

"They're *Romans*!" Togman protested. "They'll see right through you, as soon as you open your mouths!"

"Which is why *you* will go in first," Cadwal said. "The same reason you rode at the front this morning. You speak Latin and know their ways."

"Aye, I do know their ways. Like how they point hot pokers at people just to ask questions."

"All you need to do is get us through the gates."

"You just lost me my easy life I had and almost got me killed," Togman scoffed. "All I am going to do is head to some town down south away from any fighting and find me a nice woman to grow old with. What could you possibly offer me that I would risk such a madness?"

"All the coin you can find inside."

"Ah," he mused, his mouth hanging open. "The wages of five hundred men? Just to get you through the gates?"

"A fair profit," Cadwal said. "Just so we can hold the gate. The men can pretend to be some advance group of Dogs we met on the road."

"The Romans won't be ready for a fight..." Helig mused. "Their horses won't be saddled. With the rest of us pretending to be Dogs, hammers at our backs, shields in front of us..."

"We'll storm the fort," Gavo finished. "By the gods!"

His enthusiasm wasn't matched by the men though. Cadwal could see a few heads shaking in disapproval.

"But... wait," Gavo stammered, looking at Rhian with fear. "Who will be this translator?"

"I will," she said.

"Oh no! No, no, no!"

"Father, please. Let me!"

"So many years," Gavo lamented, raising a hand to delicately touch the side of her face.

"I know. But the commander might recognise me, or some of his men and let us in. And it is what I want to do. Would you allow it?"

"But..." The chief looked around helplessly.

"For years, I was a slave. They were not kind to me," Rhian said, with an edge in her voice. "A warrior's child ready to fight is a great honour for him. Isn't that right? And I would claim my revenge. Let me be an Ordo-wik!"

Gavo turned his face up to the evening sky and sighed. "So be it."

"They'll have most of their weapons stored in the principia, the main building at the centre." Togman offered. "If you can hold that..."

"Half a chance?" Brei asked.

"Aye."

"And with their big-nosed friends dead, the bastard Dogs won't be laying waste to our lands, destroying the harvest," Helig smiled.

"Great," Togman said. "But there's one very important thing you need to consider before you try this."

"What's that?" Helig asked.

"If this mad plan of yours works, and I am not saying it will, and you kill a whole fort of Roman soldiers, it'll be as good as chopping your own heads off."

"What are you talking about?" Gavo asked.

"Running around harmlessly in your mountains, you're nothing more than a mild inconvenience to Rome now. You're an enemy only in *principle*, just because you pay no taxes and make no tribute. But torch a fort and overnight you'll become a real enemy. Generally, cavalrymen are noble's sons, so there'll be a hundred important families all over the empire who've just lost their boys to barbarians. You'll have a legion marching through your land like the worst storm you ever saw. You will not have a chance against them."

There was an uncomfortable silence.

"He's right," Brei said.

"But if we just leave them be," Gavo said, looking between Cadwal, Gavo and Brei. "With the harvest gone, the result will be the same. We die either way."

"So we have no choice then?" Abuccus asked.

"We always have a choice," Helig said. "We die like slaves, or we die like *men*!"

Gavo turned around and looked at those left of the Clan of the White Stones. "We do it then?" he asked.

Cadwal saw that there was absolutely no fight in any of the men though. "Going to raid a Roman fort while pretending to be Dog?" Maccus shrugged. "Dressed as Romans in front of the gods? Are you mad?"

A couple were so unenthusiastic they even took a step back. Others shook their heads.

"I will not die with the gods thinking I am a Dog!" Abuccus spat.

"It's useless? Is that what you're saying?" Helig raged. "While we're still breathing, on our own land with weapons in our hands? I thought we were fighters? Warriors!"

Even Bevan agreed. "Let me run naked at a testudo... but not like this."

With a frown, Gavo silenced them. The stern look was enough of a reminder that it would be he who make decisions about fighting. But unperturbed, Maccus scoffed. "I am an Ordo-wik and I will *die* as an Ordo-wik!"

Although Cadwal was disappointed, he couldn't blame them as none had seen how Brei had simply strolled into Deva, or how they got back out. While they carried on arguing, he noticed Brei whispering in the Elder's ear. With a still neck, the Elder nodded in agreement. What had been agreed between them, he didn't want to imagine.

The men's discussion was ended when the Elder whacked her staff on the bedrock. The sound was like being hit in the centre of the chest with a slingshot stone and everyone jumped back into silence. With a gnarled finger, she pointed to the bound man. "Bring him. It's time."

Reacting like a barked command from Gwain the Great himself, a couple of men ran down the hill.

The Elder tried to stand, but stiff and weak from all the years that weighted on her bones, she struggled. Instinctively, Cadwal offered his hand, but she grasped him like the talons of a great but ancient bird of prey and he recoiled at the feel of the thin, taut skin stretched over bones. She didn't deign to thank him for his assistance and just rasped, "Come."

He could have done with the staff to help him up, but with blood-brother's arm around his waist, he shuffled off behind the Elder. Even with Bevan's help, every step felt like he was walking through a thicket of brambles laid over glowing embers.

At the mouth of an empty grain pit, a pile of fist-sized pebbles lay ready, and as soon as the captive's hands were unbound, he was unceremoniously pushed in. As deep as about the height of two men, it was a hard landing at the bottom.

Gripped in gnarled fingers, the Elder tipped her staff towards Cadwal, and he froze like a Roman statue wondering what, if Tegin's staff had magic enough to set fire to a whole fort, could an Elder's do to a single man? Compared to such scrutiny, he wished he was back on the horse with another day's riding to do.

"Let us see what the omens tell," she wheezed.

Gavo's men handed out the stones among themselves, some laughing as they weighed them in grubby hands. Helig stretched out and rolled his shoulders and playfully nudged the men next to him out of the way. Chuckling, they jostled around trying to get the best position, but were all whipped to attention by the first thud of the sacred staff on the ground.

Bevan handed him a stone and he ran a thumb over a jagged edge. The back was curved so it fitted well in his hand.

When the Elder was in the best position to see down into the pit, the men took position in a semi-circle around the far edge, rocks ready. On the second whack of the staff on the ground, they shifted their feet into an attack position. With the third, the cries for mercy from below became a cry of agony as a rain of stones fell.

The Elder strolled slowly around, casually looking down at the writhing and begging Dog from all angles, before signalling for the next volley.

With his bruised back, Cadwal couldn't get any power behind his throw, nor accuracy, and his rock bounced off the wall to thud harmlessly on the floor. He would have preferred to have been struck by the stone than to be the recipient of the ice-cold, condescending look of the Elder.

The third round fell and this time the Dog didn't cry out, but huddled up helplessly against the wall, he still lived. Cadwal dropped the last rock more than threw it, but just as the prisoner's arm fell away from his head, it landed square on his temple. At the loud crack of the prisoner's skull, the men cried out with joy at the good omen, but they slapped him so hard on his bruises, he almost stumbled into the pit. "Interesting," the Elder said and seeing that Cadwal was the focus of such attention, the others stopped their congratulations and nervously stepped away from him. Even Gavo. Only Bevan was brave enough to stay and help him stand.

"A very clear story," the Elder continued in a more sombre tone, gnarled fingers tapping on the shaft of her staff. "The plan will work." She waited until everyone was trying to peer into the hole, then banged the staff down again. They all jumped in alarm, some even taking refuge behind their friends' backs. She swung the staff around to indicate everyone at the pit. "But only if *every* man supports it." And with that, she shuffled stiffly off, no more attention to give to normal men.

Once she'd hobbled far enough away Helig roared, "We raid the Roman fort and kill legionaries!"

The heir to the Oak Throne and the chief of their clan they could refuse, but an omen from the gods, that they could not fight against. A few nods at first, but then their enthusiasm grew until they were cheering.

With no druid to frighten them into respectful behaviour, they had a sudden urge to empty their bladders. Sitting for days in his own soil, the Dog hadn't been the sweetest offering the gods had ever received. He was even less after they'd finished.

Bevan helped Cadwal back to the fire, where he fell gratefully back to the soft sheepskins.

"Did he die well?" Brei asked as she held out a gently steaming chicken leg.

Cadwal was suddenly suspicious. "Did you know the Elder would say that?"

The complete lack of expression on her face suggested he was right.

"What else did Tegin say to you in Dinorwig?" she asked.

It felt like half a lifetime since he'd been pulled from the bed just a day ago, but a man did well to remember the words spoken by a priest. "Power is magic, and magic is power."

"Men won't fight a battle if their hearts are not in it. But they will follow a true god-chosen hero to the end of the world. You know now how the Elder has the power to make a man into a hero," she said. "Or the *magic*, if you prefer. Gavo's men are yours now. They will follow you."

"The gods didn't choose me, though, did they?" he said. "*You* did!"

She gave him a knowing grin. "Power is magic and magic is power. This is what is means."

Cadwal shuddered with the knowledge of what the Elder had just done. "And what about the men who escaped the mines?" he whispered. "Why would the gods do that if they want men to fight?"

Brei sighed. "Maybe they just ran the wrong way."

Tossed off a cliff at the whim of a god, or dead simply because they were running in a blind panic. With his head spinning, he couldn't work out which was worse. Suddenly, the roast chicken didn't seem so tasty.

"If we fight tomorrow, then today we feast!" Gavo shouted to the cheers of his men.

"No!" Helig shouted over the din and it quickly died down to mumbles of confusion.

"But... but, tomorrow?"

"They *meet* tomorrow, so we need to leave *now*. We have to get there *ahead* of the Dogs."

"But I have less than thirty men here," Gavo said. "We have no time to muster any more."

"We'll collect more on the way," Helig beamed, full of a confidence Cadwal couldn't feel.

A glimpse at the Elder, who gave him the merest nod, and Gavo shouted, "Get ready to ride! As much supplies as you can carry. Take every weapon you can carry and call the gods to witness this fight!" A little quieter, he added, "And say goodbye to the stones of White Walls."

But then the Elder rolled her eyes back, and took a long rasping breath. It sounded like an ill man in his death throws and Cadwal wondered what kind of omen the men would think it to be if she keeled over lifeless.

"A vision?" Gavo gasped in awe.

With what Brei had just told him, Cadwal assumed it was just another ploy to get the men to do her bidding. Until he saw Brei's look of concern.

"Hear my words... For I see what the future will bring," she gasped, and the skin tingled like a dozen dead spiders were crawling down his back.

"A *prophesy*?" Maccus whispered.

"The long eye?" Abuccus asked.

"The king will die... of happiness," she breathed. "And the blood of the hero shall be on the throne."

The men, most in the process of stepping slowly away, cast confused glances at each other wondering what such words could mean.

Cadwal was more confused than impressed. Hadn't she just made him a hero? Did that mean *his* blood would be on the throne? Blood being spilled in the king's house didn't sound like the best news he'd ever heard. But he reasoned that if he got to bleed on the Oak Throne, at least it meant he'd survive the coming battle with the Romans. And after the fight there was done, he was going straight for his boys, so if it was really a prophecy, he took it as a good one.

But the Elder hadn't finished. A laboured breath, eyes still rolled up in their sunken sockets, "And that shall be the end of all. A new sun will rise..." And then she stopped.

Everyone was held in a shocked silence. Until she spasmed. Then men were bumping into each other in their haste to get away. Men who would stand strong against the Romans were terrified of an old woman. Cadwal had to admit that the performance was a powerful one though. It almost looked like a god had let go of her and she'd fallen back to the world of the living again.

He thought about asking for another performance to convince Helig to go the Dog's fort for the boys, but the way Brei was easing her to the sheepskins, as though she was lying a corpse on a pyre, he decided it might be best to hold his tongue.

FIFTEEN

S O TIRED HE could barely raise his head, Cadwal stared across the river at the ugly walls of the Roman fort. It was a lot smaller than Deva, but its wooden walls still seemed impenetrable and the platform above the gate so high that the sentries on it looked like birds perched atop a tree.

Frightened of invisible scouts in the woods, Togman had made them ride in full armour all the way from White Walls. The bottom of the shield was rested behind Cadwal's kneecap. Togman could grumble at him all he wanted, but there was no way he could hold it up. And the mail shirt was such a weight, he wasn't even sure he could stay in the saddle for the short walk up the other side of the river, never mind wield a sword.

Gavo turned around. "Are you with us? You look like you want to turn tail and run home."

Cadwal had begged to stay in the main group so someone who was capable of wielding a sword could take his place, but Brei had insisted a god-ordained hero needed to be at the head of the men. He hadn't even had the strength to argue.

The horses were almost finished as well, and as they eagerly lapped at the river water, Cadwal wished he could roll out of the saddle and do the same.

"The gods must think we've gone raving mad," Maccus sniggered, absently rubbing his shaven upper lip.

Cadwal turned to look at him. Slumped nonchalantly over in the saddle, he was practically licking his lips in anticipation of wetting his blade on Roman blood, and looked just like an Ordo-wik dressed in unfamiliar armour. Togman saw as well. "Sit up straight, Roman!" he snapped, and when Maccus sat stiffly to attention, the illusion was created again.

Riding up to to the gates with the expectation they'd be welcomed inside as friends, he felt as though he was in the grip of a fevered dream.

Under his gleaming helmet, Helig's eyes were wide with delight.

Walking behind were slightly more than fifty men, the impromptu rank swollen by disbelieving farmers and wide-eyed lads who'd joined them on the fast march from White Walls. Maybe they weren't warriors trained by Gwain the Great, but a few were old enough to remember the Black Year and had waited many, many moons

191

for revenge. Warrior or not, everyone in the land was deadly with a sling shot. With leather cords looped loosely around their wrists, and pockets bulging with stones, they were ready for the battle of their lives. Even so, the responsibility of bringing them here weighed heavier on Cadwal than the mail shirt. He tried not to think of how he'd never before been the leader of anything more than a few sheep raids over the border. And that the last fight he'd been in, he'd been the first to fall and his wife had been killed.

The scar on the back of his neck itched, but he rested the urge to stick a finger inside the helmet to scratch it.

"Be safe," Bevan said as the four of them in Roman armour, making half a contubernium, rode on ahead. A blood oath sworn to give his life to protect Cadwal's, he wasn't too happy to stay with the main group and watch his blood-brother ride off alone. Cadwal hoped that the debt wouldn't need to be paid here.

Gavo groaned as Rhian kicked her horse to ride up beside Togman at the front, hilt of a small sword poking out of the back of her shawl. One day, if the gods allowed it, Owyn and Arwel would be fighters for the tribe, but he didn't know if he'd have the same courage to allow a daughter to ride off towards men of Rome.

He watched as a couple of the guards, spears held pointing up but ready to be angled at chests in a heartbeat, walked casually down the slope to greet them.

Togman greeted them with the stiff Roman salute.

With the memory of the useless key still fresh in his mind, it was hard to trust a man who'd been happy to let him die in the darkness for a profit of a few coins. Despite getting them out of Deva and leading them through Dog land, the smith was with them not for honour, or a sense of what was right, but just to loot the wages of slaughtered soldiers. Cadwal couldn't help the uncomfortable feeling that all Togman had to do to get his old life back, was to shout out a warning. Fifty Ordo-wik heads on sticks might be enough to find himself forgiven, and back at his forge again.

Cadwal could only hope the coins Togman would find inside would be worth more than his old life.

Whatever Togman said, it was convincing, and like the magic of the most powerful Elder, the large wooden gates swung open for them. No clamouring over a pile of fallen bodies filling up the ditch as he tried to scale the wall. No trying to set the gates alight under a rain of arrows. Just walking up to the fort and being welcomed in.

"Appearance is everything," Helig breathed.

From the high platform above the gate, a pair of guards watched warily, but Cadwal saw that they were looking over his head, attention firmly on those milling about at the river, not those in Roman uniforms.

Just as Brei had explained, they were expecting a band of friendly Dogs to camp by the river, and so that is what they saw.

"I can take them out," Maccus said as they rode under the platform.

"Walk up casually," Togman said. "Maybe they'll think you've just come to look at the view."

Maccus scoffed unconvinced.

"Remember when we rode up to White Walls this morning?" Cadwal added. "You didn't think it was me, did you?"

"Aye," he nodded. "Some magic, that."

"Shut your ugly faces!" Togman seethed.

Rhian gave a little wave to a man she recognised. She was the best part of the plan. Seeing the girl who stood next to the commander of Deva when auxiliaries needed help with Latin, would lull anyone to drop their guard. No one could expect what was about to happen.

"Salva," Togman called in greeting. Full of willow powder from Gavo's supply, it was good to hear him talk without hearing the crack of pain in his voice.

They pulled up in front of a tough looking man, square jawed, and nose crooked from being broken several times. Cadwal wished he knew the name of the man who'd done that so he could speak his name to the gods. Arm out and a nod without breaking eye contact was the only greeting the man gave. But then he noticed Rhian and the beginning of a little smile curled up at the side of his mouth. She returned a dainty wave.

Cadwal's heart beat so hard, he worried the nearby men could hear it jingling his shirt mail.

Directly in front, at the end of two long and thin buildings, Cadwal saw what must be the principia, where all the Roman's heavy weapons were kept. He itched to gallop straight there.

Maccus dismounted and made a show of stretching his painful legs. He was supposed to be a cavalryman though, so should be well used to long stints in the saddle. Cadwal cringed to think their cover was about to be blown. A couple sniggered as Maccus tried to stand up straight, but didn't give any indication that anything was unusual.

Appearance is everything.

Maccus wandered disinterestedly to the steps beside the gate and started to make his way up to the rampart, whistling a tune. Cadwal looked on in amazement; the mad bastard was actually enjoying himself!

With the four riders in, the soldiers at the gates began to close them.

Cadwal's heart rose to his throat. Now or never.

While Maccus made his relaxed way up the ladder to the platform above the gate, a couple of Romans helped Rhian down from her horse, smiling at seeing her again, even though she was merely a slave.

Helig swung down and a Roman looked puzzled as to why he was unsheathing a sword. He didn't get to call out an alarm as the first guard fell over the railings above, his screams cut off as he crunched to the floor.

As everyone turned to look, there was a long heartbeat of utter stillness. For the Romans, that moment was filled with a wave of shocked incomprehension. For the Ordo-wiki it was a breath of pure ecstasy, knowing that a fight to be celebrated for generations was about to begin.

In a glorious arc of blood, Helig slashed the soldier's throat, and it began.

Maccus yelled at the top of his voice, awakening the gaze of the gods, and the second guard was barrelled over the rail by his shoulder barge.

"Cover the gates!" Helig bellowed. "And take the towers!"

The commander was already running desperately to the principia. They had to let him go as, if the gates were closed, they'd all be dead. Helig's battle cry was one of pure joy and utter madness, and just a few heartbeats was all it took for the whole fort to be full of panicked shouts as confused Romans clamoured out of their barracks to find out what was happening. None had the thought that a fully armoured Roman on a horse in a cavalry fort was a threat. A few in reach of Cadwal's blade had no idea who had killed them. Some were even unarmed.

With his left leg tucked under one of the protrusions on the saddle, he could lean out further with the sword, and his long blade had a better reach than the Roman's shorter stabbing ones. None got past him and Helig to the gates.

The blood curdling cries of the warband as they charged up from the river, raised the fine hairs on the back of Cadwal's neck. Then, in a torrent of bloodlust, they were streaming in, with Gavo at their head. The fort's defenders may have been the best trained soldiers in the whole world, but shocked and unprepared, they were no match for the half-crazed Ordo-wiki pouring in screaming for slaughter.

Helig tore after the commander, screeching like a deranged banshee. Cadwal followed, Togman alongside, knocking dumbfounded soldiers out of the way, and cutting down all those they could reach.

At full tilt, Helig managed to run the commander down, but not until he was too close to the principia to pull up in time. Helig's horse shied away from slamming into the wall, and he was pitched head first out of the saddle, his battle cry cut off. He got to his feet but had dropped his sword in the fall, so fell on the commander to pummel him with his fists.

Cadwal and Togman reigned in, and with the horses turning nose to tail, they danced in a tight circle in front of the principia door, hacking at the desperate men still coming from the barracks, trying to get inside to the stash of weapons.

Only the blood rush and the protrusions over his thighs kept Cadwal in the saddle. He couldn't see Gavo, but every soldier in the fort was a well-trained fighter and for those caught without a sword, lengths of wood were soon in their hands thumping against Cadwal's leg. Something hard bounced off the metal chains covering his chest. There were too many to fend off and he turned the horse, buffeting men away. But then, in a wave of fury, iron blades, and hammer heads glinting in the sun, the screaming band of Ordo-wiki fell on them.

Cadwal revelled in the cries of terror and exaltation, and hacked down at whoever he could reach. The slashing of sharpened metal into unprotected flesh, the arcs of blood as vital veins were slashed, the horse staggering over prone bodies, it was everything an Ordo-wik warrior dreamed of.

Above, screaming as wildly as Helig, Maccus ran along the rampart, stopping to choose a few targets with his sling. The guards in the corner towers and on the walls, were bombarded with sling shot stones from Gavo's men. Forced to take cover, they couldn't shoot arrows down.

Gavo, back on his horse, charged past and from behind, Togman shouted, "For my cock, you bastards!"

Helig was still on the ground, still locked in a fierce grapple with the commander, who was landing plenty of punches. From horseback, Cadwal couldn't reach down far enough with the sword, and although he had no idea how he would get back on again, he dismounted and stood poised with the tip of the blade pointed at the commander's face. The commander saw him, but instead of twisting out of the way, he grabbed the blade and jerked his head up to cut his own throat. As his blood pooled on the packed earth beside him, he stared up with a look of angry defiance.

Shocked by such an unexpected action, Cadwal was slow to move. Helig reached over him to cut a Roman in the head and then, as their own men swarmed around, Bevan helped Helig lift him back on the horse.

"Bastards," Gavo cried from close by as he chopped into bewildered men. They had a few moments of killing gifted for free as in the confusion Romans mistook the clean-shaven men in familiar uniforms as defenders, not their butchers. Some Romans tried to get themselves into an ordered formation but were so bewildered at seeing what they thought was their own cavalry bearing down on them, they didn't even raise their weapons. Helig and Gavo charged through, knocking them over like a child's game.

Still screaming, Maccus took men down with his whistling sling stones, while others up on the wall with him rained stones at speeds high enough to knock a man down.

"Desito! Desito!" Togman cried and in case any were from Gaul and spoke the tongue of the land, called, "Surrender!"

The sight of Romans getting rounded up and cut down like pigs in a pen was the most incredible thing Cadwal had ever seen, but then the ruckus seemed to quieten and the unnatural strength which had sustained him began to pour out like a burst water skin. The sword seemed as heavy as the trunk of an oak, and he was helpless to stop it falling from his fingers. The reins in his hands became ephemeral as mist and no matter how tightly he thought he grabbed onto them, he slid out of the saddle as though it was lathered in fat.

For a moment he thought it was Bevan's arms he was falling into, the scared face twisted in concern, but it was Gwen who caught him. He slumped lightly into her arms. But then she was pulling him, trying to get him to move towards whatever she was pointing to on the horizon. They were in a long and thin barley field, her flowing dress catching the ripening ears. The sun struck beams through the motes of dust.

"Almost..." she smiled. "Almost there."

Slowly, Cadwal was looking up at the deep blue of a late evening sky. Swallows streamed overhead. The air was full of the smell of iron and shit. "What happened?" he asked.

"Sleeping," Togman laughed. "While we were killing Romans. Again." Worryingly, the smith looked unhappy and not like a man who'd just taken part in an incredible victory.

"Here he is!" Gavo exclaimed. His ruddy face was covered in dust and spattered with blood. Cadwal was relieved to see his beaming smile. He shouted, "The hero lives!" and a cheer came from below. "You mad bastard. You did it! We took the fort! A Roman fort!" The chief laughed, shaking his head in disbelief.

Cadwal was happy to stay lying where he was, but Gavo pulled him up into a sitting position and the bear hug he gave was like being back in the midst of the fighting again, struggling for life. "A hundred bard's songs I have heard in my years." "But for the rest of my days, I will only listen to ones about what we just did here."

Bevan held a water skin to his lips and drank until he coughed. "What happened?" he asked.

"Brei says you fell off your horse because you're exhausted," Bevan said, patting him affectionately on the shoulder. "You fought until you couldn't hold your sword. Gwain would have been proud."

With a giddy feeling so strong he worried he was about to faint again, Cadwal saw that they'd carried him up to the platform over the gates. Several dead men were with them and for an awful moment he thought he'd been set on top of a pyre and was about to be consumed by the flames. But the others were the fallen who'd been brought up so the gods could see what heroes they were.

"Seven of ours, it cost," Gavo said. "But we did it, we took the whole fort! The Dogs won't raid with them now, so the land is saved! Like the Elder said, you truly are a hero."

Higher in the sky than the swallows, crows were circling, readying for their feast of flesh. The dead were mostly farmers who'd joined them on the way, but they were Ordo-wik all the same. Cadwal wanted to honour them, but could only think about the boys and that when the Dogs turned up, their fort would be almost empty of fighting men. It would be a simple thing to hide in the woods until the column had passed and then it would be just him and Helig against whoever was left in the fort. "Where is Helig?" he asked.

"Running around like a boy pretending to be a king," Gavo said, but a little sheepishly, added, "But if he does take the Oak Throne, maybe don't mention I said that. But we won!"

"I don't know why you think you've got so much to celebrate," Togman said. "All you did was catch an undermanned fort off guard. They're trained all day every day to operate as a *unit*. You surprised them, that's all. And you will pay for it very, very dearly."

"Bah," Gavo scoffed. "You only came for *coin*, what would you know?"

"What coin?" Togman asked. "There's nothing here. Only a few denari."

"Will that keep you fed?" Gavo mocked.

"For a while, maybe. But it's not what I risked my neck getting you in here for."

To diffuse the building argument, Cadwal interrupted. "You fought well. You didn't need to. Just getting us in the gates was all I asked."

"You don't think I remember my fallen brethren from Boudica's last day? With a sword in my hand again, it all came back, and I was glad to take blood. I spoke my kins' names today. That was almost worth a king's gold."

King's gold. A thought snapped Cadwal to attention. "You can *have* a king's gold," he said and watched the smith's expression cloud from thoughts of heroism to ones of profit. "What gold?" he asked guardedly.

"Helig will go to the fort of the Dogs for my boys. With all their warriors *here*, their fort will be undefended. If you help him, you can take as much gold from their king as you can carry."

"And we'll just walk straight in, shall we? Because forts... you know, they exist for the *sole* reason of preventing that."

"You fought the Romans hand to hand for some coins. I offer that you fight some women and children for gold."

Although Togman nodded, he didn't look convinced. "I will speak to Helig about it."

Cadwal should have been happy that two excellent fighters would be going to free Owyn and Arwel, but they were the two men he trusted least in the whole land.

"I will go as well," Bevan said.

"For the gold?" Togman asked, already worried about his share of the spoils.

"For Cadwal's boys!" he scoffed. "For honour! How long have you been with the Romans? You sound just like one."

Shaking the platform as he bounded up, the eldest son of Gwain was filthy and covered from head to toe in other men's blood, but otherwise seemed utterly unfazed from the fight. He exuded such an air of confidence that Cadwal's belly lurched as his concerns obviously weren't about how to reunite a pair of young boys with their father. "I know what we're going to do," he beamed, sweeping his arm out over the fort. "Cadwal gave me the idea."

"And that will be what?" Gavo asked with more than a hint of scepticism.

"The fifty of us are safe inside here with the walls around us..."

It was even worse than Cadwal had feared. Never mind not thinking about how to ride around the horde of the Dogs on the way to their fort, he wanted to fight them.

"It's closer to forty now, if you care to notice..." Gavo said, nodding at the row of bodies.

"...We could hold it for a moon," Helig continued. "But imagine if the Dogs come tomorrow and we get them assembled out there in front of the gate."

"Maybe now is not the time for glorious heroics," Gavo said dismissively.

"Listen," Helig snapped. "First, we rain the stock of the big Roman spears we found down on them to thin their numbers and spread panic, and then riders swoop in from both sides to cut them down. It will be an easy slaughter. We'll kill dozens of their fighting men in one go. And we won't have to worry about raiding this year or the next."

Helig was pointed excitedly into the fort so didn't see Gavo roll his eyes. "Rhian says that maybe they'll be two hundred," the chief shrugged. "There's only forty of us who'll be fighting tomorrow, so even with Roman horses and weapons, there's far too many to face in an open battle."

"We'll shock them like we just did the Romans," Helig smiled. "We scared them so much they just fell to their knees."

Gavo shook his head. "This time, they'll all have a full assortment weapons and they'll only be off guard for a moment."

"We'll have Roman uniforms on. They'll be confused!"

"And how many heartbeats would it take you to realise a man throwing spears at you is an enemy?"

Cadwal held onto the rail and looked at the other side of the fort walls. At the inside.

"We just walked right in here and killed nearly a hundred Romans!" Helig protested. "Most of the men can't even count how many!"

"That wasn't about numbers," Gavo said, his voice raising.

"No?"

"Like our new friend here says, we won because we caught them unawares."

"Bah," Helig exclaimed. "Gavo, listen to me. We can kill dozens of our worst enemies in one single fight. Our lands will be safe!"

"Your lands are far from safe," Togman shrugged. "The legion will have them soon enough, "They will not easily forgive what you've just done here. I told you, these were equites you killed."

Cadwal looked at the sheer steepness of the insides of the perimeter wall and the sturdiness of the gate. Helig was right about killing Dogs. They had an opportunity that no Ordo-wik had had since the Dogs had first crept off their boats and set foot on these lands. They'd be free of the Dogs for a generation. And when he got the boys back, he'd be bringing them back to a much safer place. Like usual though, it seemed Helig was looking at it the wrong way. It would surely be better to bring them *inside*.

"They are *my* men!" Gavo roared. "I am not a king's heir who can throw unknown faces at a fight. A bunch of bastards they may be, but I've known every one of them since they were a babe or a boy. Even our hero here, I remember running around with soiled swaddling. So when I say *no* you cannot use them for a bad plan, I mean that while I stand and breathe, I forbid it!"

"I am the son of Gwain!" Helig spat.

"I know well who your father was," Gavo sighed. "But now is not the time for you to try and be him."

Helig was right. As much as he wanted to saddle a fresh Roman horse and ride to the Dog's fort, they had to fight. The idea was simple. If they could lead the Dogs inside, they'd be trapped between walls. They could be rounded up like pigs in a pen. "Wait," Cadwal managed to say.

"Listen!" Bevan shouted. "The hero will speak!"

"What are you thinking?" Gavo asked, noticeably more respectfully than how he addressed Helig.

The shadow of the idea was in his head, but it wasn't attended by the words to describe it, especially as the chief of White Walls and the next king of the Ordo-wiki waited for him to speak with the wisdom of a druid. Or to hear a plan they thought was touched by the gods. "Pig pen," he mumbled.

Gavo stammered for a moment before making a childish noise with his lips, just about recognisable as that of a horse. "Well, it was nice to have a hero while it lasted," he sighed. "Did the gods get your mind in payment for this plan?"

"Let him speak!" Bevan said, a brave statement in such company.

"Why do you put pigs in a pen?" Cadwal asked.

"Well..." Gavo said, a little flustered. "Maybe this isn't the best moment to discuss animal keeping, seeing as there's two hundred Dog warriors on their way. But, so they don't rut around the fort eating everything."

"So they are trapped," Togman helped.

"Ahh..." Gavo said with a look of expectation as he realised Cadwal had thought of something.

"Helig is right," Cadwal nodded with due reverence. "The forty of us could hold these walls for a moon and keep the Dogs out. But we can't stay in here."

"So..." Helig said. "We bring them inside... and then what?"

Cadwal pointed down into the fort. "If we pulled down the buildings just inside the gate, archers on the walls would have a clear sight of every man. And with the gates closed behind them..."

"They'd have nowhere to run," Helig finished.

All gone, Cadwal thought. "And then we can go to the Dog's fort," he said, but couldn't turn quickly enough to catch Helig's expression.

Gavo blew his cheeks out. "Pigs in a pen."

"All for slaughter," Helig grinned.

"There are enough bows here for every man. Let's do it!" Helig said.

"Bows?" Bevan asked. "Who's fighting with bows?"

Gavo pointed down into the fort. "We're like buzzards up here looking down on helpless field mice."

"There's no honour in shooting a man with an arrow," Bevan said stubbornly. "It's not right. What will the gods say when I stand before them after killing men from a distance with *arrows*?"

"You can speak to the gods tomorrow if you want to fight forty against two hundred with a sword," Gavo said.

"The Dogs are owed no honour," Cadwal added.

"It's *dirty*," Bevan insisted.

"Aye. I agree," Gavo nodded. "No one should kill a man with a weapon made for an animal, but these are *Dogs*. They don't fight with the old rules any more. Like the bastard who tried to burn down our fort, and the ones who stripped Crow Hill."

Bevan shrugged.

"If it all goes wrong," Gavo continued. "I'll be right there with you in front of the gods to explain that you were just following orders. And it's a very honourable thing to obey your chief."

Bevan laughed.

"And you'll have to shave," Cadwal added.

"You want us to fight such a battle in front of the gods with shaved faces?" That's a lot to ask, even for a blood brother!" Bevan said, but with a smile.

"We need to look just like Romans. Any long moustaches and Roman uniforms on or not the Dogs will see who we are."

"Right," Helig said, enthused. "We're turning this fort into a pig pen! We need picks, shovels, buckets, and the horses harnessed to pull the buildings by the gates down!" He shouted men to him as he slid down the ladder.

Gavo rolled his eyes as he watched him leave.

The boys would have to spend another night alone, but for that, Cadwal had a chance of killing all those who'd taken them. It was something none of his ancestors could have imagined.

SIXTEEN

"Almost two hundred," Helig announced nervously.

"Just as you said," Gavo said to Rhian, his eyes glowing with admiration.

From the top of one of the square gate towers, they watched the Dog vanguard wade across the river. In a ragged line, they began to make their way up towards the fort.

"Four to one?" Helig chuckled. "But we are Ordo-wiki and they are Dogs. That makes it a little more even."

The chief tilted his head back and his smile turned into a cavernous yawn. Brei had insisted that Cadwal rest, and he'd slept all through the night, but everyone else had worked until after dawn to turn the fort into a giant trap for the approaching enemies. He turned to look at the giant trench they'd dug across the middle and hoped the thin covering of reeds and scattered earth wouldn't look as obvious from the ground as it did from up on the tower.

Gavo rubbed his ruddy face. "We beat the Romans yesterday. These bastards will be easy." The sight of so many blood enemies so close, gave a strained edge to his voice though. Not from fear, but from restraining the burning rage to fight. Any loved one lost in a fight or raid, a missed father, a son's headless body carried home... the chances were that they'd died at the hands of those milling about below.

Sweaty palms wiped on the tunic again, Cadwal gripped the hilt of the short Roman sword at his hip to mask the shaking of his hands. It seemed as unreal as being ready for a battle wearing Roman armour.

An Ordo-wik army before a fight, screaming at the tops of their voices for the gods' attention, bashing weapons together and the wailing carnyx was the loudest noise in the world. Here, it felt as though a cry was about to burst from his chest of its own accord.

Togman stood beside them, the plated armour over his shoulder gleaming in the sun, a stack of heavy spears laid at his feet. Gavo's men manned the towers at the corners of the fort and waited on the ramparts, bows, spears and rocks at the ready. With naked faces and wearing Roman tunics, they were all ready to fight in a way they'd never imagined before.

Cadwal rolled his shoulders, the bruises all down his back and sides still terribly painful, and wished again that he didn't have to wear the heavy chain shirt. Brei had insisted that he dress like a Roman so everyone who'd had to bear the shame of having their faces shaved and wear the clothes of the enemies, could see their hero doing the same.

"I want that cocky bastard," Helig announced.

He didn't point, but Cadwal assumed he meant the man at the head of the column. The way he held himself, puffed up chest and a confident swagger, singled him out as their leader. The white fox skins draped over his shoulders looked familiar, but he wore no torc, was clean shaven, and had his hair cut short in the Roman way.

Cadwal had his own targets down there and made two wishes. Firstly, that those who'd lived with the Clan of Crow Hill for a moon were among them. The second was that they'd somehow be spared an arrow or spear so it would be at his hands their deaths would be met. With such anger and hatred in his heart, four to one felt easy odds. But he caught a glimpse of something in the back of a wagon coming down to the ford that fluttered his heart with a new panic. Stepping over the spears and piles of rocks soon to be smashed on heads below, he stood as close to the edge of the platform as he dared and squinted.

"What is it?" Gavo asked, concern in his voice.

It wasn't plaited in the usual intricate way, but her long straw-blond hair was unmistakable. "The teryn of Crow Hill," he said as everything inside his body felt like it was slipping out as though his belly had been slashed open.

"Minura?" Gavo asked. He swung around and with a finger waving at his men as threatening as the tip of a sword, shouted, "Don't shoot at the wagon. It's the *teyrn*. Bleddyn's daughter!"

The message was quickly relayed along the walls. The few nods and some affirma-tive 'Ayes' wouldn't have meant much to Cadwal, but evidently the chief knew his men well enough to trust that such casual gestures meant their solemn agreement. Helig though, looked like he was trying to refrain from dancing a jig. If she was here, Helig had no reason to go to the Dog's fort.

Cadwal tried to see who was in the wagon behind. If he were to see two little heads bobbing up and down, he would call the whole battle off.

"Time to go," Gavo said as he made his way to the ladder, but paused a moment to squeeze Rhian's arm. "I know, I know," he sighed, as he looked at her with pleading eyes. "But you stay up here. *Safe*. Do you hear me?"

"I do, father."

As he felt with a foot for the first rung, he whispered, "I've never been so proud."

The long barrack buildings had all been torn down and the wood and tiles taken away so that now the area behind the main gate was just open ground, marked by lines of straight foundations of the building they'd pulled down. It looked a lot different from when they'd ridden in the day before, but Cadwal counted on the fact that no Dog had ever set foot in a Roman fort before, so would have no way of knowing anything was amiss.

"On my command. No one else's!" Gavo called out to his men. "Or you can walk the wilds for the rest of your days. Yesterday with the Romans, that was only practice! This is the *real* fight!"

There were a few laughs to cover the nerves or the excitement, but then they turned back into Roman legionaries on guard duty. Cadwal carefully followed the chief down the ladder. Gavo grinned at him as they walked across the cleared space, but his eyes were stone cold. The words of the Elder had created the magic to get them inside the fort, but now it was simply about fighting men. And he was ready for battle.

"Halt!" Togman called down to the Dogs from the platform, then shouted some commands in Latin. Rhian called down in the native tongue. "Welcome, our friends. Leave your weapons outside. We welcome you as allies inside the fort to drink our wine. But you must lay down your weapons. It is Roman law." And by her own volition added, "Corotica, just as you did when you came to Deva to make these very plans."

Through the gates, Cadwal saw riders reluctantly dismount, scabbards were unbuckled, bows set down next to shields. A few slings were unwound.

"That's my girl." Gavo smiled as they pressed themselves carefully along the wall, mindful not to step on the reeds that covered the deep pit.

Gavo and Helig got on their horses while Maccus and Bevan helped Cadwal into the principia. Once the door was barricaded, he pushed him up the ladder and onto the roof. On the warm tiles, Brei lay waiting, bows and dozens of arrows beside her. Cadwal lowered himself down just in time to see the first Dog step cautiously inside, and instead of blood, his heart pumped pure hatred. It took every last effort to stay calm and not charge into them, screaming for vengeance at the top of his voice. He was impressed that none of Gavo's men had broken their act.

About fifty Dogs had filed inside. Sixty... More. Some of them looked around with distrustful glances, just as the Romans had done to Gavo's men the day before. Distrust of strangers was a way of life. With their clean faces and identical tunics, the Dogs at the head of the line didn't give them anything more than a cursory look.

Cadwal noticed a few of Gavo's men nudging each other, maybe a reminder to concentrate on not looking like cats eager to pounce. Down in front of the principia, he watched Gavo wave the guests welcomingly to him, but a shout of warning came from near the gate. A few arms pointed to large panels above the gateway. They were obviously a non-Roman innovation, especially the spear points nailed to them.

Their leader cast an accusatory look, which blossomed into a glorious one of shock when Gavo lifted the war horn to his lips. The note it made poured through Cadwal like the deepest surge of ecstasy and all the little hairs on his body stood on end. Togman cut the ropes that held the heavy wooden panels up. Made from the barrack's roofing timbers, and hinged just above the entrance, they swung down with enough force to knock men aside as though they were children's toys and impaled anyone unfortunate enough to be standing in the reach of its swing.

Twanging of bow strings releasing arrows from strings. The whoosh as the feathers hissed through the air and the dull, wet thuds as they pierced their targets and the screams of wounded and dying enemies were sounds sweeter to Cadwal's ears than any song the best lyre player could play.

Maccus and Brei started firing down into the panicked throng, but Bevan made sure Cadwal was balanced safely on the roof before loosing his first arrow.

Cadwal's wrist was still weak from when it had been struck by the instructor in Deva's arena, but he shot off one arrow after another, not even bothering to see if he struck anyone. With their shields left outside, the bastards were helpless.

After a few moments of dumb shock, those at the front of the group, yelling with fear and rage, ran for what they thought was safety. The ditch was carefully covered so they didn't see until the first men fell into it. Those behind with quick enough reflexes to stop were forced in by those pushing from behind. If not impaled on the sharpened spikes at the bottom, they were crushed by those falling in behind. It was such a glorious sight that both Helig and Gavo cried out with delight.

Gavo, large hammer in his hand, was ready to smash anyone who made it out and shouted with joy as he rushed to cover the left flank. Helig kicked his horse into a charge to the other side, shrieking at the top of his voice with what sounded like a terrible madness.

The terrified Dogs, standing on the crushed bodies of their friends to make it to the other side of the ditch, were more afraid of the rain of arrows, until they were trampled on by the horses.

Their leader was lucky though, and, using the bodies of other men to stand on, managed to haul himself out. A few more followed, but cautiously, as they knew no safety waited for them on the other side.

Brei, kneeling over the apex of the roof, picked her targets with precision. But then a riderless horse ran below. Helig's. From where he was, Cadwal couldn't see what had happened, but more and more men were making it through the ditch, and he watched with horror as a Dog pulled himself up into the saddle. But no sooner had he grabbed the reins, he was pitched off backwards with one of Brei's arrows in his chest.

But Cadwal was shimmying down the ladder, ignoring Bevan's calls for him to come back. Out of the principia, down on ground level, the noise and the smell were more intense. With his short Roman sword, he jabbed at those trying to crawl out of the ditch but saw Helig against the far wall, the Dog leader standing over him, Helig's hammer in his hand.

Cadwal limped over, Bevan calling out a warning behind. The Dog had lifted the hammer almost high enough to strike, but another man was crawling out of the ditch in front, an arrow he'd pulled out of someone's body clasped in a hand. Cadwal could stop to kill him, but the Dog leader was a heartbeat away from killing Helig. The man in the ditch lunged, but Cadwal dodged to the side and dived, blade first at the leader's back. Sword in his spine, he crumbled like a new-born lamb and the hammer dropped harmlessly to the ground. The relief that the man who held his blood oath was saved lasted a heartbeat as from behind he heard the blood brother's cry. He turned and saw Bevan on his knees, the arrow sticking out his belly.

Helig rolled to his feet, grabbed his hammer and, stepping over Bevan without noticing him, resumed his berserk war cry along the ditch, swinging killing blows with the same hammer that had almost taken his life a moment before. He missed the man who'd stabbed Bevan though. A smile twitched across the bastard's face as he pulled himself free of the pit. He picked up Bevan's sword and swung it.

Cadwal had no defence. There was no mercy to beg, no bargain to make, only fate to face. The blade seemed to move so impossibly slow, Cadwal almost laughed at how easy it would be to duck under it and casually slip it out of the man's grasp but his body wouldn't move. He felt like one of the statues Rome was famous for and all he could do as the sword kept drifting closer was to twist slightly out of the way.

He'd come so close, had done so much to get here and was only a few moments from being able to go for the boys. The gods were crueller than he had ever imagined.

The sword stuck with its length across the centre of his chest.

All sorts of lights flickered before his eyes. He was dimly aware of the shocking metallic clash, loud enough to make his ears ring. Then he was laid out on his back staring up at the clear blue sky.

He couldn't breathe.

It felt as though a horse was lying on his chest.

With a rasp like an old dying man, he managed to drag a tiny bit of air past his lips, but it burned like breathing in fire.

Hands from those trapped in the ditch grabbed at his tunic, pulling him in.

He dabbed his fingers into the gaping wound and held his bloody hands up to see his life blood all over them. But they were covered only in dirt. Confused, he tried again and in the sweetest relief, realised the chain mail had protected him. Another desperate and burning gulp of air, and he rolled over and dragged himself over to Bevan. The arrow was gone from his belly and for a moment Cadwal was ecstatic to think he'd been mistaken, but then he saw the hole punched through the chain shirt. And the Dog he'd stabbed in the thigh with it crawling away.

"You paid me back," Cadwal gasped, a hand over his blood-brother's oozing wound, but Bevan's eyes were staring up at the sky. Hopefully, the gods were looking down on him and would know him for the hero he was.

All Cadwal could do was focus on drawing in one breath after another. His only fight now against the encroaching darkness. He could hear Helig's distinct scream from the midst of the fight, engrossed in his bloody harvest.

But then he saw Dax.

Hunched over, he ran against the far wall.

The chaos of the battle stilled, and everything went strangely quiet. Cadwal saw nothing but him.

Sword clenched in a weak hand, he got to unsteady feet, and with all the breath he could manage, he rasped, "*You!*"

Despite his panic, Dax stopped.

Heaving in another breath, he croaked. "Remember me?" as he hobbled over. Terrified, Dax shook his head.

It took Cadwal a moment to realise Dax thought he was being addressed by a Roman soldier. He smiled. "Take my name to the Otherlands with you, bastard. I am Cadwal ap Madog. Of Crow Hill!"

The recognition hit Dax harder than a hammer. He cowered, terror on his face, like two little boys being dragged away from their chained father.

Killing him with the sword was too clean a way for him to die. Cadwal wanted him to suffer, to rip his guts out and watch him writhe as he watched every last man of his tribe die. But at least it wasn't just with the terror of death he died. He went to the Otherlands wrapped in the madness of thinking he was killed by a dribbling ghost in a Roman uniform.

As though he was in a dream, Cadwal saw what a mess he'd made of the body from hacking it so much. He sucked in another desperate breath and looked around. From the ramparts, Gavo's men still fired arrow after arrow. Only a few Dogs were left standing. Helig and Gavo rode up and down in the cleared part of the fort like heroes from a bard's song, swinging hammers and felling unarmed men as easily as a farmer reaping wheat.

A group of Dogs had huddled together against the wall using the bodies of their friends as protection, so they crashed into them with the horses and the archers picked off those left exposed.

"Open the gates!" Helig bellowed and Gavo followed to help those outside. Jumping down from the walls, most of the archers ran after them, swords drawn and hammers raised.

It was over. The depth of satisfaction from watching the Dog's blood seep into the ground was so profound, Cadwal had to use the sword to help him stand. He trod carefully over the soft bridge of arrow-filled bodies filling the ditch. He was heading out as well. Owyn and Arwel could have been brought here, as Minura had been, and he needed to find out.

Rhian, face flushed and hair dishevelled, ran to him and patted his body to see where he was hurt. Brei caught up and cupped his sweaty face in a hand. "I thought you were dead!"

The tips of her fingers bleeding from the bow string, she helped him pull the mail over his head and Rhian gasped at the sight of the angry red line over his ribs. In some places, the skin was pricked with spots of blood where a few broken metal rings had pierced it. With the shirt off, it was much easier to breathe.

A drift of bodies blocked both sides of the gate, so over cracked skulls and chests struck through with the fearsome Roman javelins, he stumbled over. The grass outside wasn't much easier to walk over as it too was covered with the dead, sprawled out where they'd died fighting or fleeing from the mounted Ordo-wiki who'd ridden them down.

The gods couldn't have been anything but impressed, but they were the least of his concern.

Halfway down to the river, a single Dog was left standing. One arrow had gone all the way through a shoulder, another stuck out of the top of his leg. As he hobbled around, a couple of Gavo's men closed in like crows around carrion. Cadwal didn't give him the honour of watching him die.

With one of the horses twisted gruesomely in its harness, the wagon was going nowhere. He pulled the cover back, and like a cornered cat, the teryn screamed a wild cry and lurched forwards trying to bite his arm. With her hands bound behind her back, she couldn't do too much, but he was pleased that the leader of his clan fought like a real Ordo-wik.

"I'll cut you loose," he said, but she was making too much noise to hear. Showing her the spatha only made her even angrier.

"It's *me*!" he said, but the teryn couldn't see beyond his Roman clothes, so he grabbed her by the hair and held her down while he sliced through the ropes.

Rubbing her chafed wrist, then wiping the sweat from her face, she looked up confused. He supposed the swollen black eye and the split lip were a part of the reason she was so afraid.

"Minura, it's me. Cadwal ap Madog!"

The horn blew from the wall and they both snapped around. But whoever had it, wasn't warning of an incoming threat and tried to play a tune. Her head swung from side to side like an owl as she saw all the bodies spread from the gate all the way down to the river. "Cadwal?" she gasped, open-mouthed, as she recognised him. "By the gods!" she said accusingly. But then the full realisation of the enormity of what she was seeing hit her. "What have you *done*?"

"There's some story to tell," Maccus grinned as he sauntered up.

As Maccus took Cadwal's hand and placed it on his head, Minura asked, astounded, "You took a Roman fort?"

"Aye," Maccus beamed. "We did."

Cadwal was about to point out that it wasn't a common girl he was talking to, but she didn't seem too offended his glib reply.

"Where are my boys?" Cadwal asked.

"Boys?"

"My *boys*!"

"Did you see *me* before you started firing?" she asked Maccus in a tone more resembling the teryn Cadwal knew well. And feared. One of her eyebrows rose. Under normal circumstances, the gesture would indicate that someone's attitude needed a swift change. But if he wasn't interested in the opinions of the gods, then a teryn's mattered even less.

"My boys!" Cadwal repeated sternly.

If she was outraged about Cadwal caring more about the children than her, at least she didn't put words to it. "They're back at the fort."

"They live?"

"Yes!" The eyebrow that was once the terror of a whole clan raised again. "But I think you have a story to tell!"

"Later!" he said, but perhaps a little harsher than he'd intended. She didn't snap at him, though. Perhaps she understood that men who'd won such a fight were elevated to a higher, more equal social standing. It was only an idle thought though, he really didn't care.

He looked back at the fort, and the devastated enemies spewing out of its gates. More dead foes to his name than Gwain himself. More than any Ordo-wik who had ever lived. He was a real hero. Maybe even call him 'Great' and his name would be sung long after his face was forgotten. He couldn't care less and dismissed the thought quickly, as he was nothing until he had the boys.

There were other wagons on the far side of the river. Ignorant of the killing, a horse was lazily grazing at the riverbank. Cadwal managed to get into the saddle and rode off.

Over the ford, bodies of slain Dogs were scattered along the track and a couple of overturned wagons had their contents scattered out, but there were no boys. He called their names into the trees but got no reply.

Half a dozen riders came back, heads of those who'd fled tied to their saddles. Cadwal waved them over and they obeyed his command as though he was Gavo. But they'd seen no children.

Despondent, he rode back to the scenes of jubilant celebration in front of the fort and tethered the horse to the teryn's wagon. The men all wanted their fill of his god-touched hands on their heads. With a hundred Romans and nearly two hundred Dogs dead at their hands, they had a lot to celebrate.

One man absent from the congratulations was Helig. Cadwal found him with Minura, deep in a heated conversation. More interested in rescuing his boys than being polite to a teryn, Cadwal interrupted them. "We ride?" he asked, staring straight at Helig.

"At once!" Minura snapped. "My father is in great danger from Derog!"

"To the Dog's fort," Cadwal said without turning away from Helig.

Helig visibly blanched, and Cadwal was sure that even worse than arguing about the blood oath, he'd *forgotten* about it. He couldn't even look Cadwal in the eye.

"Tell me you refuse," Cadwal demanded.

"I..." he stammered. "The teryn is here!"

"And my boys are *there*." Cadwal held up his palm to show the mark. Again Helig turned away. "You forgo your oath?"

"What is this?" Minura snapped but both of them ignored her.

Helig looked pitiful, like a child knowing he was about to be beaten, his last defence to plead for mercy with his eyes. "We have to..."

"Tell me you *refuse*!"

"I will be king..."

"An honourless one," Cadwal said as he turned away. In his heart, he'd known it would come to this, but the man who would have the Oak Throne dismissing a blood-oath to his face was still an aching disappointment.

The euphoria of the battle wearing off, he limped back towards the fort but the pain in his chest and the sense of despair made it feel like he was drowning in the dark river again. The grass looked as inviting as any bed and when he lay down it was a little less painful to breathe.

Gwen was before him. So close he could almost reach her, but infuriatingly not quite.

"Come," she breathed. She strode casually and carefree towards the rising sun, streaks of light coursing through her long, free hair. Cadwal had never felt happier and smiled at the thought of what they'd do together when he caught her. But then she said, "Hurry..."

The rising sun. *East.* Hurry. Suddenly Gwen was gone, and he was looking at the long line of a palisade wall atop a mountain. The Dog's fort. He woke with a start, water dripping off his face.

"Your friend said you should sleep," Togman said. "But I think you'd rather be somewhere else."

Cadwal snorted some water out of his nose. "How long was I out?"

Togman shrugged. "Long enough."

Cadwal looked around. Gavo's men were sprawled out around the gates, almost indistinguishable from the dead Dogs. They'd dragged some huge amphoras out of the principia and had drunk enough of the strong Roman wine that they were already half unconscious. After such an unimaginable fight, he couldn't blame them for their celebration. But none would be in any fit state to ride to the fort of the Dogs.

He pushed himself to his knees and saw Bevan's body being carried up to the platform above the gate. He thought about joining his blood-brother up there but was sure he didn't have the strength to get up the steps. In the fight, he'd let Bevan die to save Helig. If he could have that moment again, he'd choose differently.

He limped over to Gavo. Rhian was tending his badly twisted hand. "Broken," he snarled. "I didn't even notice." To Rhian he smiled, "Leave me, I will be fine. Go to him." He nodded to Abuccus.

At first Cadwal couldn't see why Abuccus needed help. In one hand, he had a huge Roman goblet full of wine but was spilling most of it down his chest. But then Cadwal realised the slick mess on his front wasn't glistening with just Rome's finest vintage. He moaned. With all the blood and other things oozing out of a deep wound in Abuccus' guts, all the bandages from the fort's medical supplies wouldn't help him see the next dawn.

In a blood covered finger Abuccus turned one of the coins someone had found in the principia. Ones he'd never get to spend. "So that's the emperor's face on the front?" he asked.

Rhian knelt next to him. "Yes, that's Vespasian."

"How do you know?"

"That's his name written around the sides."

"Ah," Abuccus mused. "Guess it's a bit late to start learning to read. But what's wrong with his head? He looks like a pig!"

"That's what he looks like."

"Am I rich now?"

"It's called a denarius. It means 'ten donkeys' You'd get one or two for a day in the legion," she said sweetly.

"I earned these on the day we killed every last legionaries in the fort," he smiled and he rubbed his thumb over Vespasian's ugly likeness. "If he hears about what we've done here, those fat jowls of his will wobble when he shouts 'Ordo-wiki' around his villa."

"He will," Rhian agreed, but Cadwal knew that as momentous for the men as a tribe taking a Roman fort was, it was nothing compared to what Boudica had done, or what Arminius did to Varus' legions in the forests of Germania. It would rile the legion in Deva, but an emperor wouldn't be kept awake at night by the loss of a less than half-full auxiliary fort at the edge of the empire.

Cadwal grasped Abuccus's cold hand in both of his. "You fought well. You are a hero."

"No pity for me," he grinned, shaking his head. "I fought with Cadwal the Great, killing Romans and Dogs. I die with the music of our enemies calling out for their mothers. And now I drink with my friends and brothers in the sun... in the middle of more bodies of my enemies than I can count. Is there a better way to die?" He tried to take another gulp wine and Cadwal helped hold the goblet to his lips. "Three hundred of them for twelve of us." Abuccus shook his head in disbelief.

Cadwal flinched as he realised Abuccus already counted himself among the dead.

"The grandchildren of our grandchildren will sing songs about today."

"It's not over yet," Cadwal said quietly.

"It's not?" Abuccus said, making to get to his feet.

Looking out over the trees to the hills beyond there was one more fight to come. Only then would he allow others to call him Great.

"Where are you going?"

"To get my boys."

Abuccus chuckled, "I hope the gods were watching today, or they won't believe me when I tell them what we did here." He dribbled more wine down his chest. "Can I ask you to do something?" he asked seriously, giving Cadwal's hand a squeeze.

"Anything."

"Every now and again... if you think the gods are near. Could you speak my name?"

Cadwal gripped his hand tight. "I will not speak your name," he said. "I will *shout* it!"

When he looked up, he saw Togman waiting. He helped Abuccus' hand to his head a final time, then walked over.

"Not bad for a slave," the smith shrugged. "Ready to get my gold?"

Men fight to defend their land, for honour and to show the gods their bravery, so discussing such a fight for gold seemed dirty. But not as bad as the heir to the Oak Throne reneging his blood-oath. Cadwal nodded.

Caught up in their revelry only Rhian noticed him tying ten of the Roman's horses together and told him to wait as she ran off to get them some supplies. "Come back safely," she whispered as she packed a saddle bag with food. She took his hand and rested it on top of her fine hair. After what they'd just done, in the mess of bodies they stood in the middle of, her touch seemed too soft, too delicate.

As they set off, the afternoon sun was halfway from horizon to zenith, so if they ate in the saddle and had no trouble with the horses, they had just about enough time to get there before dark.

SEVENTEEN

I T WAS FULLY dark as they steered the horses into a stand of woods at the foot of Bastard's Hill. Cadwal dismounted stiffly and tried to force his stiff and weak legs to get him up the lower slopes. The smith's strong hands dragging him back made him feel as helpless and panicked as a fox in a snare.

"We tried fighting in the pitch dark once," he snarled. "It's no fun. You want to live to see your boys, you have to wait until first light!"

Ruefully, Cadwal admitted he was right; a warrior shouldn't fight blindly. Gwain had taught him that lesson well.

Togman laid a few Roman cloaks on the ground, and, with only a little pressure on his shoulder, Cadwal crumpled to his knees.

"Sleep," Togman said, as he set to tethering and feeding the train of horses. "And come the dawn, we will take what is ours."

Cadwal wrapped himself up in the most comfortable position he could find for his bruised chest. He was sure he wouldn't sleep for a moment, but a few heartbeats later, Togman was nudging him gently awake. He shivered in the damp air but his heart was soon hammering at the thought of being so close to the boys.

With his bad wrist, he didn't trust that he could swing a sword properly, so set a small dagger at each hip, and around the still swollen joint, wound a slingshot cord. The pouch, full of a dozen or so stones, he tied next to the dagger on his left hip. Blades or rocks, he didn't care how he would kill anyone who he found standing in his way.

"Ready?" Togman asked, hefting two coils of rope over his shoulder.

His body said no, but his heart screamed yes.

They felt their way up the steep slope through the wet bracken and heather, but didn't get too far before Cadwal was completely out of breath. When he stumbled, Togman reached back to help him up as though he was a blood-brother, not a man who'd sold him as a slave only a few days before.

In the first bruise of light over the south-eastern horizon, they could just about make out the long line of the fort's wall, but the ends were lost in either distance. In the dew-damp grass, they shimmied forward on their bellies, and lay with their heads just above a low ridge, listening for the footfalls of any guards. All they could hear was the disinterested bleatings of sheep and the songs of birds.

"We probably killed them all," Togman mused.

Cadwal almost chuckled but with a sickening sense of being in the grip of a fever, he saw that the wall wasn't even the height of a man.

"Won't be needing these, then," Togman mused as he dropped the ropes.

Cadwal simply stepped over the wall into the fort, and with breath steaming in the morning air, squatted down to get his bearings. A few houses were nestled out of the wind against the inside of the wall but none were the size of a king's. The rest of the huge expanse inside was just open grass and it looked more like a giant sheep pen than a hillfort. They could run around until the sun was fully up and they still wouldn't have made a full circle.

"Fire?" Togman whispered, unsheathing his sword.

Cadwal nodded, and with a dagger in hand, jogged the short way to the first house. Chickens from a cluster of little huts clucked nervously as they approached. They crouched beside the door for a few moments, but no one came out.

"Careful with the women or children," Cadwal whispered. "They might be from Crow Hill."

There was just about enough light to see Togman nod.

"Cover the door. We need to be quiet."

Inside it was pitch dark.

"Biticus?" a nervous girl asked. When no reply came, she wailed, "Who is it?" At the bed, with a hand firmly pressing down on the woman's throat, Cadwal growled, "Scream and you will die."

She chose to live.

"Are you Ordo-wik?" Cadwal asked.

Understanding who he was, she froze.

"*I* am!" another young girl gasped. "Who are you?"

"Cadwal ap Madog, of Crow Hill."

"By the gods," she cried, shuffling towards him. "How can it be! I saw you led out in chains."

"Don't move!" Cadwal snarled at the women in the bed as she tensed. "And this one?" he asked.

"She's a bitch!" the girl hissed.

There was a sudden movement, but it was predictable and Cadwal easily twisted her wrist until she dropped her knife. The girl fumbled for it and slammed it into the woman's chest.

"Is there anyone else in here?" Cadwal asked.

"No," she gasped. "But the men have left to raid our lands with the *Romans*. We have to go and warn the king!"

"Ssh," Cadwal said. "No one is raiding. And no one is coming back here, either."

"How..?"

"You two playing lovers reunited, or do we have a king to kill?" Togman growled from the doorway.

"Do you know where my boys are?" Cadwal asked.

"Probably over at the king's house on the other side by the gate, over the hill. I think they're kept in a shed outside. They keep them locked up because they kept trying to escape."

"How many guards does the king have?" Togman asked.

"Tonight? I don't know. What happened?"

"I'll tell you a fine story later," Cadwal said as he knelt to blow on the embers in the fire pit. When a bunch of kindling caught, he held the flames up to the reeds above the door. The roofing didn't take too long to catch.

In the light, Cadwal could see the girl was Bera.

"My sister is in the next house!" she said. "They are cruel. I can hear her crying at night."

"No!" Togman said, but despite being so close to the boys, his short glimpse of slavery meant he couldn't leave an Ordo-wik in chains. At the next house, he pulled the thick hide from the door and hissed, "Fire! Fire! Get out now! Bring water!"

A man with a sagging belly and hair that had gone mostly white, grumbled as he stooped under the low hanging thatch. He cursed at the glow coming from his neighbour's house and called for the others inside to get up.

One swing of Togman's big sword and the man was dead before he hit the ground. His wife followed and died at the man's feet without even seeing the blade that cut her down.

"Gleva," Bera called inside. "Come out."

A timid face appeared at the door, and when she saw Bera, the sisters ran to embrace.

"Go straight down the hill to the trees," Cadwal said. "Wait for us at the horses."

They ran away towards freedom without a backwards glance.

They didn't torch this one. One house on fire was an accident, two of them burning was a raid and that would cause men to look for intruders. Togman dragged the bodies back inside to earn a little more time before the alarm was raised.

By the time they'd run around the pond to the crest of the hill in the middle of the fort above the pond, the house was fully in flames and people were shouting. Reassuringly, mainly women.

And then the horn blew from the gate. A long note of warning.

The king's house was by far the biggest. It had other full-size houses crowded around it as the others had chicken coops. There was an animal pen ringed by a rough fence and in the corner were a few smaller buildings. "Over there," Cadwal said with breathless anticipation.

"The king first," Togman said, grabbing his arm to hold him down.

"What? Why?"

"He's probably unguarded."

"I don't care about that!" Cadwal snapped.

"Well, I do!" he hissed. "I'm here for gold, remember?"

Cadwal scoffed.

"And didn't you give me your word?" Togman asked.

Cadwal cursed him as they loped over to the houses. From the doorway of the biggest, a man ran out. "What's happening?" he asked sleepily, mistaking them for one of his own tribe.

"Fire!" Cadwal called. "Everyone out!"

"Where?" he began but found that he couldn't speak too well with the point of Togman's sword lodged in his throat.

Another man came out, but stood up quickly when he saw the dead body. Not much can be done to disguise the sound of a sword slicing through flesh, sinew and bone and a half-decapitated body slumping to the floor. Someone from inside called out worriedly.

Ducking under the door, it took a moment for Cadwal's eyes to adjust to the light of the fire. When they did, he was confronted by a boy a few years older than Owyn with small bow pointed directly at his chest. It was less than half the size of a real one and was useless as a weapon, apart from defending the inside of the house, which it would do pretty well.

"Wish you had that chain shirt on now, huh?" Togman asked.

Without it, he had absolutely no defence. He'd got so close. He was in shouting distance of the boys. And he'd failed because of one man's greed for gold. It was all he could do to stay on his feet.

"I would hear your name and the reason for your trespass before you die." On the large bed lay the fattest man Cadwal had ever seen. No wonder he hadn't ridden to join the Romans with his men, he'd have needed a cart to get him there, not a horse.

"I am Cadwal ap Madog of Crow Hill," he said proudly. If this was his last moment of life at least he could sow pain in the heart of his enemy. "We've killed every one of your men at the fort. The Romans too."

"Take him alive!" the fat man ordered but Cadwal wasn't sure who there was to obey. The young boy looked absolutely terrified. Cadwal hoped his trembling fingers wouldn't slip off the draw string by accident.

"Cadwal?" a girl gasped. "Kill this bastard!"

"Drop the knife," the king said in a weak voice.

Cadwal let the dagger slip out of his hand but made sure it landed point first into the rug. Slowly, in a pose of submission, he dropped down to a knee.

"You dare..." the fat man started but was interrupted by Togman's dagger whooshing above Cadwal's head. It slammed handle first into the boy's chest but was enough to shock him, so the loosed arrow landed harmlessly in the thatch.

Cadwal snatched up his dagger and lunged forwards, but the boy was both fast and old enough to know he was fighting for his life and managed to smack Cadwal on the side of the head with his bow. With his good hand, Cadwal grabbed his hair and with his dagger against his throat, the little body went limp.

"He's just a boy," the king pleaded, a hand of chubby fingers held out in a bid for mercy.

"He beat your boys!" the girl cried.

Cadwal recognised her voice. It was Velua, the teryn's servant. In one fluid movement, he pulled the boy's head back and drew the dagger across his exposed throat. He twisted out of Cadwal's grip, but slumped to the floor, choking on his own blood.

"Now *you*!" Velua snapped as the king whimpered. "By the gods, I have dreamed of this," she spat. She leapt at him but the chain around her ankle held her back so all she could do was claw uselessly at his face. Cadwal approached with his dagger aimed at the king's quivering expanse of flesh.

"He's had me every night for a quarter of the moon. He is *mine*!" she cried, but the king grabbed her hair and before he could hurt her, Cadwal sank his blade into the side of the king's fat neck. Velua pulled it back out and rammed it to the hilt under his chin. "I thank the gods for granting my wish," she said as she stared into his eyes. "I sacrifice this *pig* in their honour!" She twisted the blade and after a few choking sounds, the king of the Dogs was dead.

"You could have waited until he told us where his gold is," Togman moaned.

"In a chest behind his bed," Velua said.

Excitedly, Togman leapt over and pulled the plush covers back. When he'd got the lid open, he gasped at the treasure inside.

"He rubs it on his body," Velua said, disgusted, but Togman was mesmerised.

Cadwal left him ogling his fortune. His treasure was outside. He kicked down a flimsy gate into to foul smelling little yard of goats and strode to the rough little shacks standing against the perimeter fence. He pulled the door straight off. Inside, he could just about make out two filthy but perfect little faces. They lit up his heart like the sun.

"Da!" Arwel squealed as he crawled out. Owyn followed a little more cautiously. Cadwal pulled them to him and cried out with the happiness of holding their cold bodies close to his. The sun hadn't yet risen over the horizon, but it had in his heart.

"Hurry up!" Velua shouted as she ran, bloodied knife in her hand, into another house. Screams followed.

Cadwal had to pull Arwel off him to go to the other shed. He broke the doors off and snapped, "Out now!" but the figures huddling at the back, stayed where they were.

"*Nicely*!" Arwel said.

He sighed. "I am Cadwal from Crow Hill, Arwel's Da. Do you remember me? I've come to take you home."

A few faces poked out. "Home?" one asked in a pitiful voice.

"You just to have to be brave for a little longer," he said. "And run really fast. Are there any more of you anywhere?" he asked, but Owyn, dumb with shock, couldn't answer. "Is there anyone missing?" he snapped, shaking him by the shoulders.

"*Nicely*!" Arwel cried.

With all the people attending the fire they couldn't get out the way they came in, but the perimeter wall around the king's house was more than twice the height of a man.

"Going through the gate then, are we?" Togman asked, voice strained from the effort of holding the chest.

"Who's that?" Arwel asked.

"He's our friend."

"He looks scary."

"He's even worse when you get to know him."

Velua came out of the next house with two barely dressed girls in tow but she'd had the presence of mind to collect some old shields. Cadwal took one and handed it to Owyn. "Hold it out far away from your body. If it catches an arrow, it can poke right through."

They were probably heirlooms of the Dog's ancestors, the nicks and scuffs in the paint probably made by Ordo-wiki spears and hammers. Now they would be used to protect them. It was almost a shame their king didn't live to see such a thing.

"How many guards on the gate?" Togman asked.

"How should I know?" Velua snapped. "You think I got to stroll around their nice fort?"

Owyn just about managed to hold a shield. Cadwal set Arwel on his left hip and covering him a little clumsily with another shield, they ran down the gentle slope towards the gate, trying to unwind the sling shot cord from his wrist. He was out of wind after just a few steps

If it was just him and the boys, they might have had a chance of sneaking up and surprising the guards, but with half a dozen girls banging shields together, and Togman grunting with his heavy chest of clinking gold, they arrived like a farmer at sowing time, trying to scare away the birds.

The horn blew. Three times. Attack. Those at the fire would be running towards them in a few moments.

A girl screamed as a sling shot stone smashed into her shield. Arwel cried in terror into Cadwal's ear and he felt the warm flush of his son's fear run down the side of his leg.

"Futuo!" Togman cried. Waddling along with the chest, he couldn't hold a shield. Velua screamed as a stone whacked into her thigh.

"Futou!" Togman spat as one slammed into the front of the chest causing a shower of splinters. The impact made him stumble and he tripped head first over it, spilling the shiny contents out. Cursing, he held the empty chest in front of him, and shouting insults and threats to gods Cadwal didn't know, ran to the steps at the side of the gate.

As he set Arwel down, Cadwal saw the guards had spotted him standing still and unarmed. Before he unwound his sling cord, he made sure Arwel was safely behind the shield and stepped to the side to draw the guard's aim away. Only then did he place a stone on the leather pad. A stone buzzed a hand's width past his head. A miss. Half a chance!

Warrior calm, he thought, and ignoring the pain it caused in his chest, began whirling it around his head. He'd slung his first stones when he was younger than Arwel so the movement felt as natural as breathing.

He thought of the broken Crows at the bottom of the hill and the curses he'd offered the gods. All he needed now was for one stone to find its target. It wasn't that much to ask for.

The pain in his wrist flared up and the flick at the release wasn't as smooth as it should have been. It was a good shot, though, and as the stone flew Cadwal decided that if the gods guided it to the chest of the guard, he would think about forgiving them. From the pitch of the guard's cry, he judged he got him hard enough to break skin, if not bone. He didn't go down, but neither did he sling another stone.

The second was about to fight Togman, so with Owyn leading Arwel, Cadwal helped the other girls drag Velua to the gate and tried to lift the bar. It was a heavy beam of wood, and he needed a couple of half-maddened girls to help him with it.

As it swung outward, the second guard fell from the rampart. The girls screamed as he crunched to the ground.

"Run!" Cadwal shouted.

Some of the younger boys were so shocked they milled around rather than dash down the hill for their lives.

"Come on!" Cadwal snapped, pulling the arm of the most confused one. "Back to Crow Hill."

With Togman's help, he dragged the gate brace up and wedged the big doors shut with it to give them a few moments head start. He had wanted a chest of gold in his arms but it was Velua he carried.

Nearing the trees, he wasn't sure where the horses were but as they got close, they began whinnying. It was almost as though Epona herself had come to help them home.

"We're really going to escape?" one of the younger girls asked as she shepherded the bewildered children along.

Bera came out of the trees with her tear-stained sister. "Cadwal," she said accusingly. "These are *Roman* horses."

They lifted Velua into a saddle and looked at her heavily bleeding leg but there wasn't time to do anything about it.

"I can ride," she said through gritted teeth. "I am not going to die in Dog lands."

Owyn sat in front of Bera on the second horse, and, with Arwel bundled up in front of Cadwal, they ran as fast as they could.

"You're hurting me!" Arwel cried, and Cadwal realised how hard he was gripping his youngest son.

When the horse began protesting its need to slow to a canter, Cadwal reined in at the crest of a low hill to see if any Dogs were chasing. The light of the rising sun caught a trail of thick smoke billowing from the top of the hill. At the thought that there probably weren't enough people left alive up there to put it out, a mad laugh burst from his chest. It lasted until he saw Owyn's blood-covered body, when it turned into a scream. He muttered a few words of gratitude to the gods as he realised it was Velua's from behind him.

She was worryingly pale faced, and her head was lolling as though she couldn't stay awake. Her whole leg under where the stone had hit was covered in blood. Togman cut off a length of his tunic and tied a tourniquet around it. She would either live or not, but she had to ride as they wouldn't be stopping to rest.

The further they rode away from Bastard's Hill the more the belief he'd finally got the boys began to seep into Cadwal's heart. The road ahead began to blur. He had them safe, but no matter where they ran, or how fast, they could never get any closer to Gwen.

An arrow through the chest would have hurt less than realising he'd never get to share them with her. The pain felt fresher than the day he'd found her headless body sprawled out in the grass.

Arwel kept protesting he was being held too tight and once or twice Cadwal almost lost his balance turning around to make sure Owyn was still with them. There was still something in him that couldn't believe this wasn't just some dream. That really all he had to do now was keep riding to the fort and the nightmare would be over.

A few times he was worried the ailing horse would keel over with exhaustion but he didn't stop pushing the poor animal until they met the scouts sent out to look for them. Arwel cried out in fright as they pulled up, but the men whooped with joy as they vied for Cadwal's hand to press to their heads again.

The high walls of the fort were still intact but with smoke coming from a few places inside, it would soon be burned to the ground. Near the gates, still smouldering in the mid-morning sun, were a dozen piles of ash. Cadwal hoped that when he saw them again, the fallen Ordo-wiki would forgive him for not standing witness.

He nudged the horse into the river and pushed Arwel out of the saddle. "Da!" he cried laughing as he splashed in the water.

Cadwal slid off and knelt in the water with him. The current that pushed them a little downstream was nowhere near as strong as the urge that had forced him to the little slave shed on Bastard's Hill all the way from that terrible morning at Crow Hill. The water was too cold and they were both already shaking almost uncontrollably, but Cadwal dunked Arwel's head under and rubbed his face. The grime he was covered in was Dog's dirt and he wanted it washed away. And maybe with it would go some of the hurt and pain.

Some of the bruises on his little chest were Cadwal's from where he'd held him too tight.

Velua wanted to join them and Togman gently lowered her in. "I was so close..." he lamented as he gently washed the dried blood off her leg to better assess the wound.

"To what?" she asked.

"To having all I ever dreamed of in my hands."

"That's nice of you to say," Velua breathed. She opened her hand to reveal a sweaty clutch of gold rings and coins. She'd been holding them so tightly for so long, they'd marked her skin. Togman's expression was one of utter delight.

But there was not enough gold in the world to equal Cadwal's happiness. He pulled Owyn in with them and began washing off Velua's dried blood. Bringing the pinkness back to his skin was like bringing him back to life, even though he stood as still and silent as a statue. But the muck would wash off, the marks on their skin from ropes and whips would heal, they'd put weight back on and soon they'd be his boys again.

He hugged Arwel again and would do the same with Owyn when he was ready. And Gwen would be happy. And when the day came for him to stand with her again, he'd be able to say that he'd looked after them. Promise kept.

EIGHTEEN

LOOMING ABOVE THE rocky bluff, indistinct through the thick sea fog, Brei could just about make out the north facing ramparts of Dinorwig. The aroma of wood smoke and horse dung was welcoming. It meant safety, security. Life carrying on as it always had.

The noise of a hundred unseen horses riding up to the walls would worry the guards, and preferring to be greeted with cheers rather than sling shot stones, she asked Gavo to blow his horn. No enemy would announce their arrival in such a way, but then Bleddyn hadn't shown great judgement of who was a friend and who was foe. Her back burned almost as much as her hatred for the king.

With his head as clouded as the sky after drinking so much wine, "Eh?" was all Gavo managed to reply. Eventually, the chief found it somewhere in his clothing and after a couple of attempts, got a rasping toot out of it.

The horn on the wall blew in response, a plaintive note that would rouse any man from the deepest stupor to get weapons ready and listen for shouted commands. A few men in the line lifted their heads at the sound.

On the horse next to her, little Arwel squirmed around in front of Cadwal. "That's where the king lives?" he asked in awe. "Up there?"

Brei smiled at his sweet curiosity and Cadwal, coming slowly awake, managed a nod.

"Are we going to meet him?" he asked.

His father was still too tired to speak, so she said, "We're going to drop all of those stinky heads at his throne." She smiled at the thought of what song a bard could write about Bleddyn being buried under the heads of his enemies.

"Are they all going to welcome us? Because Da is a hero?" Arwel asked uncertainly at the sight of a row of men on the walls, unwound slings and spears at the ready.

"They are," she said. But now she hoped it was simply a time for kings rather than heroes.

Helig rode at the head of the long line of horses, and in the twisted world they found themselves in, she rued the fact that instead of being richly rewarded, he would more than likely be banished for disobeying Bleddyn. She also tried not to think so much that death was the only punishment for such a man riding back up to the gates.

"You need to go with your brother to the back," she said to the wide-eyed Arwel. "These types of hellos aren't for children." To Cadwal, she said, "We don't know what reception is waiting for us." She hoped he'd understand what that implied.

Gavo did though. "Come here, you little monster," he grinned, and nudged his horse close enough to reach over and pull Arwel out of the saddle. "I think it's time for you to start learning how to be a warrior."

"Now?" he asked, with incredulous excitement.

"Wouldn't you like to meet the king as a warrior instead of just a little boy?"

"Oh yes! What do I have to do?"

"The first job..."

"Yes!?"

"...Is guarding the baggage horses at the rear!"

Brei laughed as the chief turned his horse and pounded back down the track, Arwel's little voice whooping off into the mist.

"You too, Owyn," Cadwal croaked.

"Yes, father," he replied with a face so serious, Brei had to stifle a laugh.

As they came in sight of the guards on the wall, Helig raised his arm to show that they approached in peace.

Brei looked at Cadwal again. Keeling over in the saddle, clean shaven like a child, the thought of the three hundred dead to his name, and everything else he'd done since being captured from Crow Hill, almost defied belief. But she couldn't help recalling the imposing stature of Gwain. Almost a head taller than any other man, back and shoulders as straight and wide as an Old One's standing stone, hair cascading down his back with the moustaches of the thirteen Dogs he'd taken woven into his own locks. To the marrow of his bones, Gwain knew he was a hero and lived like one. If Cadwal was going to rouse people away from the command of the king and face the wrath of Rome, he needed to be as radiant as the sun. Men couldn't simply be *told* he was a hero, they had to be shown. Slumped on the back of his horse, it looked like he'd been drinking for days, and the mead had caught up with him. It wouldn't work.

Helig slowed to let Brei pull up beside him and quietly said, "I was less nervous against the Romans and Dogs than I am now. I could be king in a few moments."

Brei wasn't too sure about that.

"And being banished probably won't help," he mused.

"Banishment needs to be proclaimed to our faces," she said, although that would be a fine point to argue with the men on the wall.

She shifted nervously in the saddle.

Up the hill and around the end of the spiral outer rampart, they came to the open space used by the traders who weren't allowed into the confines of the fort. Ahead, the path narrowed to single file between the high banks that wound towards the gate on the other side.

"I am Helig, son of Gwain. I have great news for the king!" he shouted to those on the wall.

"You are not welcome here!" came a thin voiced reply.

Helig turned to look at Brei. "Derog giving orders?"

"Not good," she agreed. She didn't need to say it was more disappointing than the even worse scenario she'd imagined on the ride from the fort, and she gritted her teeth at the sight of a man who had conspired to let the whole land perish for his false glory.

"At least it means he's still alive for me to kill," Helig shrugged. "So I'll take it as a good sign."

"Helig!" she warned. "If Bleddyn is dead and Derog sits on the throne, he is *king*. You can't just go and fight him. The whole fort will be fighting each other as soon as you free your hammer.

Gavo pulled up with his men behind. None dismounted despite the disrespect it was to stay on a horse in front of a king.

"We would like to speak to the *king*," Helig shouted.

"I am his heir!" Derog called back.

Helig cursed.

"Get the heads out now!" she ordered.

"Here?" Gavo asked.

"Quickly. Now! The more people see them all the better."

Helig shouted the order and severed heads soon started rolling on the ground.

"Dogs!" Helig shouted. Another sack was emptied. "Warriors. Two hundred of them!"

She could see Derog wave his hand dismissively, but the sacks kept coming and the quickly growing number of people on the wall started cheering their appreciation. Helig played with this and waved them up to a cheer before another half a dozen heads were dumped. Derog called out for them to stop, but those spreading out either side of him couldn't believe what they saw. Sack after sack was dumped out until vacant-eyed heads were rolling over heads, piling up.

Finally, they were done and Helig stood like a farmer in a very successful harvest of macabre cabbages. "This is what we have done to the Dogs!" he bellowed.

The crowd on the wall, which now included women and children who'd run over to see what was going on, bayed to the skies in delight. "But that is not all!" he boomed. From inside his tunic, he pulled out the bright red insignia of the cavalry that had been stationed in the fort and shook it out. "We took the fort on the Chief river! Every man! A hundred Romans."

The crowd were too stunned to shout.

"Order the gates open!" Brei said.

"That's for the king to command," Helig said, confused.

"Exactly."

A beaming smile spread over his face, like a sun coming out from behind a cloud. "Open the gates!" he bellowed in a clear and confident voice.

A cry of assent went through the crowd as people ran off to the other side of the fort to welcome them in. As Brei had hoped, Derog was helpless to stop them.

As they rode between the steep banks and ramparts, Brei forced her horse next to Helig's and they rode around the narrow, slightly rising curve with feet and legs pressing together. "Derog is not the biggest problem," she said with a hint of iron in her voice she hoped Helig would catch.

"He is dead. I have sworn it."

"Listen to me. *Look* at me," she said with authority. "I don't say this as a mere friend, or your father's wife. I talk as counsellor. To the king."

"I am listening," Helig said, calmer.

"There are many men in the fort who will be horrified at the thought of going against the will of the gods by standing against Bleddyn."

"I am aware of that."

"You can't just walk in and kill him."

"Watch me!" he said with worrying determination.

"You will start bloodshed. And if that happens, Rome has already won. It's the legion we have to fight, not each other."

"I swore to the gods," he growled.

Nothing Brei had seen in the last few days had had the touch of the gods about it. The unimaginable victory at the fort she'd just put to fire had been conceived, fought and won by men. Brave, courageous ones, but men all the same. But whatever had happened in the Otherworld, the fear of the gods could still sway a man's heart. "Then as someone instructed in the Laws and Ways, and sister to Tegin, I command you not to touch Derog. Or even threaten him to his face."

Infuriatingly, he just shrugged. "I am bound to my word."

She wanted to scream. Or hit him with something solid to make him see sense. In real exasperation, she raised her voice and spoke words she knew would give him pause. "The scar on your hand marks the value of such a bond."

A betrayed blood-oath turned to bad blood between two men wouldn't normally be too much of a concern. They would fight each other to the death, of course, but that would be it. Between the man who would be king and one who was now called Great, it could be the end of everything. She heard the words of the Elder like a whisper.

From the look he gave, for a moment, she thought he was going to strike her but with the outrage on his face fading to impudence, he asked. "So what shall we do?"

She sighed with relief at his change of attitude. "The first thing is to make sure you're not banished."

"Killing Romans behind the king's back might not have been the best way to go about that," he sighed.

"No. But bringing his daughter back might help address the balance. But what we *have* to do now is get an army together. We can't do it behind his back any more. The final fight has begun."

Around the tight turn before the gate, they both looked up. Maidoc's skull had been set next to Gwain's. The old hero and the future king, both dead before their time. If Helig was to act too rash in the next few moments, there would be a lot more heads to go up there.

Inside, they dismounted and the cheering crowd were all desperate to know what had happened. Brei waved one of the women to her and snapped, "Go and get Tegin, now! Hurry!"

Gavo helped Cadwal slip out of the saddle, and with an arm around him, they made their way up to the door of Bleddyn's big house. Behind, the train of horses kept coming in, and the women holding babies were forced further and further back.

A couple helped Velua out of the saddle.

"I will come to you as soon as I can," Brei said, but wasn't sure if the poor girl understood. "Tell Conna to put a poker in the fire," she told those carrying her.

The teryn, ready with the plan of Helig revealing her at the right moment, had the cowl of her cloak pulled over her head. Helig strode purposely to Bleddyn's house and Brei had to run to catch up with him.

Helig ducked down under the low lintel first but waited for Cadwal inside and took over from Gavo in helping him walk. In the strong smell of smoke and old sweat, she followed them along the three fires burning in the long hearth. She hadn't expected to be grateful that Bleddyn was still on the Oak Throne, but it meant the traitorous Half Seed wasn't king. With pallid skin and the way he had keeled over to the side, like a boat in the mud at low tide, he was clinging onto life with the ends of his yellowed fingernails. If Derog's poison made men sleep, maybe he'd given the king a half dose. It didn't matter, she only needed Bleddyn to live for a few more moments. Just long enough to affirm Helig as heir, then his task on this earth was done.

Nervously, Derog took a seat at the end of the bench to the king's right, gripping it with white knuckles so if Helig wanted to move him from the privileged position at the side of the king, he'd have to rip him off.

The house was full of Bleddyn's closest men, all desperate to know what momentous events had taken place without the king knowing, and the air crackled with curiosity.

Helig chose to stand in the most confrontational spot in the whole house, right between Bleddyn and Derog. Brei took her place at his side.

"I will give you a moment to explain," Bleddyn growled. "But know this; I ordered you to stay." His voice was slurred, as though he had partaken of Rome's strong wine with Gavo's men. A bit of drool glistened at the side of his mouth, which helped give the impression of a giant slug rather than the glorious leader the tribe needed now.

"You defied me and you will answer for that. You too," the king added, casting a dark glare at Brei.

"And you are not his heir," Derog added petulantly from behind, but he spoke to Helig's back as his brother paid him no mind. She saw how Helig's fist clenched next to the hilt of his sword though and so she slowly moved her hand to touch his wrist. When he didn't respond, she dug in her nails.

With the king's finger raised, silence fell. "What have you done?"

"We killed two hundred Dogs!" Helig announced proudly, just under a shout.

The men didn't wait for the king to speak and let out a resounding cry of joy. After many moons of worrying about encroaching enemies, with the Romans building forts, the news of such a devastating blow came with a huge release of pent-up fears. Some of the braver men came to slap Helig on the back and fought to have him touch their heads with his palm.

"And the Romans?" Bleddyn asked when they'd calmed down.

"We killed every man there," Helig announced. "And burned it to the ground. We have more than a hundred horses and all of their weapons."

The gasps of disbelief soon erupted into another resounding cheer.

Bleddyn, however, far from rejoicing, hung his head. When enough people had noticed his finger held up for silence he said, "You have brought the end to us all." Absently, he tried to wipe away the drool but only smeared it across his face.

"There's more!" Brei said

"More?" someone asked incredulously.

She waved the teryn over. With the shawl pulled over her head, she weaved her way through the crowd but, kneeling before her father, pulled it back.

"Minura!" Bleddyn gasped, suddenly alert. "How? How did you do this?"

"How?" Helig asked, baiting the question in front of everyone. He raised his hand to point at Cadwal. "This man." Everyone looked at the unassuming man, who was humiliatingly shaven-faced and not quite standing up straight. Black rings shadowed his eyes.

"This is the stranger you brought in?" Bleddyn asked, but his accusing finger was quickly withdrawn so he could cover his mouth with a hand.

"Fifty of us he led into the fort," Helig shouted proudly. "Straight through the open gates, and we took a hundred Romans. The next day we killed two hundred Dogs." He pounded his chest with an open palm and bellowed, "Cadwal the *Great*!"

In the shouts of the tribesmen no one noticed that Bleddyn had started to cough.

"Am I banished?" Helig asked.

Bleddyn gave a clear shake of his head, which was greeted with yet more cheers. "And Brei and Cadwal?"

Again, the king shook his head but held both hands in front of his mouth, eyes full of fear.

Brei knelt beside him and pulled his hands away. They were covered in dark clumps of old blood. Realising the urgency, she shouted, "Is Helig your heir?"

The king though was racked with coughs. He tried to clear his chest but so much blood came up it seeped through his fingers.

"Healer!" Derog shouted into the crowd, ignoring Brei.

"Am I your heir?!" Helig shouted desperately.

"Do something!" Derog shouted into the confusion, but as terrible as is the death of a king, Brei knew that if he couldn't breathe, nothing could be done.

"Father!" Minura cried, trying to hold him. He pushed her away and slumped out of the throne onto floor, convulsing as though some maleficent spirit had control of his body. He coughed and spat up even more blood, making the most horrendous noises and clawing at his throat as though he was trying to rip it open.

Then, in the utterly silent house, the king lay still.

"Get him out so the gods can see him!" Gavo shouted. A few men cautiously approached and hauled him out.

Brei followed them back out into the damp air, thinking that with the land covered in such thick fog it was an inauspicious day for a king to die. The women and farmers not allowed in the king's house cowered away in shock. A moon ago, she would have celebrated him dropping dead off the throne as a gift from the gods. Maidoc would have been king and an army would have been readied before the pyre had been stacked. But the old bastard couldn't do anything right. It was even beginning to rain.

Watching his lifeless corpse dragged across the mud, with Derog of all people next in line, it felt as though the ground she was standing on was giving way.

Her brother, Tegin, chalk dust on his face giving him an otherworldly pale pallor, stood forlornly at Bleddyn's head as though he'd known to be there.

"He's dead?" Minura asked.

"He is," Brei shrugged.

"There's nothing you can do?"

Brei didn't think his daughter needed to know he'd drowned on his own blood just as a man lost in the sea. "No. Sorry."

Heulwen, probably not understanding what had happened, danced a new straw doll up and down Bleddyn's chest. Or maybe she understood perfectly... and Brei wondered if she was seeing a vision about what the legion was about to do on the lands of the Ordo-wiki.

"I thought he'd be younger than that," Togman said as he limped next to her, hand still grasping his crotch.

"That's not Derog," she said. "That's the *king*!"

"Oh," was his only response.

Helig came to stand on the other side, and grinding his teeth, his look was one of thunder. Whatever he chose to do now wouldn't only be his fate, but that of the whole tribe as well.

Cadwal stared at the dead body. Somehow, he couldn't think of it as the king lying in the mud, even though he'd been on the throne only a few moments before. Kings were supposed to be more than mere men and shouldn't die as easily as others... but then he recalled how easy it was to sink his knife into the Dog king's fat neck.

Gavo helped him back inside, and he slumped gratefully on one of the benches to the side of the hearth. But Derog didn't allow him a moment of rest. He stood before the throne and with arms open welcomingly wide, triumphantly shouted, "My people."

From the doorway, Helig bellowed, "Nooo!" But Derog sat down.

Men stepped out of Helig's way as he stormed towards his brother, and despite being in the king's house, Cadwal thought he was about to unstrap the hammer from his back.

Gavo saw too and stopped him with an arm across his chest. "Calm, you fool!" he hissed. "Think about where we are! And he was named as Bleddyn's heir!"

"No," Helig growled. "It will not be."

"It *is*!" Gavo said and nodded over to the side of the house. Cadwal turned to where the chief was looking. Back in the shadows, away from the light of the fire, Tegin had taken a watching position, the top of his staff lost in the smoke hanging under the thatch.

At the sight of the druid, Helig hesitated and Gavo used the moment to pull him down to the bench. "The only way to kill a king is to get him to challenge you to a fight," the chief snarled." Derog, against *you*? He's a bastard, but he is no fool. He'll never do that."

Helig was still livid and spat, "We have *truth*."

"Aye, maybe. But what good is saying anything without proof? You'll get half of us killed, boy! And then where we will we be?"

From the huge throne, Derog announced, "Bleddyn named *me* heir, so by the words of the old king's words, *I* am king!" His voice didn't have the strength of any of the other men in the house though and the rumble of approval wasn't exactly overwhelming.

"No!" Helig roared, and Cadwal saw that it was only Gavo grabbing the hammer strapped to his back that kept him on the bench.

Derog's eyes narrowed. "The gods have witnessed this. I am king!"

"This is not the time of gods," Helig snarled. "This is the time of *men*!!" He cast an arm over those assembled around the hearth, trepidation clear on every face. "All of us! What we do now is by our own hands."

Cadwal wondered if anyone else felt bitter chill pass through them at the gods being denied in the king's house. But Derog seemed more concerned with his earthly powers than those of the Otherworld. "I am the rightful heir. *Me*, not you. Bleddyn decreed it."

Far from taking Gavo's sage advice, Helig broke free of the chief's grip and stood back up. "I defy the old king!" he shouted. "I defied him when he was alive and went to Deva with our hero and fought the Romans and Dogs. And I defy him in *death*!" He spread open his arms and tilted his head up. "Let the gods judge me for that." He peered expectantly at the apex of the roof supporting poles but in the silence there was no message from above. "Seems they've changed their minds," he beamed to a few nervous chuckles.

At the back, Tegin still stood, passively watching what was happening. No one else seemed to have noticed.

"You defy the king and the gods," Derog snapped, his hand resting on the head of Gordd-ap-Duwia, which was set against the side of the throne. "That is a terrible crime. And *for* it, I banish you!"

Cadwal groaned. If there was to be any plan for even the slightest chance of mustering a defence against the legion, it depended on all the fighting men of the land not killing each other about who sat on the Oak Throne. Had any other man in the last hundred years made such a statement from where Derog sat, Helig would have been manhandled out of the fort by a dozen men, never to return. Instead, he burst out laughing.

"Banished!" Derog called out again, but to his clear astonishment, no one stepped forwards to do his bidding. His supporters, and those who'd honoured Bleddyn and now saw a king on the throne, looked furtively at each other. Cadwal saw some nervous fingers flitting close to sword hilts, but no one dared to draw.

He recalled the Elder's prophecy. The king will die... of happiness and the blood of the hero shall be on the throne. But Derog was on the throne and he was certainly no hero.

Helig waited, playing with the nervous silence, stepped slowly around the back of the throne.

Derog looked around nervously trying to see what he was doing.

"The gods require only a few things from men," Helig said as he reappeared on the other side. He spoke quietly, and as the men strained to hear, the tension increased. "But they are *law*! Courage, he needs... but more than that, everything has to be done with *truth*."

Several voices murmured agreement.

"To lie to the gods is to have your soul forgotten forever. No man may speak his name. The king is dead. He lies outside, body still warm, so the gods watch us now. Would you speak a lie before their gaze?"

"I am king!" was Half Seed's only response.

"Truth," Helig smiled. "Did you kill Maidoc?"

Derog's mouth opened but as his confidence drained away, he seemed to shrivel up on the throne.

"Did you poison him so that he died in his sleep? And tried to do the same with me? The king, even? Speak, for the gods wish to hear!"

"I... I," he stammered. "No." There wasn't really anything else he could say. The gods might strike him dead for lying, but to speak the truth, the men would drag him outside and rip him to pieces.

Helig snarled like a dog ready to bite, but Derog had lied in front of the gods and he clearly hadn't expected that. And so Minura, striding with the confidence of a king, pushed Helig aside. Cadwal wondered what it was he saw on her face. Grief? Her father had just died in front of her, so her puffy eyes were perfectly understandable.

But what else was it? Hunger? Lust? Greed? He'd seen Helig change over the days and sacrifice even his honour to sit on its well-polished seat.

Minura turned to face the crowd and with a forced smile, said, "Not the return I was envisaging. Slave to queen in one day."

No one laughed.

Cadwal couldn't work out if she meant any humour in such words. But he supposed that if you were going to make the gods laugh, you might as well do it properly, and a three-way fight for the Oak Throne was much more interesting than simply two.

In a measured tone, Helig asked, "What are you doing, cousin?"

"Have you all forgotten that I am the *daughter* of the king," she asked. She pointed at Half Seed, and with haughty disdain said. "And he is only the last born of his brother."

"I am the son of Gwain!" Derog protested. "The *first* line."

"The *dead* line," she snapped, but then remembered who she was talking to. "Sorry," she said to Helig.

Minura had invited the Dogs into Crow Hill as friends, and as far as Cadwal was concerned, that meant she should be kept far away from any power. Helig had betrayed his blood oath and abandoned Owyn and Arwel as slaves... and what Half Seed had done... If Cadwal could help it, none would take the throne.

His blood on the throne and the king dying in happiness... With a shiver so strong he almost cried out, he realised the king had coughed to death holding the daughter he thought he'd lost. In happiness, just as foretold. Goosebumps covered his arms.

But as Gavo had said, there was nothing Helig could do to get Derog to fight him. One of the biggest men and fiercest fighters in the land could beat his little brother with his eyes closed. But if Derog wouldn't dare fight Helig, he might agree to face a man who could barely stand... With a heavy reluctance, he said, "I would speak."

"Give the hero some room!" Maccus shouted and leaned over to help him stand.

From behind, a spindly arm offered him a stick. "Hold onto this," Tegin said, and Cadwal almost cried out in shock as the druid had been on the other side of the house. Gathering himself, he clamped a sweaty hand around the worn wood of the sacred staff.

Maccus cowered away.

He didn't have the strength to shout, so banged the staff on the floor. A dozen men cursed in fear and all took a step or two back.

In the sudden silence, Cadwal said as loud as he could, "I have no proof, so ask me for none. But I *know* the truth. This bastard who calls himself king in front of us was in Deva... But not with me. He was there to make a deal with Rome... for the Dogs to take all of our land apart from Mona, where he would sit and call himself king. The lives of all of us here... just so he can claim an island as his kingdom, paying tribute to Rome. Sitting on a throne made of our bones."

In feigned outrage, Derog spat, "Without proof, how can you make such an accusation of the king?" He'd turned a shade paler though and gripped the edge of the throne so tight his knuckles were even whiter than his face. Cadwal could see the effect of his words. "Call yourself king, I spit on your name," he shouted and staggered forwards a couple of steps. "I call you a liar and a traitor. I shit on your name and will never speak it."

Derog twitched, a look of the purest hatred on his face. "Banished!" he shouted, but Cadwal thudded the staff on the floor again, and with the bones tinkling above no one dared to follow the order.

He knew what power he held. He took it, wrapped it around himself like a cloak. Appearance is everything. Power is magic and magic is power. Holding the druid's staff, he knew at that moment is was more powerful than the throne.

He took another painful looking step closer, holding onto the staff a little more than he needed to, remembering the frail gait of the Elder as she hobbled around, and stood himself right in front of Half Seed. His hand shook enough to disturb the bones on top. "If you want to be king here, you will have to face me with hammers in our hands. Fight and kill me, and the new hero of the Ordo-wiki won't spit at the sound of your name."

Derog leaned forwards. "You are almost a cripple. It wouldn't be fair."

"You are Half Seed, the Runt," Cadwal spat. "It will be fair."

Some men chuckled and he made such a convincing show of his legs threatening to give way that Maccus overcame his fear and held onto his arm to support him. Two leaves. He was staking his life on Half Seed looking, but not seeing.

Helig's life too.

"And if you win, Helig will be banished. No one will question your claim."

And as he'd hoped, Derog took the bait. "Done!"

"What!" Helig protested. "You can't make such a deal!"

"Why?" Cadwal asked. "You will fight me?"

Minura beamed with a greedy and expectant grin, and Helig was about to say something else, but was interrupted by a red-faced Brei as she stormed between them. "What are you doing? I haven't even started the rites for the dead king and you're already fighting over the throne! What's wrong with you!?"

"My counsellor," Half Seed said, but she ignored him as her eyes ran up the staff Cadwal held, widening as they got to the dangling finger bones at the top. Her brother standing quietly at the side gave a shallow nod.

"You know what you're doing?" she asked Cadwal.

Cadwal hoped so. He nodded and Brei took a step back, pulling Minura with her. He heard the teryn's protests as she was led away from the throne.

"We fight," Derog said.

In reply, Cadwal banged the staff on the floor for the third time. He hoped he wasn't as weak as he'd made it seem, as it wasn't for show he needed Maccus' help to get outside.

"Use Gordd-ap-Duwia!" Helig shouted at Derog, mocking his brother's diminutive stature.

"That is for smashing the heads and bones of our enemies!" Helig retorted over his shoulder. "I will not strike one of ours with it!"

Cadwal was disappointed with such a good answer.

Back outside in the weak light of the overcast day, Cadwal squinted. He stood where the old king's body had lain just a few moments before and thought again about the hero's blood on the throne.

Helig offered him the hammer off his back. "You better not lose," he warned.

"Why?" Cadwal asked. "Will you kill me?"

One to one, a sword would have been easier to fight with, but he was an Ordowik, a man of the hammer, and so that's how he would fight. Or with one in his hand, die.

The shaft felt natural and familiar in his hands, the balance good, but the weight was all wrong, like the very first time Gwain had thrust one at him and expected him to swing it all day. Not much older than Owyn, it had been impossibly heavy to wield. Fingers, wrist, and arms all protesting, he was weaker than he'd thought. No matter how much he wished the Runt dead, it was going to be a hard fight.

Derog took his shirt off and showed off his young, hairless torso proudly to the sky. The fog still lingered. The gods wouldn't be able to see properly.

The crowd formed into a tight circle, men jostling for the best view. Cadwal wondered how long it had been since they'd seen a king fight... probably the day Gwain died.

Without thinking about it, he drew the warrior calm around him and the deafening roar of encouragement became just a faraway distraction merely tugging at the edges of his perception. He didn't care who was shouting for him, who for Derog, all there was in front of him was someone he needed to kill for the good of the tribe.

He looped the strap at the end of the shaft around his still swollen wrist.

Derog, too young to have been trained by his father, took a hammer in one hand and a long sword in the other. Having two weapons made him look like a hero of old, but it took a lot of skill to wield both effectively. Cadwal hoped such arrogance would be his undoing.

Someone blew the carnyx to attract the gods' attention, if they hadn't already noticed the king's death, and Helig roared one of his mad battle cries.

Cadwal shifted his weight from one painful foot to the other while Derog circled around so easily, it looked like he was dancing. But beyond the runt's fierce expression, Cadwal could see fear.

Half Seed's first strike was almost lazy in its predictability, and the hammer swinging over his head was easy to dodge. But then came the thrust of the sword. Aimed at Cadwal's midriff, left-handed, it was neither fast nor accurate and was easy to twist away from, but it put him off balance for the next hammer swing. Coming right at his head, he had to roll out of its way, and it thudded into the ground near his hip. A hand span closer and it would have hit him.

The head was sunk a little in the ground and when Derog couldn't pull it out on the first attempt, Cadwal took the opportunity to kick the handle out of his grasp. Gavo's men cried out in delight. Derog left it, but swept the sword through the air in front of Cadwal's face with both hands. Off balance for a moment with the momentum, Half Seed was an easy target. If Cadwal could have struck any part of his body, the fight would have been over. The little bastard was still fast though, and what Cadwal hoped was going to be a killing blow, found only air.

It must have been the most pathetic fight any of the onlookers had ever seen.

He stood near Derog's discarded hammer, keeping it out of reach, but as the Runt gripped his sword it looked as though he was enjoying himself. Small and young, he must often have been overlooked when men were getting groups together to patrol the borders or launch a raid in enemy land. Now he was finally fighting for everyone to see.

Derog's blade arced again in a blur. Blocking the blows with the hammer shaft held in two hands, Cadwal was struggling for his life. A leg gave out and he was down on a knee, handing Derog a real advantage, and the cries of the crowd echoed his own panic.

The sword flashed so close to his ear, he heard its terrible swoosh. Another slash and pain like being splashed with cold water shuddered through him. Derog's blade had caught him just above the hip.

"Da!" he heard Arwel cry out and saw his youngest trying to run out. Only Gavo's firm grasp held him back.

Derog saw too and the next slash didn't come, for killing a man on his knees was a dishonour, even for a man such as he. He took a step back, allowing Cadwal back to his feet, and into that space Arwel twisted out of Gavo's hands and jumped in front. "Don't hurt my Da!" he wailed, little arms out protectively.

Panting, Derog looked down the length of his sword at Arwel, the little boy his deal had made a slave.

"You'll have a chance to be a hero one day," Gavo smiled as he pulled Arwel away.

Cadwal pushed himself back to his feet and felt the notches and splinters on the shaft where the sword had hacked. The hammer felt lighter. Blood ran down his chest. For a moment he felt the sun on his face, a fresh wind stirring the grass and dandelions, and the sound of the sea far below.

Arwel cried out desperately again, and it took Cadwal back to the morning the Dogs had taken Crow Hill. Derog had made his deal before that, so maybe he knew the plan and had let it happen. He'd never hated a man so much before, not even a Dog. Even they had more honour. Derog had to die... and at that moment Cadwal didn't care if it cost him his life.

And then he swung.

There was no way Half Seed could defend himself from the strength of the blow. It was as if Camulus himself had swung Gordd-ap-Duwia. All Derog could do was dive under its deadly arc. But instead of struggling to slow the swing, Cadwal put even more strength into it and pirouetted around, despite an awareness somewhere in his mind of Gwain expressly forbidding any action that turns your back to an enemy. Derog was no true fighter though, so he dragged the hammer through the air, the speed of it straining his arms and shoulders, the strength coming from somewhere beyond himself.

But when he came around again, Derog was closer, his sword thrusting at Cadwal's chest. A novice fighting mistake that would kill both of them.

"TAAAMMMM!" he screamed as it sliced across his chest.

The hero's blood on the throne. But instead of pain as the heavy head of the hammer pummelled into Derog's side, he was filled with ecstasy. The impact was so gloriously hard that the last of Gwain's sons was broken almost in half with the sound of snapping wet sticks. His crumpled body rolled to the feet of the onlookers, where he lay motionless, like a discarded straw doll.

Then Cadwal was looking at the sky again, the sun of a summer's day on his skin.

"Shout it in battle," Tamm laughed. "You bastard!"

But it wasn't a grassy slope he lay on, he was held aloft by dozens of hands presenting him to the gods as the victor, until Brei's commands cut through the men's voices and her healing hands were inspecting the wounds. "Go find Heulwen. I need yarrow. *Yarrow*! All of it!"

Owyn and Arwel were crawling over him, nuzzling their faces into his neck, Arwel mewling, "Don't die, Da. How can *we* rescue *you*?" His little hands were covered in fresh blood.

On the churned ground beside him, Derog was still gasping for breath, but Cadwal knew the blow he'd struck was fatal. He only had the time left for the blood to empty from his ruptured veins and fill his belly.

"Give him some light!" someone called, but Helig's massive form was looming over them both. "You were on my throne, little brother," he snarled, not a trace of compassion in his voice.

"Father always looked over me," Derog gasped. "Never me. Just because I was smaller."

"And you hated us for that? Just because you were born a runt?"

"You wouldn't understand."

"No," Helig nodded. "I wouldn't." He laid a large foot on the side of Derog's neck. Speaking loud enough for all to hear, he said, "You die now. Your last words. Either I hear the truth from your lips, or your name never leaves mine."

Derog coughed. He only had a few breaths left.

"Did you make a deal with Rome?"

"Bastard..." was the only response.

Almost shouting, Helig addressed the nervous men. "As long as a man's name is spoken, he still lives. I command this as my first words as king: no one will ever speak this bastard traitor's name again. Let it be forever said that Gwain only had four sons."

Derog coughed again, starting to choke now.

"Feed him to the pigs," Helig commanded.

"Pigs?" someone asked, horrified.

"What less honour for a man who kills his own brethren for Rome?"

Derog was so small it only took one man to drag him away. He was still alive, and Cadwal hoped he'd last long enough to die in the stinking mess of a pig pen, rather than in the light of day.

Brei was tending his wound with a cloth to stem the bleeding. He tried to hold Arwel but his arms were so weak, it felt as though they weren't really there.

And then he was being carried inside.

"In the sun," Cadwal gasped. "Leave me in the light!"

"You're not going to die!" Brei snapped.

He was set lying on a bench near the hearth, his head near the Oak Throne.

Gavo knelt by him, resting a big hand on his shoulder. "It's deep," he said, "But I trust Brei."

Helig came in and Cadwal watched as he picked up Gordd-ap-Duwia, the muscles of his arms bulging under the weight of it. Raising it over his head he proclaimed, "I am king."

Most of the men roared their approval.

"No," Cadwal said, but in the noise of the crowd only Brei heard him.

"Shh," she breathed.

"Not king," Cadwal said and Brei's eyes hardened as she turned from healer to counsellor. "I killed the king," he gasped. "The second one today."

"Wait!" Brei shouted with her special voice as Helig took his seat, the heavy hammer resting across his knees. "Wait!" she repeated, and the jubilation of the crowd died down.

"My counsellor?" Helig asked.

"No," she said. "Derog was the king. Cadwal killed him. By right, the throne is *his*!"

"Cadwal killed the king!" Gavo shouted.

The bloodlust of the fight was beginning to wear off and the pain was starting to take root, but Cadwal forced himself up.

Hero's blood on the throne. He could almost touch it with his bloodied hand. But he knew what the prophesy meant now.

"He was fighting for *me*!" Helig protested.

"No!" Cadwal shouted, despite the pain.

"A hero fights for his king!"

"I fought for the *tribe*," he gasped. "For the *children*!"

A dark look of hatred fell across Helig's face, the same expression Cadwal had seen when they'd camped near White Walls and after they'd taken the Roman fort, when honour was replaced by something else. Something dirty. The same lust for power that Derog had sold the tribe for. "I fought the king with honour," Cadwal gasped.

"And I thank you for that."

"*I* claim the Oak Throne."

"As is his right!" Gavo shouted. "A hero for a king!"

"Silence!" Helig bellowed.

"Will you fight me?" Cadwal asked, tasting blood in his mouth.

Some men laughed, but Helig saw no humour. "I am Helig ap Gwain. The last of the hero's sons!"

"We have a *hero*," Gavo shouted, pointing down at Cadwal.

"Are you forgetting that Bleddyn sat there for thirteen years?" Brei asked. "*Minura* has a right before you."

"You are my counsellor," Helig pleaded to Brei.

"No," she said. "I am the *king's* counsellor."

Heulwen pushed her way through the men with a bunch of herbs clenched in her small fist, but not quite ready for having his wound treated, Cadwal managed to get to his feet. The whole of the house was silent.

Without looking, he held his hand out. He knew Tegin would be waiting to hand him the staff. The power was his. He took it. "Look at your hand," he said to Helig.

Helig looked down at the cut on his palm.

"A mark of a blood-oath should be a mark of honour." Cadwal raised his own palm up. "But yours is a mark of shame."

"How dare..." he started, but despite the pain it caused, Cadwal hit the staff down on one of the stones lining the hearth. He looked at the man who had betrayed him and left Owyn and Arwel at the mercy of the Dogs. "If you'd had honour enough to keep your blood-oath, you could have kept your precious throne. But I am a hero now, a king killer, and have the power to deny you. Stand up."

The glare of utter hatred could have withered a whole testudo formation before it, but with gritted teeth, Helig growled, "*I* am the king!"

Cadwal hit the staff of the stone again. "Stand up!" he shouted.

A man giving up on his dreams is never a pleasant sight, and Cadwal couldn't help a little sympathy, even for a man of such dishonour.

Shoulders hunched, Helig reluctantly stepped away and Cadwal looked at the empty throne. If he was to sit on it, it would be covered with his blood, just as the Elder had said.

Little Heulwen was pressing the yarrow to the wound on his side and with one hand on her delicate shoulder, the other grasping the sacred staff, limped with her to it. He stood at one of the arms and turned to address the men.

"Keep still!" Heulwen chided.

"Why don't you sit here?" Cadwal asked her. "You can reach better then."

So intent on holding the herbs to his cut, she didn't even notice where it was she was sitting.

Helig was skulking away through the men, but Cadwal called out for him to stop. "Do you want Gwain's blood on the throne?" he asked.

"You wish to toy with me?" Helig asked. "I am the last!"

"Are you?"

When he saw Heulwen on the throne, he gasped a curse.

"Will you claim your daughter now that Bleddyn is dead?"

Mouth hanging open, he stared. "You mean it?"

"Would you like me to make a blood-oath?'

The look of disgust fell across Helig's face again.

The men looked around nervously.

"The legion will come," Cadwal said, cringing as Heulwen poked him a little too hard. "It will be the last fight, and, for us, there is only a choice between execution, slavery... or the chance to die bravely in front of the gods. Nothing else."

"That's an easy choice!" Maccus laughed.

"But there's no Dog to take over our land now, so there could be a new treaty with Rome. Not for those who'd destroyed the Roman fort... but..." he placed a hand on Heulwen's head. "It is said that the children are the future. And Heulwen is Gwain's blood, not Bleddyn's."

A few men huffed in disbelief, but Helig snapped, "It is the truth. Heulwen is mine. I claim her."

Cadwal turned to look down at Heulwen, still totally engrossed in her task of healing his bleeding with the herbs. "You are queen now," he said.

"Keep *still*!" Heulwen snapped, and a few men laughed... and then they began to cheer.

EPILOGUE

O F ALL THAT Brei had seen in the last half a moon, in her life even, no single act took as much strength or bravery than Cadwal standing up to leave the embrace of his sons.

Forcing himself up, he looked at her, his drawn face a mask over the turmoil that must have been raging inside him. "They could have no better counsellor," he told her evenly. "Be safe."

Brei had mourned babies that had been born breathless, but she couldn't imagine how it would feel to walk away from the boys you'd hoped to see grow into men.

To cover the cracks threatening to tear her heart apart, she smiled.

"You be brave," Cadwal said to them all. "And you be good."

"We will," Owyn said formally, but Arwel wailed, "Daaa..." and his cry shattered what was left of her heart.

"And speak my name when you remember me," Cadwal added.

"We will," Owyn nodded.

"A man is not dead while his name is still spoken," she said. Gods to hear or not, she would speak it every day.

"Thank you for giving me the throne," Heulwyn said. "It's very nice. I put flowers on it."

Cadwal smiled and nodded respectfully to the queen.

"But it's for Gavo now."

"What?" Cadwal exclaimed. "You can't just give it to any one..."

"Gavo the cat," Brei interrupted.

"The fire is always burning, so he likes it there," Heulwyn added.

The Queen of the Ordo-wiki held Brei's hand, straw doll in the other. Nothing Brei had learned on Mona had prepared her for advising a seven-year-old queen, but with Heulwyn betrothed to Owyn, if they survived what was coming, they would live in a world that would not resemble the old.

Thirteen days they'd had to talk about the new future coming. Thirteen days to give a lifetime's advice to his children. Thirteen days until the end of the world marched in, five thousand strong. Thirteen days to decide who left, who stayed and who was to die. Thirteen days for a man to teach his sons all of the names of those who needed to be remembered. They'd sung, drunk, danced around the fire and made love as though every one of those days was the last. And now it was.

As the men started to ride out the women wept, and it was a heart wrenching chorus of keens to mourn the end of an age.

Gavo pulled away from a tearful Rhian. As she checked the bindings of the splint around his broken wrist, he ran his shaking fingers running through her hair. He couldn't wield a weapon but his men would fight with more heart if he was with them.

When the last had walked out, the gates weren't closed behind them. Brei shuddered at the thought of what men would be the next to come through them.

"We should go now as well," Togman said.

"I'm sorry," Rhian sobbed.

"Ssh..." Brei smiled. "I understand."

After ten years of being a Roman slave, and knowing what they did to recaptured ones, Brei knew why she would go south with Togman, Minura and most of the other girls too afraid of what the Romans would do to them when they rode into Dinorwig.

"I will return when..." she started.

"When it's safe," Brei finished.

In tears, she nodded. "Are you sure you won't come with us?" she asked one more time.

"I will paint my face with clay and hobble around in a dung smelling cloak so they will think I am some old hag," Brei said.

"Eiw," Heulwyn snickered.

"Exactly!"

It wasn't much protection, and if the Romans found her out, they would not go easy on her. But she would survive. As long as the Praefectus Valerius didn't find her. She had her children now and if she saw the next dawn, she planned on living in this new world. For the children.

The sloping land between two points of higher ground formed a natural amphitheatre and it was here Cadwal had chosen to stand the unordered mass of Ordo-wik fighters. A little over six thousand had come for the last fight. It was more men than he'd ever seen together. And it was nowhere near enough.

On the horizon, jabbing into the grey-green sea he could see the eastern finger of Mona, the land of the druids... where Half Seed would have been happy to be king, once most of his tribes people had been killed or enslaved. He shuddered involuntarily at how close Gwain's last son had come to bettering him in the fight.

He'd survived and won, but there would be no living through what was assembling on the road below.

He'd asked the gods to influence the trajectory of a stone in flight. Getting them to make an entire Roman legion to drop dead where they stood might be a bit much to ask.

His life and those of his kinsmen were now measured in heartbeats.

The long column of Roman soldiers marched on the track below. Each man in unison, stomping five thousand left feet on the land of the ancestors, then five thousand right. It gave the effect of a giant insect, as though they were about to fight some dread monster instead of just unimaginably well-trained and heavily armoured soldiers. Like some kind of forest of trees planted in straight lines, each man carried a long spear and Cadwal wondered if Togman had hammered any of the sharp tips at his forge. Or if he himself had pumped the bellows for them.

At regular intervals through the ordered horde, men rode with the arching plumes of horsehair over the crests of their helmets. Apart from the strange order they walked with, it was these that elicited the most fear as they looked unlike anything known to the tribe. Some carried poles with golden disks nailed to them. But for what reason, Cadwal couldn't begin to imagine. He thought about asking Brei, but with a punch to the guts remembered he'd already spoken his last words to her.

A single man rode at the head. With a blood-red cloak spilling over the back of his horse they looked joined in some frighteningly otherworldly way. Spots of light flashed off his armour. His head was turned towards the assembled Ordo-wiki, but he showed absolutely no concern. He didn't even need to shout any commands to his men.

"The governor of Britannia," Gavo growled from beside him.

Brei had said his name was Gnaeus Julius Agricola. It seemed strange that the head of a force of such death and destruction would have the name of a man, not a god. It suggested he had a life of friendships and hardships, a family of his own.

Agricola. It was the name of the man whose hands held the destiny of Owyn and Arwel.

The boys. Thirteen days is all he'd had at Dinorwig with Owyn and Arwel, trying to teach them all he could about the new world they would grow up in. In the old one, enemies on all sides, it was easy to die, and many lives were given for such things as pride, honour, and the right to call the land your own. But in the one they were about to live in, they'd have to find a new way to survive, one with treaties, tributes and taxes. Someone else's laws and someone else's gods.

He could still feel the tugging of his shirt in Arwel's clenched fists as he left, and Owyn's stern expression, less than that of a young boy and more of a man who had some understanding of the horrors of the world.

After the battle was over, the legion would go on to Dinorwig, where Brei would find some way for the women and children to come to terms. Subject to the cruelties Rome. But alive. He trusted no one in the world more than her.

And as though the legion assembling before them wasn't a demoralising enough sight on its own, the wind dragged a squall of rain up the hill. Several men nearby groaned. There wasn't much glory to be had when the gods were pissing on you.

Men put so much stock into the will of the gods, and yet Cadwal saw they'd done nothing for the tribe. He might be about to meet them, but they would have to earn his forgiveness.

To his left was Gavo, strands of loose hair blowing around his head. With lines of woad paste over his cheek, his face had looked fierce, but the rain was streaking the blue, so he looked like he'd had an accident in a blackberry bush. And then he saw the chief's eyes. In them was the same sinking sorrow that was leaking into his own bones. He knew what was coming. They shared the knowledge that it was less an army they faced, more their executioners.

They'd come to this barren mountainside not to win a great battle, but to die.

Tegin had exchanged his staff for a spear. The iron tip would be more useful in battle than the tinkling bones. An Elder could whisper words that made sense only after they happened but a druid couldn't tear asunder the ground under the legion's feet. Cadwal imagined there were many hoping for such a thing, but they would be disappointed.

A boy threw up and apologised profusely.

"You all right, lad?" Helig asked.

He nodded.

"You don't have to pretend to be brave."

The boy looked at him, confused.

"You're with all of your clan and tribe and so you're just as brave as the rest of us. Here, take this," he said, handing over the hefty bulk of Gordd-ap-Duwia.

Wide-eyed with the honour, the boy took the scared hammer, but in his scrawny arms, the weight of it looked more like a burden than a weapon.

When Helig took it back, he held it aloft and shouted, "We are Ordo-wiki. We are *brethren*!"

The hundreds of heart-felt cheers roaring from all around pricked the hairs on the back of Cadwal's neck.

"They look like mean bastards," Gavo said.

In the legion below, Cadwal couldn't see any fresh-faced recruits training for their first kill in the men below. He thought some had grey in their short beards.

Cadwal tried to take a deep breath but the still wound on his chest from Half Seed's blade were loath to allow it. It must have been the rain in Gavo's eyes as there was no way a chief would cry in front of his men before a battle.

The Romans stopped marching, and in an ordered and well-practised way that no Ordo-wik could imagine fighting in, arranged themselves into the straight lines and square shapes of their roads and buildings. Nothing natural. And there were so many of them.

"My name is Maccus! If any of you bastards are still alive this evening, sing that for me."

"My name is Prasto," someone else shouted. And the last time the wind would hear them speak their own names spread through the crowd.

Cadwal shouted his own name too and was glad the boys would do him the honour of speaking his name to keep it alive in the new world. "Tamm!" he shouted. "Drust, Bevyn, Abuccus..." And from all around men shouted the names of all who had ever been lost.

"Gwen!" Cadwal called at last... and had a strange, goosebump inducing feeling that she heard him.

A piercing shout came from one man in the legion and the first row turned their shields to face them. The second row lifted their shields and clamped them on top, and it was as though they had made their own fort on the side of the hill. A testudo.

Cadwal's belly turned over and the calling out of names stopped.

"We charge?" Gavo asked.

Maybe Togman had the best idea, as wherever he had gone with Rhian and Velua, tomorrow they would wake up alive.

"We need to break their wall," Helig said. "Get it open, and we can get in."

"Charge it with horses?" Gavo suggested.

"They won't get past the first volley of spears," Helig dismissed.

"So what do you suggest? Send men in to take spears in their shields and chests and run the horses in over them?"

Realising that they were still waiting for him to come up with a plan, Cadwal was glad of the rain on his face.

"Then let the horses go free," Gavo sighed. "If we can't, let *them* live on this land until the days our names are forgotten!"

Then came a roar. Cadwal turned back and saw the legion was charging up the hill. The noise like countless Ordo-wik bones being raked along a pebble beach was five thousand sets of Roman armour clinking and rattling and five thousand shields rubbing against each other.

Agricola was at the head of his men, a cruel smile on his face, tip of his sword pointed directly ahead.

"Bastards!" Gavo barked, but then sounded more like a chief. "It's not *when* we die!" he shouted. "It's how!!" To Cadwal, he added, quieter, "I will run down this hill a free man."

"Chaaarge!" Helig shouted, and an answering cry rose through the Ordo-wiki.

Maccus pushed him forwards and so Cadwal found himself running down the hill, a step behind Gavo. "If anyone lives through this," the chief shouted as he made his way over the rocks poking up through the swathes of heather. "Rhian is not marrying any bastard from my band!"

Maccus laughed but Cadwal didn't think there was too much chance of that happening... then he slammed into Gavo's back so hard all the air was forced out of his chest. He landed in the damp heather, ears ringing, with the chief lying flat across him. Pulling himself out from underneath, he saw a huge javelin pointing straight up to the sky. Its end had gone through the chief's shield, through him, and was embedded in Cadwal's shield.

Men ran over them, some not bothering to jump, and so he pushed himself up and got swept up in the melee. He didn't get a chance to say a word to the chief, his friend. A few steps away, Tegin lay dead like an ordinary man.

Cadwal ran, spear raised, hammer banging against his shoulder. For a long moment, there was nothing but the sound of his breath in his ears, and all he thought of was Gwen, and the hope she'd be happy with what he'd done. But the strange silence was shattered with the cacophony of hundreds of shields bashing together, grunts as men heaved forwards with all of their might and the clashing of metal.

Maccus, teeth bared and growling like a wolf, swung his hammer at a shield but it held. Before he could pull it back again, swords stabbed out of the gaps between the shields and found soft flesh.

Men slammed in from behind and Cadwal was forced up against the wall of shields.

The world was filled with a mix of hysterical war cries, and pain-filled shrieks of terror. He heard Helig's distinctive half-mad wail, and the cracking of wood as the last son of Gwain managed to swing Gordd-ap-Duwia into Roman shields. For a brief moment, he opened a gap, but in a heartbeat, the soldier behind slid his shield down and replaced it. As impenetrable as the walls of Deva once again.

One man tried to pull a shield down and lost his fingers.

If the gods were watching, instead of pissing on them, bravery they would have seen in an abundance, but glory they would have not.

Overhead, stones were loosed from slings, but they bounced harmlessly off shields.

And there was so much blood. The heather was awash with it.

Face full of the testudo, Cadwal tasted iron and bile and a strange silence settled around him like the first snow.

"Over here!"

He looked up and saw a way through the wall of Roman shields.

"Over *here*!"

Tamm's big hand reached out and grabbed his arm and pulled him through the snarling faces of the Roman front line.

"This way!" Tamm called. His voice sounded close and so far away at the same time.

The further through the legion's ranks they went, the calmer it got, until the men were merely standing, holding their shields above their heads, looking almost bored as hundreds of men died a few steps away. And the pouring rain lightened into a bright summer's day.

And then they were on the other side. Birds were singing and the rain had stopped.

"Here, brother," Tamm called. "Someone is waiting for you."

"Cadwal," Gwen said, her hand held out towards him. He took it. It was soft and warm and the perfectness of the short years they'd had together poured into his heart.

"The boys..." he said. "I looked after them."

"You did," she soothed. "I know. They will be fine men. And they will speak our names."

She offered a horn and Cadwal took a long swig of the finest tasting mead that had ever passed his lips. When he handed it back it was still full to the brim.

She took his hand. Where there had been two scars, now was just smooth skin.

"Promise kept," she beamed.

"Cadwal the Great," Tamm smiled and slapped him on the back with a big hand. It didn't hurt.

Gwen pointed up. Cadwal followed her gaze to see the horde of the ancestors in the clear night sky. Another six thousand just joined. Black sand underfoot.

Gwen pulled him to her. He smelled her hair. And smiled with a happiness his ancestors had never known.

THE END

AUTHOR'S NOTE

I am sorry about the ending. But it had to happen that way as Brethren is based on a true story and it's what happened to the Odovice / Ordo-wik tribe on an exposed hillside in Wales some two thousand years ago.

The surviving text the story is based on is Tacitus, The Life of Cnæus Julius Agricola. Taken from the Perseus Digital Library. Open source.

Such was the state of Britain, and such were the vicissitudes of the war, which Agricola found on his crossing over about midsummer. Our soldiers made it a pretext for carelessness, as if all fighting was over, and the enemy were biding their time.

The Ordovices, shortly before Agricola's arrival, had destroyed nearly the whole of a squadron of allied cavalry quartered in their territory. Such a beginning raised the hopes of the country, and all who wished for war approved the precedent, and anxiously watched the temper of the new governor.

Meanwhile Agricola, though summer was past and the detachments were scattered throughout the province, though the soldiers' confident anticipation of inaction for that year would be a source of delay and difficulty in beginning a campaign, and most advisers thought it best simply to watch all weak points, resolved to face the peril.

He collected a force of veterans and a small body of auxiliaries; then as the Ordovices would not venture to descend into the plain, he put himself in front of the ranks to inspire all with the same courage against a common danger, and led his troops up a hill. The tribe was all but exterminated.

The story ends on a Welsh hillside and it also began on one. I consider myself Welsh, but haven't lived there for a very long time. A few years ago I was being buffeted by the wind up on Dinas Bran, Crow Hill in Brethren, and had a revelation that I knew hardly anything about the pre-Roman people's who called this exposed hill their home. Some research in the shelter of the medieval castle ruins and I found the passage from Tacitus you've just read.

A little while later, while walking the Camino in Portugal in a ghostly mid-winter dawn, the story of Cadwal came to me. Five years later the book is finally published. And I sincerely hope you enjoyed it.

If you did... there are a couple of things you can do.

First, is to leave a review on Amazon and/or Goodreads. Nothing helps an 'indie' book get noticed by the algorithm better than a verified review.

Second, you can get a free book, the prequel to Brethren, set seventeen years earlier, when you sign up for my newsletter. Roughly once a month you'll get an email about exclusive offers and information on the forthcoming second book in the Foundation of the Dragon series, tentatively titled 'Bastards'. It's set around 300 years after Brethren, but in the same familiar places of present day North Wales, as well as England and western Europe. It will partly be a modern re-telling of the ancient Welsh epic the Mabinogion. And like Brethren, will also be based on a true story.

www.robbpritchard.co.uk

ACKNOWLEDGEMENTS

Writing, by itself, is a solitary affair. Writing a book, however, is a collaboration.

For bringing Brethren into the world, I owe a debt of gratitude to Hal Duncan, author of the unbelievably amazing Vellum and Ink, who in his manuscript review, basically taught me how to write.

Marina Kosenkova, my best friend, for late night questions on grammar, punctuation and the meaning of life. Joseph C. for going above and beyond in his line edits. (Who is speaking here?!) Kristina Spiel for the honest and often delightfully acerbic feedback. Sorry about the ending... Shahaf Galil for putting the knife in Cadwal's hand in the opening lines.

Dr Mark Gallaway for being the first ARC reader to finish and routing out a few cheeky typos trying their best to hide in the text.

Meghalee Mitra for the final edit.

And some of the best beta readers, all of whom had some influence on the development of the book. Victorique Crawford, Siri Gusdal, Rachael A, Lauren Miller.

I must have seen hundreds of Youtube videos about self-publishing and writing, in general, but the best resource for me, by far, is the 20BooksTo50k Facebook page. The resources, mostly free, put out by Craig Martelle are absolutely invaluable to an indie author.

For historical advice and the brilliant FB page on the fort of Caerhun, David from `facebook.com/Caerhun`

To Joe Morgan for letting me walk around his garden... which is Dinorwig hillfort!

For going way beyond the call of duty, I owe massive thanks to Sasa Juric for the work he did on that gorgeous cover.

And lastly, but definitely not least, to my awesome Mum, Carol Pritchard, typo finder extraordinaire!